RE-VISIONS

New Perspectives of Art Criticism

Edited by
Howard Smagula
Felician College

Prentice Hall, Upper Saddle River, NJ 07458

Library of Congress Cataloging-in-Publication Data
Re-visions new perspectives of art criticism/[edited by] Howard Smagula.
p. cm.
Includes bibliographical references and index.
ISBN 0-13-779364-2
1. Art criticism—History—20th century. I. Smagula, Howard J., 1942– II. Title: Revisions.
N7475.R4 1990
701'.18'09045—dc20 90-40950
CIP

Editorial/production supervision and
interior design: Tage Publishing Service
Cover design: Patricia Kelly
Manufacturing buyer: Herb Klein

A Pearson Education Company
Upper Saddle River, NJ 07458

Printed in the United States of America
10 9 8 7 6 5 4 3 2 1

ISBN 0-13-779364-2

Prentice-Hall International (UK) Limited,London
Prentice-Hall of Australia Pty. Limited, Sydney
Prentice-Hall Canada Inc., Toronto
Prentice-Hall Hispanoamericana, S.A., Mexico
Prentice-Hall of India Private Limited, New Delhi
Prentice-Hall of Japan, Inc., Tokyo
Pearson Education Asia Pte. Ltd., Singapore
Editora Prentice-Hall do Brasil, Ltda., Rio de Janeiro

Contents

Preface

By the beginning of the 1980s, it was evident that an increasing percentage of new art was effectively challenging many of the assumptions of modernism. This could be seen in the architectural work and writings of Robert Venturi and Michael Graves; the resurgence of narrative, figurative oil paintings; and the use of traditional sculptural materials and processes such as bronze casting and stone carving. Furthermore, this aesthetic countermovement was not limited to the visual arts. Virtually every form of cultural expression such as music, literature, dance, and theater had its "Post-Modern" advocates whose work challenged and in many cases clearly refuted longstanding modernist conventions.

Ironically, it was the triumph of Modernism that fostered the revisionist spirit of Postmodernism. Architectural clones of International style buildings had sprouted up in every locality throughout the country. Downtown Phoenix looked no different than Seattle or Portland, Maine. And virtually every museum throughout the country featured similarly abstract, modernist art in its collection.

By 1980, it had become clear to many artists—and contemporary critics—that present day social and economic orders had transformed the way we worked, played, and thought. The Industrial Age, characterized by the movement of the assembly line and mechanized tools, was supplanted by the Electronic Age where digitalized data moved invisibly through wires and satellite transmitters almost at the speed of light. Work and leisure activities were dominated by huge multinational corporations—some with the political and economic power of small nations—who provided employment and were happy to sell us goods and services to amuse us during our nonworking hours.

Entertainment has emerged today as one of the most profitable new industries of postindustrial society. Video cassettes, compact music disks, and cable and satellite television communication links provide us with a vast cultural menu of performances and events. These programs range from televised tours of the Louvre Museum to Rolling Stones concert videos. Rather than reinforce the historic chasm between elitist culture and popular entertainments, the burgeoning media and electronic delivery systems seemed to foster a synthesis between "high" and "low" art. Recently, performance artist Laurie Anderson's recording of *O Superman* reached number 2 on the British Pop Charts.

In response to these changing social and economic realities, contemporary criticism places new importance on theoretical discourse. With the focus on theory has come a blurring of what was once clearly defined academic disciplines. Philosophers, sociologists, literary critics, and political scientists now freely cross traditional departmental lines and produce writings that cannot be categorized as belonging to any one camp. What they do create is usually referred to as "theory," not the theories of any one discipline but theory per se. The work of the French Structuralists and Post-Structuralists have been in the forefront of this intellectual movement; and the work of Michel Foucault best characterizes this trend toward interdisciplinary synthesis. The warps and wefts of social theory, political history, classic philosophy, and contemporary aesthetics are so interwoven in Foucault's work that "pure" philosophy, social history, and aesthetics can no longer be extracted from the text. These disciplines coexist in an interdependent and mutable state of theoretical discourse and speculation. The influence of the French School on literary and art criticism is deep and far-reaching. In many ways, the specialization associated with the Industrial Age has led to the de-specialization of the Information Age.

One of the most prevalent characteristics of recent criticism is the fact that works of art are now viewed and interpreted through specific ideological or critical perspectives. Often several viewpoints are combined by critics or art historians (or by philosophers and social historians) and brought to bear on works of art. In order to spotlight the broad spectrum of critical avenues at work today, I have included a representative selection of the most viable and stimulating concepts: sociological, political, feminist, psychoanalytic, Post-Structuralist, ethological, and economic. The final essay theorizes about the efficacy and validity of critical theory itself and thus brings the anthology full-circle to a speculative and open-ended conclusion. Future criticism may well rely on the ability to synthesize many modes of enquiry in order to arrive at meaningful truths and significant personal insights.

In terms of acknowledgments, I am grateful to the students who were in my graduate seminar when I was a visiting professor at San Francisco State University. Their interest in the structure of various critical perspectives was an important catalyst in the creation of this book. Conversations with my good friend and colleague Steve French about the field of criticism have always proved stimulating and have provided me with an ongoing source of valuable ideas and important references. I would also once again like to thank Bud Therien, my executive editor at Prentice Hall, for his expert help and guidance in the publication of this anthology. Tony Caruso, the production editor, kept things moving efficiently and pulled everything together with great skill and engaging humor. It is my hope that *Re-Visions* contributes to the understanding of criticism and that this fosters increased dialogue between artists, critics, and viewers.

1

The New Art Criticism

Howard Smagula

Along with the emergence of a Postmodern aesthetic in art, one hears much today about the validity and relevance of what might be called the "New Art Criticism." Certainly, these two contemporary phenomena are in large part symbiotic and ideologically intertwined. Partly in response to the appearance of mysterious and baffling works of art, a new set of analytic criteria has evolved to adequately deal with work that defies classification by traditional modernist standards. Formal elements such as composition, line, and color are either nonexistent in many of these new artforms (earthworks, conceptual art, performance art, and media works) or are transformed beyond recognition. Over the last two decades we have witnessed profound changes in the form, function, and meaning of art. Responding to both internal and external forces at large in the world, the criteria and methodology of criticism have evolved in concert with these new manifestations of art.

Much of this new criticism is characterized by the importance it pays to *sociocultural* perspectives and its reliance on *theory* (to a large extent literary theory). Rather than address traditional critical issues such as an art work's visual style, quality, iconography, and meaning, contemporary criticism is more likely to focus on the work of art's ideological, economic, political, and social ramifications. Instead of viewing the work of art as an expression of individual creativity (or perhaps "genius" if the artist is well-established in the canon of recent history), the new criticism has for the most part focused on the social process and interaction between producer (artist) and consumer (viewer or owner). Replacing the terminology of formalist criticism—quality, attribution, style, and connoisseurship—with a new set of linguistic labels such as ideology, class, gender, sign, and signifier, the new art criticism reveals its origins in the disciplines of the social sciences and literary theory.

The emergence of this new critical sensibility can also be attributed in large part to late-sixties liberalism, which questioned and rejected many of the accepted political and social assumptions of the day. But the roots of this far-ranging sensibility extend back in time much farther than the heady social experiments of the 1960s. Ideas previously associated with European Marxist intellectuals were introduced to England in the 1930s by scholars fleeing the terrors of Fascism. By the 1960s a tight cadre of young English critics were espousing the merits of a sociocultural purview of art.

Because of the permissive climate of this period (the Beatles Era), previously "tainted" left-wing social ideologies—that earlier might have gotten an intrepid critic or art historian black-listed from teaching positions or publishing contracts—were no longer viewed as socially destabilizing and dangerous. The type of Marxist art criticism practiced in the 1960s was rightly perceived as less concerned with political revolution and more involved with a reinterpretation of art in terms of social, economic, and cultural parameters.

In order to better understand the ideological foundations of the New Art Criticism, it is necessary to briefly define the beliefs and methodologies it sought to reform and supplant. Formalist art criticism emerged in Europe at the end of the nineteenth century as a revolutionary movement that sought to lift the veils of "mysticism" and social "myth" which older criticism imbued art objects with; and, in their view, prevented viewers from clearly perceiving a work of art's place in social history along with its unique visual characteristics. Heinrich Wolfflin's writings typify this early formalist approach perhaps better than anyone else and establish its analytic foundations.

As is often the case with innovative and supplantive theories, eventually they assume the authoritative stature of the concepts they seek to replace and finally collapse under the weight of ever narrowing points of view. It appears that within the seeds of revolutionary critical thought is the genetic predisposition toward eventual obsolescence.

The writings of Clement Greenberg exemplify formalist art criticism of the postwar era. Greenberg was adamant in his beliefs about art and pursued the truth (his version) with uncompromising vigor. There was little room in his formalist ideology for opposing aesthetic concepts. Greenberg championed an "official" art of smoothly machined abstract hermeticism in which nothing existed outside of the pure sensory experiences the work of art made us privy to. Greenberg's model of art making was conceived in no less than Olympian terms. He wrote:

> The avant-garde poet or artist tries to imitate God by creating something valid solely on its own terms, in the way nature itself is valid, in the way a landscape—not its picture—is aesthetically valid, something given, increate, independent of meanings, similars or originals.

It is easy to realize why socially conscious critics of the late 1960s and early 1970s rejected many of the tenets of late formalist thought and why some of them came to view this once dominant form of criticism as a form of "secular religion" that branded as heretics artists who refused to make strictly avant-garde, abstract art. As early as 1944 (when the prevailing modes of artistic expression were less numerous than today) Greenberg, writing in the *Nation,* pronounced with solemn conviction, "The extreme eclecticism now prevailing in art is unhealthy and it should be counteracted, even at the risk of dogmatism and intolerance."

No doubt even in the early 1940s Greenberg had a prescient and frightening vision of the Modern world veering toward a multiplicity of aesthetic visions and a plurality of beliefs rather than the monotheism formalism championed. The power of socially relevant concepts over established authority and a burgeoning internationalism ensured that the lock hold of formalism was on the wane.

Appropriately the social and political upheavals that preceeded World War II played an important role in the dissemination of social and political viewpoints about art. German and Austrian art historians such as Frederick Antal, Francis Klingender, and Arnold Hauser immigrated to England and brought with them strong Germanic traditions of scholarship, precision of thought, and perhaps most important, a keen personal awareness of social history.

One of the most significant European scholars to influence the new methodologies of art criticism was Arnold Hauser. His ideas, expressed succinctly in the lead essay of this book, *Sociology of Art,* functioned as a blueprint for a host of critical inquiries which began to gain acceptance in the late sixties and early seventies. Primary to Hauser's beliefs was the notion that a work of art was not a hermetic organization of shapes and colors that could be systematically analyzed and interpreted, but a form of communication that draws its meaning from our own social milieu and beliefs. Along with other scholars writing from this perspective of historic materialism, Hauser was instrumental in stimulating a reassessment of art criticism from sociological, philosophical, and economic perspectives.

Despite the political and ideological "thaw" taking place in the late sixties, art historians affiliated with established institutions resisted the intrusion of these new methodologies and for the most part dismissed or ignored the work of sociologically based analysis as irrelevant to their discipline.

During the late fifties and sixties, art critics writing for a popular audience in the better English journals were instrumental in popularizing the radical social and cultural theories of historians such as Hauser. (At this point in time, America was not a significant player in this debate—the witch hunts of McCarthyism had significantly destroyed any vestige of left-wing sociopolitical thought, at least in the professional art world.)

The inspired writing of John Berger, an English writer and art critic, established a beachhead for the type of critical thinking that linked the production and consumption of art to issues of social control, economic manipulation, and the effects of mass communication on our perception of art. Berger's classic book, *Ways of Seeing* (an excerpt of which appears in this anthology), was made into an immensely popular BBC television series in the early seventies and had quite an impact on the way an entire generation of art students approached the analysis of art (it was later televised in America as well). With great clarity and forceful example, *Ways of Seeing* presented Hauser's challenging concepts to a much broader audience and thus effectively challenged the supremacy of formalist art criticism.

Using direct quotes from a respected art historian's monograph on Frans Hals as an example, Berger convincingly argued that formalist art history and criticism were covertly engaged in a process of "mystification." According to Berger, ". . . the art of the past is mystified because a privileged minority is striving to invent a history which can retrospectively justify the role of the ruling classes, and such a justification can no longer make sense in modern terms." Berger's essay goes on to explore the sociological/cultural dimensions of art and artmaking from an essentially Marxist point of view. Acknowledging his ideological debt to Walter Benjamin's *The Work of Art in the Age of Mechanical Reproduction,* Berger also shows how the invention of the camera has changed the way in which we have come to view art and the way reproductions interact with the world. All of Berger's writings about art are based on the firm conviction that the making of art and the viewing of art are basic human activities that cannot be fully understood outside of the context of broad social and economic concerns.

It is impossible to pinpoint with any degree of precision the beginnings of The New Art Criticism in America but certainly the writings of Lucy Lippard would warrant her inclusion in anyone's list of early practitioners of nonformalist criticism. Her book, written in 1973, *Six Years: The Dematerialization of the Art Object From 1966 to 1972,* set the stage for criticism that played down traditional analysis in favor of documentary reportage. *Six Years* was an exhaustive compilation of nontraditional art being made in America during this time period: the enormous earthworks being built in the southwest, site-specific environmental sculpture, performance, and conceptual art. Lippard called these works "dematerialized" forms of art because she felt that they stood in direct counterpoint to the consumer products of most galleries, commodity items destined to became status symbols for wealthy collectors. Most of the artworks featured in *Six Years* could not be owned, at least not in the same way as Modernist sculpture and paintings.

Lippard's critical methodology in this book related to her concept of "dematerialized art." No analytic discourse ruminated on the meaning of this diverse collection of challenging objectless art works. Information about the sites, conceptual schemes, or events was compiled and presented without the interjection of personal bias or preference. It was as if Lippard felt that the volumous analytical discourse of the formalist past could most effectively be exorcised by its opposite—pregnant silence.

Six Years was the materialization of Clement Greenberg's worst nightmare. The specter of "extreme eclecticism" that haunted this critic in 1944 was by 1973 a hard-core reality that would not vanish no matter how vehemently formalist critics protested the "deterioration" of art. Certainly this period—1966 to 1972—was an important watershed for the future development of a pluralistic art and The New Criticism.

Lippard's primary focus today centers on the concept of art as a form of political activism and intervention. Her contribution to this anthology, *Hot Potatoes: Art and Politics in 1980,* outlines the dilemma faced by artists whose work is deemed "political" and the problems criticism faces when it seeks to justify and interpret an art of political conscience. Lippard firmly believes that ". . . art and progressive politics as currently defined can't get together in America because they come from opposite sides of the tracks." Committed leftists view the work of most professional artists as hopelessly rooted in the values of the ruling class while most artists, even those engaged in the most "elitist" type of work, vaguely identify with a romanticized notion of themselves as workers. Rejecting the sixties notion that the business of art was art, Lippard defines and describes what she believes is a growing awareness: that our actions and our art are greatly determined by our social standing in the world.

If one of the guiding principles of the New Art Criticism is the desire to position art and artmaking firmly within relevant social and cultural contexts, certainly the issue of feminism occupies a significant place in the critical spectrum. In many ways this critical perspective represents one of the broadest sensibilities at work in the field of art criticism. Most of the women who have entered the field of art making or scholarship since the early 1960s express, to one degree or another, a consciousness of feminism in their work. For example, although Lucy Lippard's and Jane Gallop's essays in this collection deal with politics and psychoanalytic criticism respectively, both essays inherently embody feminist points of view.

Joanna Frueh's article, *Towards a Feminist Theory of Art Criticism,* specifically addresses feminism's contribution to the disciplines of art history and art criticism. Frueh maintains that feminists can be instrumental in the unification of these related but separate disciplines—history and criticism—two fields of study she finds unfortunately at odds with each other. This author believes that feminist art criticism has the potential to join the supposedly incompatible modes of art historical and art critical practice by pursuing old questions in new ways—a sensibility inherent to feminism.

However, while Frueh believes that feminist criticism has many able practitioners and offers much in the way of relevant insight, she also finds that feminist art criticism is methodologically underdeveloped in comparison with feminist literary criticism. In an attempt to formulate a conceptual basis for art criticism, Frueh outlines the three "critical" stages of development of literary criticism and offers it as a model that might advance the cause of feminist art criticism.

Ultimately, the author advocates a feminist challenge to conventional (male dominated) academic art history and criticism. Frueh calls on feminist scholars to risk the charge of being intellectually "soft" in their academic pursuits in order to achieve the breakthroughs feminism is capable of securing, nothing less than the repossession of one's mind and body and the realization of an intellectual freedom heretofore unknown in the field.

In *Second Generation Art Criticism and Methodology,* Thalia Gouma-Peterson and Patricia Mathews also offer insight as to what direction feminist criticism might pursue in the future. Similar to other contemporary feminist art professionals, they believe that we have recently passed through what might be called first-generation feminism. This stage of consciousness has been successful in exposing the methodical discrimination of women and winning well-earned recognition for both historical and contemporary women artists. Second-generation feminists, however, usually reject the strict biological determinism of artists such as Judy Chicago and Nancy Spero—the "celebration of otherness" as one feminist critic puts it—in favor of postmodern strategies based on the theoretical disciplines of poststructuralism, semiotics, psychoanalysis, and political ideologies such as Marxism.

At this heady juncture of politics and concepts things tend to resemble physicist Werner Heisenberg's theories regarding certain electrons that appear to bounce forward and backward in time. The Postmodern world is rife with theory and counter-theory, and much energy is expended in the establishment of one ideological stance against another. In their article Gouma-Peterson and Mathews present a balanced survey of contemporary feminist attitudes acknowledging the advantages of a "Postmodern" approach as well as the dangers contained therein. Noting the rejection of all authoritarian discourse by some Postmodern critics (including feminism) and the rejection of "nature" in favor of "culture," some feminists have begun to view Postmodernism as yet another male dominated strategy to exclude women.

Psychoanalytic approaches to art have also played a significant role in the methodology of The New Criticism. With the recent popularity of figurative and image-laden art works, psychoanalytic studies of art and the art making process have assumed a position of heightened relevance. Jane Gallop's essay, *Psychoanalytic Criticism: Some Intimate Questions,* probes the psycho-sexual dimension of art criticism from a Freudian perspective. Rather than theorize about the interpretation of obvious sexual subject matter (or Freudian interpretations of images that might be read as sexually significant) Gallop advocates a far more interesting and provocative approach to the psychoanalysis of art. The interpretation of sexually oriented subject matter in art is deemphasized by Gallop, instead she argues that subject matter in art is in itself sexual in nature. Gallop distinguishes between two different ways in which psychoanalytic art criticism can be related to concepts of sexuality. The most obvious linkage is the appearance of sexually representative imagery. The second and more critically engaging connection is that our perception of subject matter (of any kind) conjures up what she refers to as "the erotics of engagement," the notion that sexuality lies in the *encounter* with, not the object of our perception. Gallop believes that the richest legacy of Freudian analysis of art lies not in our presumption of important, sexually relevant details, but in our attention to "peripheral, insignificant trivia," which have the possibility of surprising and enlightening the critical observer. The work of the psychoanalytic art critic is primarily viewed as a process of asking intimate questions of the artwork and translating answers into words. This process is what Freud called "interpretation" and attests to the desire on the part of the psychoanalytically oriented critics to understand what moves them.

Donald Kuspit also employs psychoanalytic methodology in the formation of his critical posture. His essay *Artist Envy,* focuses on some of the potentially troubling aspects of the relationship between the psychoanalytically oriented critic and the artist. Kuspit maintains that the trained psychoanalyst cannot help but envy the power and the illusionary "magic" of the artist. Although Freudian psychoanalysis historically aligned itself with the methodologies of science and medicine, it assumed a dependent relationship with the process of art. Kuspit writes: "Psychoanalysis, while wanting to free itself and us from illusions, knows that because we are always in a condition of projecting our unconscious expectations on the world we are always in a condition of illusion." This "illusion" is closely connected with the kind of vision art makes available to us. Thus, despite psychoanalysis' disdain of nonscientific methodology, it knows it needs knowledge of artistic illusions in all of their social and cultural manifestations. Furthermore Freudian thought acknowledges the visual as more primitive and in some ways more powerful than the verbal (Freud for instance, placed primary significance on the infant's preverbal closeness with the mother). Kuspit's provocative analyses of these aspects of psychoanalytic thought give the reader a glimpse of some of the dichotomies that energize this interpretive discipline of critical thought. Although verbal *interpretation* might unlock the conscious intellectual meaning of works of art, their monumental *silence* binds them intimately to our deepest feelings.

While the European heritage of Marxist thought forms the backbone of Arnold Hauser's and John Berger's intellectual and cultural sensibilities, recent scholarly thought is careful to categorize this form of political and economic analysis as *classic* Marxism. By the time Berger's essay, *Ways of Seeing,* was published in 1972 an important group of French scholars from a variety of disciplines had already formulated a host of complex interdisciplinary theories that questioned the ability of standard Marxist doctrine to account for the societal changes they were witnessing. Basically these scholars posited that with our entry into the "Post-Industrial Age," the structure of capitalism had undergone profound changes.

French theorists such as Roland Barthes, Michel Foucault, Jacques Derrida, and more recently Jean Baudrillard, essentially believed that classic Marxist thought had now become an inadequate means of analyzing and interpreting a society in which old style methods of industrial planning, manufacture, capitalization, distribution, and consumption had greatly changed. The Post-Industrial or Postmodern Age, they argued, had brought about significant new social changes in terms of the meaning of production and consumption, largely through the forces of potent new technologies such as the computer and sophisticated communication networks. Work places and work processes, for example, were so transformed in this new age that Marx himself, were he to return, would scarcely recognize them for what they were: information factories designed to gather, interpret, and process the raw material of our time—data.

Our collective appetite today for "information" in the form of work related statistics and verbal text, as well as our leisure time consumption of television, print media, and packaged music on disks and tapes shows no signs of diminishing. We are so awash in a sea of media and consumer products that the boundaries between goods and information has become blurred. Roland Barthes, a French semiologist has even argued that in our age automobiles and fashionable articles of clothing function more as media-generated signs (which endow the end-user with the illusion of power and security) than as objects which express a traditional utilitarian function. Barthes hypothesized that an examination of late capitalist modes of production and economic exchange must now take into consideration a "process of verbal abstraction" that refers not to the commodity itself but to its *sign.* The mass media, seen as an invention designed to serve capitalist interests, now presents the concept of an automobile to us essentially as a means of achieving various goals—freedom, power, sexual conquest—rather than as a means of transportation. The contemporary world, as interpreted by Barthes and other linguistic philosophers, has been transformed by media intervention into abstracted patterns of signification. Following the formula put forth by these semioticians, the linguistic sign is divided into several related components, and advertisers manipulate these language components toward their own ends. For instance, the word "car" would be the *signifier* in this equation and its meaning (power or social status) as defined by advertising becomes the *signified.* The third component would be called the *referent,* which is the "real" or actual automobile. Semiologic theory maintains that language has been purposefully abstracted in the media in order to fulfill the needs of multinational capitalism.

If, as thinkers such as Barthes point out, items as basic as clothing and automobiles no longer mean what they once meant, what were the ramifications for complex social-cultural categories such as art and literature? In the world-view of these theorists, contemporary life has assumed a phantom nature and Byzantine complexity. It would follow, they reasoned, that the nature of art and artmaking are likewise transformed in this brave new world of the media and multinational corporations.

Fredric Jameson, a prominent commentator on the subject of Postmodern society, believes that these developments have not generated a new *style* of art but rather the emergence of a new culture based on the profound social changes and economic imperatives which now inform our life. One significant result of this new culture is the disappearance of a sense of history and tradition which guided all earlier societies. Consequently, Jameson maintains, we now live in a state of "perpetual present" and have to deal with perpetual change.

Jean Baudrillard, a French sociologist by training, also writes about this displacement of time and place we see manifest in the world today. Baudrillard's theories have captured the imagination of the American artworld perhaps more forcefully than any other poststructuralist thinker (poststructuralism is what Americans call the theories of French scholars such as Foucault, Derrida, Baudrillard, etc.). Although the writings of Foucault and Derrida are singularly influential in American literary circles, artists and art critics have adopted Baudrillard as their "patron saint" largely because of his unique perceptions of modern culture and his interest in the role visual "simulation" now plays in our world. What has particularly intrigued art professionals is Baudrillard's vision of an end to culture and art as we have come to know them, thus paving the way for the creation of radical new forms and philosophies of art. Also, his emphasis on simulation has been widely adopted by art critics as the conceptual justification and impetus for a variety of art works based on communication theory, mass media and the "appropriation" of historic images as aesthetic symbols. A number of contemporary artists are also fascinated with Baudrillard's concept of the "simulacra," his terminology for the profusion of culturally generated images that constitute our paradigm for reality in the Post-Industrial Age. Some artists used his writings as conceptual blueprints (or at least as theoretical vantage points) for the manufacture of physical art objects that were exhibited and sold in galleries. Artists such as Sherrie Levine, Haim Steinbach, and Peter Halley (a contributor to this anthology) have claimed Baudrillard as one of the primary influences on their work.

Although Baudrillard may be somewhat of a prophet to these vanguard artists, he admittedly remains a reluctant one. During a lecture tour of America in 1986, Baudrillard was interviewed for *Flash Art,* an international art magazine, and questioned about his following in the world of art. His interviewer cited the fact that leading critics made extensive use of his texts to comment on the work of some new artists and that the artists themselves often referred to his ideas as the conceptual basis of their art. Baudrillard replied that he was pleased that this work operated in systems outside of the university. However, when queried specifically about some of the "appropriationist" art being produced under the umbrella of his socio-linguistic cultural theories, he was less than enthusiastic.

> Generally speaking, the play on quotations is boring for me. . . . The infinite nesting of box within box, the play of second and third degree quotes, I think that is a pathological form of the end of art, a sentimental form. It would be more exciting for me to find something beyond the vanishing point: a hypersimulation which would be a type of disappearance beyond disappearance. . . . If only art could accomplish the magic act of its own disappearance! But it continues to make believe it is disappearing when it is already gone.

This passage illustrates the type of complex and convoluted processes of thought that have intrigued the contemporary artworld. But the very brilliance of Baudrillardian thought, with its enigmatic verbal and conceptual constructs, also creates problems for his followers. During a recent lecture at Columbia University, Baudrillard was again asked specifically about some of the artists who claimed adherence to his theories of "simulation." He replied, "In the world of simulation there is no object (that is, physical work of art). There is a misunderstanding in taking me as a reference for this work." Nevertheless his ideas—particularly as they relate to the realities of our culture—continue to be a conceptual catalyst to critics and artists alike.

Probably the most intriguing theories of Baudrillard—at least to contemporary art critics—are his concepts of "simulacra" and "simulation." Through these concepts, Baudrillard further extends Barthes's theory of the sign's precedence over the object in late twentieth century life. In *Simulacra and Simulation,* Baudrillard's contribution to this anthology, the world of Postmodern commodity culture is shown to be dominated by models of thought, or "simulacra," that are independent of any reality other than their own self-referential musings. Baudrillard defines "simulation" not in terms of any kind of fiction or lie but as an indication of how in the Postmodern world the imaginary has become the real. Baudrillard conceives of Disneyland, for instance, as the quintessential model of simulation with its elaborate play of illusions and the creation of imaginary worlds. With a wry and puckish logic, Baudrillard writes: "Disneyland is presented as imaginary in order to make us believe that the rest is real, when in fact all of Los Angeles and the America surrounding it are no longer real, but of the order of the hyperreal and of simulation."

It is no wonder Baudrillard's curious theories of "reality" have proven of such great interest to contemporary art professionals: Ever since classical Greece, philosophical concepts linking art and illusion have permeated Western thought.

Critic Kate Linker explores this Baudrillardian world of simulation in *From Imitation to the Copy to Just Effects: On Reading Jean Baudrillard,* and relates his theories to twentieth century culture and art. In this essay, Linker envisions the contemporary visual world as a cybernetic machine programed to spew out scintillating visual forms. " . . . 'sheer' images, 'pure' surfaces emanate from the image mechanism," she says, "only to slither in the glamor of the void that constitutes consumer society, their external enchantments compensating for the loss of substantive matter."

Linker's article also focuses on Baudrillard's history of the evolution of the simulacra from Renaissance concepts of the "counterfeit," to our period's "simulacra of simulation," a world dominated by complex codes and a celebration of the artificial. At the conclusion of her essay, Linker makes use of Baudrillard's theories to argue convincingly that recent "retro" styles of art—expressionism, cast bronze, and traditional hand-carved sculpture, are in fact *simulations* of earlier modes of production.

Peter Halley's art and critical writing are inexorably linked to many of these ideas about the nature of culture and art in the late twentieth century. Along with Baudrillard, Halley believes that society has undergone a sea change in terms of its relationship to the "natural" world. In his essay *Nature and Culture,* Halley interprets in the late modernist art of Jackson Pollock and Clifford Still a desire to achieve a unification with the natural world that has been lost to the process of industrialization. This type of art, Halley posits, adopted a "spiritual" posture as a means of curing the ills and alienation of the Modern world. Recently, this stance has fallen in disfavor, the author asserts, because a new generation of artists tend to view concepts of the soul and spirituality as bourgeois culture's attempts at self-aggrandizement and authoritarian control. Halley outlines the philosophic background of the Late Modern Period in order to contrast its tenets with the theories of the French poststructuralists. While he is a close reader of Baudrillard, and clearly one of his admirers, Halley interestingly acknowledges some of the troubling questions that surround his theories in terms of their relationship to art. "If indeed the postindustrialist world is characterized by signs that simulate rather than represent," Halley asks in his essay, "How can an artist communicate this situation?" Halley's article closes with a provocative query that questions the social dangers of a world dominated by the struggle to understand and manipulate a morass of self-reflective visual and linguistic signs.

Much of the critical focus and speculation of sociocultural critics such as Barthes, Jameson, and Baudrillard has inevitably focused on the nature and workings of contemporary society. Often the prognosis for our civilization—when such a position is deemed relevant—is gloomy and disheartening. Most Marxist critics believe that postindustrial culture manifests a mesmerizing and numbing alienation that extends beyond the levels of the Industrial Age. Such questions have rekindled an interest in the most basis origins of culture, art, and economic exchange. Perhaps the most speculative and unique critical perspective expressed in this collection is that of *ethology,* the study of the biological basis of human behavior. Ellen Dissanayake's essay, *Art as Human Behavior: Towards an Ethological View of Art,* discusses art making in terms of intrinsic human behavioral patterns that have been shaped and conditioned (such as humankind's anatomy and physiology) by the forces of natural selection. If contemporary linguistic philosophy—as in the work of the poststructuralists—acknowledges an inherited human predisposition for language and thus for the mental thought process itself, Dissanayake argues that artmaking and consequently art criticism must take into account the biological basis for humankind's behavioral and physiological evolution.

What role has the impulse to make art (discernable in some form in every culture) played in our history, survival, and achievements; and what bearing does this have in our critical assessment of the art process? Dissanayake addresses these issues by outlining three major aspects of an ethological approach to art: the definition of fundamental assumptions and references that such a view point demands, an attempt to define a codified "behavior of art" that has as its basis the biological imperatives of our paleolithic ancestors, and a discussion of ways in which the values of art are intrinsic to the day-to-day functions of human life. Potentially, the author believes, such an objectified view of the biological/social evolution of art can shed much light on the meanings of Western cultural traditions. Dissanayake cautions against our-all-too apparent willingness to endow these values with concepts of "timelessness" and "universality." The primary reason for studying art from a perspective of biological behavior and evolution may be to allow us the opportunity to assess art from less culturally self-referential perspectives.

Spurred by the astounding prices paid for early modernist artworks and an art market experiencing a frenzy of contemporary blue-chip sales, economic issues are playing more and more of a role in the critical evaluation of art's political and social functions. Western aesthetic and cultural traditions have conditioned us to view the connection of art and money as something unsavory and suspect. Conventional wisdom perpetuates the formula art = beauty = truth. Supposedly, through this spiritual path one is led to material transcendence. A close examination of the facts, however, reveals economic survival, greed, fear, and the acquisition of personal power are the driving forces behind the production and acquisition of art both of the past and present.

Carter Ratcliff, in his essay, *The Marriage of Art and Money,* argues that the commodity value of an art work and its aesthetic value are not separate and independent (as we have been led to believe), but intertwined and dependent. Trying to separate these two values in today's society is meaningless, Ratcliff maintains, because they are not independent entities, rather, they function as two facets of a single issue. Western identity is so defined by entrepreneurial endeavors that all aspects of our life—social, political, and aesthetic—are conditioned by economic imperatives. In Ratcliff's view, " . . . the aesthetic is an aspect of the economic and the economic is an aspect of the aesthetic." Thus, the marriage of art and money in the West is more a story of love at first sight rather than a shotgun wedding.

The essays and articles mentioned so far manifest an extraordinarily far ranging field of sensibilities, philosophies, and methodologies that have been utilized recently in the criticism of art. One characteristic, however, unites these divergent points of view, their reliance on the importance of *theory* per se. Some theories exist in seeming isolation, while others join and recombine in complexly interwoven relationships. But the acceptance of "theory" as a methodological basis is virtually universal in contemporary circles of art criticism.

This emphasis on theory has of course been rampant in the academic literary establishment for the last fifteen or twenty years and has become one of the "glamor" fields of study within the university. Naturally, other disciplines within the humanities have adapted the methodologies and language of these complex literary and social theories to the problems of their own fields of study. Recently, in the world of literary criticism, an interesting debate has erupted involving a group sometimes called the "New Pragmatists." The advocates of this position, have challenged the entire canon of contemporary theories (poststructuralism, Marxism, semiotics, deconstruction, etc.), with what is essentially an antitheoretical position. In general the stance of these "renegade" critics is far from reactionary. Instead, it appears to call for the formation of a "supertheoretical" position, one which postulates that the "central mechanism" of theoretical arguments will fail and fail in the same way regardless of the type of theory employed.

With a knowledge of this recent critical debate, David Carrier has written an essay, *Suspicious Art, Unsuspecting Texts,* that questions whether critical theories can validly represent recent developments within the contemporary art world. Carrier does not question the original texts of French poststructuralists (believing that they have an internal truth and integrity) so much as the way art critics paraphrase and apply these contextually related ideas toward specific art-critical issues. "To think that the claims of Baudrillard, or Derrida, Foucault, Lacan, etc.," he states, "can be paraphrased is to assume what they perhaps deny, that form and content are separable."

Carrier's strategy throughout his essay is to note that what critics say about the pitfalls of visual representation can also be applied to their verbal representation of those images. Even as Carrier raises questions about the validity of writers (critics) representing other writers (French theorists), he acknowledges that he in turn (through the writing of this essay) is involved in a process that represents other texts.

Appropriately, Carrier's provocative essay brings us to the conclusion of this anthology of critical theories and philosophical methodologies. Through the questioning of theories that might explicate art, Carrier brings us full circle in the quest for interpretive methodology: One is reminded of the first sentence of Arnold Hauser's lead essay, "A work of art is a challenge, we do not explain it, we adjust ourselves to it." Perhaps at this juncture of time we are left with the realization that no one theory or critical perspective can provide us with all of the answers. We may indeed be headed toward a form of "dialectical pluralism," which seeks to unite diverse concepts under something similar to a grand unification principle. Such a vision might not pit theory against theory but would ask us to conjure up an image of the whole corpus. All relevant theories united by fundamental aspects of common concern.

Howard Smagula is an artist and writer who lives in the Metropolitan New York area. His most recent book is Currents: Contemporary Directions in the Visual Arts, *published in 1990 by Prentice Hall.*

2

Sociology of Art

Arnold Hauser

A work of art is a challenge, we do not explain it, we adjust ourselves to it. In interpreting it, we draw upon our own aims and endeavors, inform it with a meaning that has its origin in our own ways of life and thought. In a word, any art that really affects us becomes to that extent modern art.

Works of art however are like unattainable heights. We do not go straight toward them, but circle around them. Each generation sees them from a different point of view and with a fresh eye; nor is it to be assumed that a later point of view is more apt than an earlier one. Each aspect comes into sight in its own time, which cannot be anticipated or prolonged; and yet its significance is not lost, for the meaning that a work assumes for a later generation is the result of the whole range of previous interpretations.

We are now living in the day of the sociological interpretation of cultural achievements. This day will not last for ever, and it will not have the last word. It opens up new aspects, achieves new and surprising insights; and yet this point of view evidently has its own limitations and inadequacies. At best perhaps, before its day is over, we may be able to anticipate some of the future criticisms and become aware of its insufficiencies without foregoing the insights that have been and may be gained within these limits.

There are still people who do not feel quite happy when spiritual phenomena, or, as they prefer to call them, the higher spiritual values, are in any way brought into connection with the struggle for existence, class conflict, competition, prestige, and the like. To deal with them fully would take us too far from our subject; here we can only remark that requiring the spiritual to be preserved from all contact with the material frequently turns out to be a way of defending a position of privilege.

Far more worthy of consideration are those who resist a sociological interpretation of spiritual achievements from a conviction that any significant structure, and above all a work of art, is an independent entity, a closed and complete system in itself, the elements of which are to be entirely explained in terms of interdependence, without any recourse to circumstances of its origin or to its influence. For a work of art undoubtedly has an inner logic of its own, and its particular quality is most clearly seen in the internal structural relations of the various levels of organization and the various motifs distinguishable in it. It is further indisputable that consideration of genetic relationships, that is, of the stages by which the artist moved from one idea or motif to another, not merely introduces a different emphasis, but is also likely to blind us to internal connections and alter the values upon which the aesthetic effect of the work depends. The factors that are most important in the actual production of the work are not equally important in giving it artistic value and effectiveness. Again, the practical aims of the artist, that is, the extraneous purposes that the work of art may be intended to serve, are not always in accord with the inner aesthetic structure that the work reveals. But the exponents of the theory of "art for art's sake"—and that is what is at issue here—are not content with asserting that a work of art is a microcosm and exerts a sovereign power over men; they maintain that any reference to actualities beyond the work must irretrievably destroy its aesthetic illusion. That may be correct, and yet this illusion is not all, to produce it is not the exclusive or the most important aim of artistic endeavor. Even if it be true that we have to loosen our hold upon reality to a certain extent in order to fall under the spell of art, it is no less true that all genuine art leads us by a detour, which may be longer or shorter, back to reality in the end. Great art gives us an interpretation of life which enables us to cope more successfully with the chaotic state of things and to wring from life a better, that is, a more convincing and more reliable, meaning.

The purely formal laws of art are not essentially different from the rules of a game. However complicated, subtle, and ingenious such rules may be, they have little significance in themselves, that is to say, apart from the purpose of winning the game. Considered as mere movements, the maneuvers of football players are unintelligible and, in the long run, boring. For a time one can find a certain pleasure in their speed and suppleness—but how meaningless are these qualities compared with those noted by the expert observer who understands the object of all this running, jumping, and pushing. If we do not know or even want to know the aims that the artist was pursuing through his work—his aims to inform, to convince, to influence people—then we do not get much farther in understanding his art than the ignorant spectator who judges the football simply by the beauty of the players' movements. A work of art is a communication; although it is perfectly true that the successful transmission of this requires an outward form at once effective, attractive, faultless, it is no less true that this form is insignificant apart from the message it communicates.

The work of art has been compared to the opening of a window upon the world. Now, a window can claim the whole of our attention or none. One may, it is said, contemplate the view without concerning oneself in the very least with the quality, structure, or color of the window-pane. By this analogy, the work of art can be described as a mere vehicle for experiences, a transparent window-pane, or a sort of eyeglasses not noticed by the wearer and employed simply as means to an end. But just as one can concentrate one's attention upon the window-pane and the structure of its glass without taking note of the view beyond, so, it is said, one can treat the work of art as an independent, "opaque" formal structure, complete in itself and in isolation, as it were, from anything external to it. No doubt one can stare at the window-pane as long as one likes; still, a window is made to look out of.

Culture serves to protect society. Spiritual creations, traditions, conventions, and institutions are but ways and means of social organization. Religion, philosophy, science, and art all have their place in the struggle to preserve society. To confine oneself to art, it is first of all a tool of magic, a means of ensuring the livelihood of the primitive horde of hunters. Then it becomes an instrument of animistic religion, used to influence good and bad spirits in the interest of the community. Gradually this is transformed into a magnification of the almighty gods and their earthly representatives, by hymn and panegyric, through statues of gods and kings. Finally, in the form of more or less open propaganda, it is employed in the interests of a close group, a clique, a political party, a social class. Only here and there, in times of relative security or of social estrangement of the artists, it withdraws from the world and makes a show of indifference to practical aims, professing to exist for its own sake and for the sake of beauty. But even then it performs an important social function by providing men with a means of expressing their power and their "conspicuous leisure." Indeed, it achieves much more than that, promoting the interests of a certain social stratum by the mere portrayal and implicit acknowledgement of its moral and aesthetic standards of value. The artist, whose whole livelihood, with all his hopes and prospects, depends upon such a social group, becomes quite unintentionally and unconsciously the mouthpiece of his customers and patrons.

The discovery of the propaganda value of cultural creations, and of art in particular, was made early in human history and exploited to the full, whereas thousands of years passed before man was ready to acknowledge the ideological character of art in terms of an explicit theory, to express the idea that art pursues practical aims either consciously or unconsciously, is either open or veiled propaganda. The philosophers of the French, and even of the Greek enlightenment, discovered the relativity of cultural standards, and doubts regarding the objectivity and ideality of human valuations were expressed again and again in the course of the centuries; Marx, however, was the first to formulate explicitly the conception that spiritual values are political weapons. He taught that every spiritual creation, every scientific notion, every portrayal of reality derives from a certain particular aspect of truth, viewed from a perspective of social interest, and is accordingly restricted and distorted. But Marx neglected to note that we wage a continual war against such distorting tendencies in our thought, that in spite of the inevitable partialities of our mental outlook, we do possess the power of examining our own thought critically, and so correcting to a certain extent the one-sidedness and error of our views. Every honest attempt to discover the truth and depict things faithfully is a struggle against one's own subjectivity and partiality, one's individual and class interests; one can seek to become aware of these as a source of error, while realizing that they can never be finally excluded. Engels understood this process of pulling oneself out of the mud by one's own bootstraps when he spoke of the "triumph of realism" in Balzac. But no doubt such correcting of our ideological falsification of the truth operates within the limits of what is thinkable and imaginable from our place in the world, not in a vacuum of abstract freedom. And the fact that there are such limits of objectivity is the ultimate and decisive justification for a sociology of culture; they stop up the last loophole by which we might hope to escape from the influence of social causation.

Apart from its external limitations, the sociology of art also has internal limitations. All art is socially conditioned, but not everything in art is definable in sociological terms. Above all, artistic excellence is not so definable; it has no sociological equivalent. The same social conditions can give rise to valuable or to utterly valueless works, and such works have nothing in common but tendencies more or less irrelevant from the artistic point of view. All that sociology can do is to account in terms of its actual origin for the outlook on life manifested in a work of art, whereas for an appreciation of its quality everything depends upon the creative handling and the mutual relations of the elements expressing that outlook. Such elements may assume the most diverse aesthetic quality, and again the qualitative criteria may be the same in spite of great diversity of outlook. It is no more than an idle dream, a residue of the ideal of *kalokagathia,* to suppose that social justice and artistic worth in any way coincide, that one can draw any conclusions with regard to the aesthetic success or failure of a work from the social conditions under which it has been produced. The great alliance envisaged by nineteenth-century liberalism between political progress and genuine art, between democratic and artistic feeling, between the interests of humanity in general and universally valid rules of art was a fantasy without any basis in fact. Even the alleged connection between truth of art and truth in politics, the identification of naturalism with socialism, which was from the beginning a basic thesis of socialistic art theory and still is part of its creed, is very dubious. It might be very satisfying to know that social injustice and political oppression were punished with spiritual sterility, but this is not always the case. There have indeed been periods such as that of the Second Empire, in which the predominance of a not very sympathetic social type was characterized by bad taste and lack of originality in art; but along with that inferior art much valuable work was being produced as well. Along with Octave Feuillet there was Gustave Flaubert, along with the Bouguereaus and Baudrys, artists of the rank of Delacroix and Courbet. It may, however, be significant that from the social and political point of view Delacroix was no closer to Courbet than to Bouguereau, that the common artistic aims of these two artists did not rest upon any sort of political solidarity.

Still, on the whole one may say that in the Second Empire the *arriviste* bourgeoisie got the artists it deserved. But what is one to say about epochs such as those of the Ancient Orient or the Middle Ages, in which a most severe despotism or a most intolerant spiritual dictatorship, far from preventing the production of the greatest art, created conditions of life under which the artist did not seem to suffer in the least, certainly no more than he now fancies himself to suffer under the compulsions of even a very liberal form of government? Does not this show that the preconditions of quality in art lie beyond the alternatives of political freedom or unfreedom, and that such quality is not to be compassed by sociological methods?

And what of examples that seem to suggest a contrary view: Greek classical art, which had scarcely any connection with the common people and only the very slightest connection with democracy? Or the "democracy" of the Italian Renaissance, which was anything but a democracy in reality? Or cases from our own day which show the attitude of the masses to art?

It is reported that some time ago an English firm published a book of reproductions of paintings of the most various sorts—good and bad, examples of popular and of more refined taste, devotional pictures, illustrations of anecdotes, and genuine pictorial creations all jumbled up together. The purchasers of the book were requested to indicate the pictures they preferred. The result was that, although as book-buyers the persons questioned were more or less cultivated, and although eighty percent of the reproductions fell within the category of "good art," thus loading the scales in its favor, not one of the first six pictures getting the most votes belonged to this category.

If we took this kind of response to signify that the great public is definitely opposed to the better sort of art and prefers the worse, we could at any rate formulate a sociological law establishing a relation—though an inverse relation—between aesthetic quality and popularity; but there is no trace of any consistent attitude to aesthetic quality in this case. Undoubtedly, there is always a certain tension between quality and popularity, at times—as now with modern art—an open conflict. Art that is worth anything is addressed to those who have attained a certain cultural level, not to the "natural man" of Rousseau; understanding of it depends upon certain educational preconditions, and its popularity is inevitably limited. Uneducated people, on the other hand, do not positively favor bad art over good; they judge success by quite other than aesthetic criteria. They react, not to what is artistically good or bad, but to features that have a reassuring or a disturbing effect upon their course of life; they are ready to accept what is artistically valuable provided that it supplies vital value for them by portraying their wishes, their fantasies, their day-dreams, provided that it calms their anxieties and increases their sense of security. One must not, however, forget that the strange, the unaccustomed, the difficult has, merely as such, a disquieting effect upon an uneducated public.

Thus sociology fails to explain the connections between artistic quality and popularity; and to questions about the material conditions of the creation of works of art it gives answers that are not altogether satisfying. For sociology is subject to certain limitations common to all those disciplines, notably psychology, which employ the genetic method to deal with cultural forms, limitations arising out of that method. It is in fact likely to lose sight, from time to time, of the work of art as such and to consider it a record of something more important than the work itself. And just as the factors psychologically decisive in the creative process are not always identical with the artistically most important factors in the work, so also the sociologically most significant features of a work or of a school are not always the ones that are aesthetically relevant. From a sociological point of view a second-rate or third-rate artist may occupy a key position in a particular artistic movement. The social history of art does not replace or invalidate art history, or vice versa; each starts from a different set of facts and values. When the social history of art is judged by the standards of art history, the facts begin to seem distorted. To counter this impression, one may point out that even art history adopts standards different from those of simple art criticism, and again from those of immediate aesthetic experience, that there is often a decided tension between historical and aesthetic values. The sociological view of art is to be rejected only if it claims to be the sole legitimate point of view, and if it confuses the sociological importance of a work with aesthetic value.

Apart from this shifting of emphasis, which, though it may confuse is easily compensated for, the sociology of art has in common with other disciplines employing the genetic method a further inadequacy in the eyes of the art-lover: it claims to derive special and unique characteristics of works of art from that which is of quite another order, from something general and artistically indifferent. The worst example of this sort of trespassing is seen in any attempt to show that artistic quality or artistic talent is dependent upon economic conditions. It would be too cheap a retort merely to assert that only a few dogmatic simpletons have proposed to derive spiritual forms directly from economic facts, that the formation of ideolo-

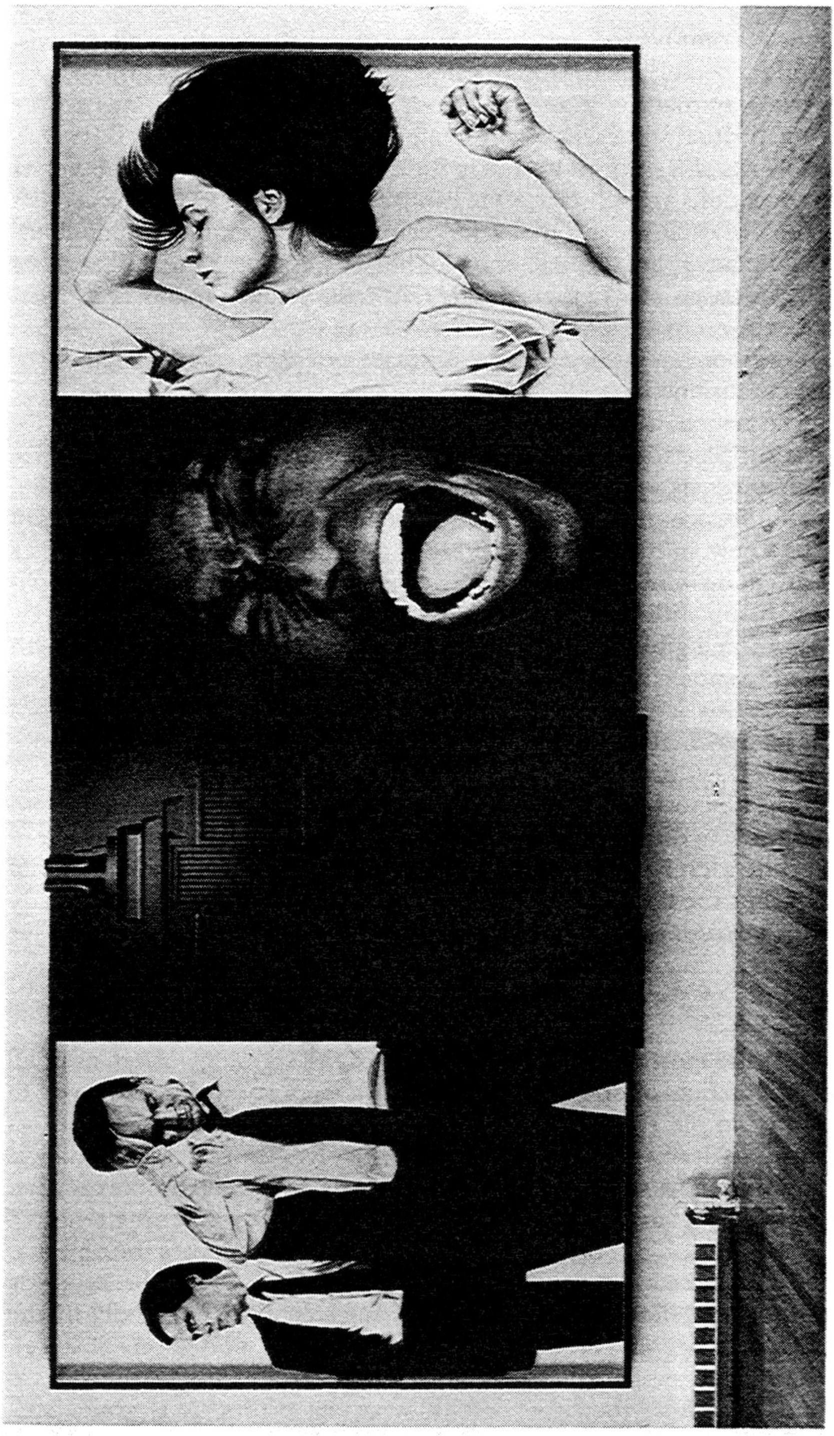

Robert Longo, *Master Jazz*, 1982–83, Mixed Media. Courtesy of *Metro Pictures*.

gies is a long, complicated, gradual process, far different from that envisaged by vulgar materialism. Complicated, full of interruptions and contradictions the way may be that leads from certain social conditions to the creation of spiritual values, as for instance from Dutch middle-class capitalism to the works of Rembrandt; still, in the end one has to decide whether or not such conditions are relevant. One can put off the decision, conceal one's position, talk of dualism and dialectic, reciprocity and mutual dependence of spirit and matter; but after all one is either an idealist or a realist, and has to face the question of whether genius falls from heaven or fashions itself here on earth.

However one may decide this ultimate question, the translation of economic conditions into ideologies remains a process that can never be completely clarified; at some point or other, it involves a gap or leap. But we should not suppose that only the transition from material conditions to the spiritual involves us in a leap of this sort; all transition from one spiritual form to another, change of style and fashion, collapse of an old tradition and rise of a new, influence of one artist on another, or even a single artist's turns of direction—all these changes are equally discontinuous and inexplicable. Seen from without, every change looks abrupt and remains, strictly speaking, unintelligible. Continuous gradual change is something of which we have only a subjective, inner experience; it cannot be reconstructed from objective data.

The leap from the material to the spiritual is immeasurable, and yet we make this leap within the sphere of social life, even within the sphere of economics. The most primitive economy is a humanly organized economy, not a natural condition; nature once left behind, we do not anywhere encounter the merely material; we may thing we are talking about material conditions, but the leap into the realm of spiritual conceptions has already occurred. The distance between natural occurrences and the most primitive economy is thus in a way greater than that from primitive economy to the highest flights of the human spirit, although every stretch of the way is broken by abysses.

One of the most obvious shortcomings of the sociology of art, as of all genetic explanation of spiritual structures, derives from the endeavor to analyze into simple elements an object whose very nature consists in its complexity. No doubt scientific explanation involves simplification, analysis of the complex into such components as occur in other complexes also. Outside the field of art this procedure does not destroy anything really of the essence of the object, but when applied to art, it eliminates the object as presented in its completeness, the only way in which it can be properly presented. If one eliminates or purposely neglects the complexity of the work of art, interweaving motifs, ambiguity of symbols, polyphony of voices, mutual dependence of form and content, unanalyzable fluctuations of cadence and emphasis, then the best of what art offers us is gone. Still, sociology is not alone in incurring this sort of loss, for all scientific treatment of art has to pay for knowledge gained by destroying the immediate, ultimately irretrievable, aesthetic experience. In even the most sensitive and understanding historical analyses of art, that original direct experience has been lost. All this is, of course, no excuse for the special shortcomings to which the sociologist is prone, nor does it liberate him from the duty of correcting the defects of his point of view as best he may, or at least of being aware of them.

The work of art is not only a source of complex personal experience, but also has another kind of complexity, being a nodal point of several different causal lines. It is the outcome of at least three different types of conditions: psychological, sociological and stylistic. As a psychological being, the individual retains not merely the freedom of choosing among the various possibilities permitted by social causation; he is also always creating for himself new possibilities in no way prescribed by his society, even though they may be restricted by the social conditions under which he lives. The creative individual invents new forms of expression, does not find them ready-made. What he takes for granted is of a negative rather than positive character: it is the totality of what cannot be thought, felt, expressed, or understood at that particular historical moment. Undoubtedly, such "blind spots" of an epoch can be established only subsequently; our actual state of affairs always has an anarchical look, as if the individual could do with it just what he fancies. Subsequently one comes to see a social law that has molded the individual choices in accordance with a unitary trend. In a similar way a stylistic line gradually comes to be recognized, along which particular modes of expression which have seemed to be freely selected fall into place. Indeed, stylistic trends, even more than sociological, have definitely the appearance of being objective regularities that impose themselves upon the individual choices; viewed retrospectively, the individuals seem to be little more than carriers of these anonymous stylistic trends.

But the history of style cannot do away with either psychological or sociological causation. It will never be possible to explain by purely formal, stylistic considerations why a line of artistic development breaks off at a certain point and gives place to a completely different one instead of going on to further progress and expansion—in short, why a change occurred just when it did. The "climax" of a line of development cannot be foretold on the basis of formal criteria; revolution occurs when a certain style is no longer adapted to expressing the spirit of the time, something that depends on psychological and sociological conditions. Change of style, no doubt, occurs in a direction determined from within; but there are always a number of possible directions, and in any case the "maturity" of choice is never fixed in advance or secure from the unforeseeable. Among the circumstances governing the occurrence of the change, social conditions are probably preeminent; but it would be a mistake to suppose that social conditions produce the forms in terms by which the artistic revolution expresses itself; these forms are just as much the product of psychological and stylistic as of sociological factors. When one considers social causation, psychology appears as a sort of incipient, abortive sociology, when one regards the psychological motivation, sociology looks like a refusal to trace events to their ultimate origins in the make-up of the human soul. From the stylistic point of view, both psychology and sociology make the same mistake: they derive what is special to art from motives of a heterogenous character, explain artistic forms in terms of something that has nothing to do with "form." Only in descriptive analysis is the uniqueness and complexity of the work of art preserved; it is inevitably destroyed by attempts at pragmatic explanation, whether genetic or teleological. In this respect psychology and art history are on the same footing as sociology.

The inadequacy, however, that we often find in the sociologist's view of art is not simply the result of the method of research which sociology shares with psychology and art history. It is also owing to the rather undeveloped language applied by the sociologist to the subtly differentiated world of art, a language vastly inferior to the far more refined and appropriate language of the psychologist and the art historian. The concepts with which the sociologist works are woefully inadequate for dealing with the wealth and subtlety of artistic production. Categories such as "courtly," "bourgeois," "capitalistic," "urban," "conservative," and "liberal" are too narrow and schematic and also too rigid to do justice to the special character of a work of art. Each category comprehends such a variety of artistic views and aims that it does not tell us much that is really relevant. What do we really know about the artistic problems with which Michelangelo had to wrestle, about the individuality of his means and methods, when we have noted merely that he was contemporary with the formulae of the Council of Trent, the new political realism, the birth of modern capitalism and absolutism? When we know all this, we perhaps understand better his restless spirit, the turn that his art took in the direction of mannerism, possibly even in some measure the astounding inarticulateness of his last works. His greatness and the incomparable quality of his aims are no more explained this way than Rembrandt's genius is to be explained by the economic and social conditions that were at once the foundation of his artistic career and his undoing. Here we come up against the definite limits of sociological inquiry.

But if there are such limits, do they really matter? If sociology is unable to penetrate to the ultimate secret of the art of a Rembrandt, are we to dispense entirely with what it can tell us? For example, are we to refuse to probe into the social preconditions of his art, and so of the stylistic peculiarities that distinguish it from the art of the contemporary Flemish painters, notably Rubens? That would be to ignore the only means of throwing light upon the otherwise unintelligible fact that two such different types of art as Flemish baroque and Dutch naturalism arose almost simultaneously, in direct geographical contact with one another, on the basis of similar cultural traditions and a long political experience in common, but under markedly different economic and social conditions. Certainly, we have here no explanation of Ruben's greatness or the mystery of Rembrandt. But then, what genetic explanation of this stylistic difference is there other than the sociological one that Rubens produced his works in a courtly-aristocratic society, Rembrandt his in a bourgeois world, with its inclination to inwardness? That Rubens, unlike Rembrandt, went to Italy and absorbed the spirit of Italian baroque is rather a symptom than an explanation in itself. Mannerism was in fashion at the turn of the century in the northern provinces as in the southern, and at first Protestant tendencies were to be found in the South just as much as in the North. But in Flanders, in consequence of the Spanish rule, there was an ostentatious court, an aristocracy accustomed to appear in public, a magnificent Church—all things that did not exist in the sober, Protestant Holland that repelled the Spaniards. There, on the contrary, we find a bourgeois capitalism, liberal and without much feeling for prestige, and so ready to let its artists work according to their own fancies, and starve as they pleased. Rembrandt and Rubens are unique and incomparable; not so their styles and their fates. The various turns and changes that we detect in the course of their artistic development and the story of their lives are by no means without parallel, and do not incline us to attribute the difference of type in their art simply to individual disposition and personal genius.

Sociology possesses no philosopher's stone, does not work miracles or solve all problems. Still, it is more than just one departmental discipline among many. As was theology in the Middle Ages, philosophy in the seventeenth century, and economics in the eighteenth, it is a focal discipline in our day, one upon which the entire world-view of the age centers. To recognize the claims of sociology is to decide in favor of a rational ordering of life and for a struggle against prejudices. The idea upon which this cardinal position of sociology is founded is the discovery of the ideological character of thought, a discovery made in several different guises, during the past hundred years, in Nietzsche's and Freud's exposures of self-deception no less than in Marx's historical materialism. To get clear about oneself, to become conscious of the presuppositions of one's own character, thought, and will is the requirement upon which all these different thinkers insist. Sociology endeavors to probe into the preconditions of thought and will which derive from a man's social position. Objections made to such research are mostly due to the fact that correct estimation of these social connections is not a purely theoretical matter; men are inclined to admit them or deny them on ideological grounds. Many of those who will not hear of sociology exaggerate its deficiencies in order that they need not become conscious of their prejudices. Others resist sociological interpretation of everything in the spiritual realm, not wishing to give up the fiction of a timeless validity of thought and a meta-historical destiny for man. Those on the other hand who accept sociology as simply one means toward more perfect knowledge have no reason to minimize either its undeniable limitations or the extent of its unexplored possibilities.

Arnold Hauser was born in Hungary in 1892 and became a British citizen in 1948. He was a leading figure in the field of the philosophy and history of art. Incorporating elements of sociology, economics, and philosophy, Hauser brought new insights to the fields of art history and criticism.

3

Ways of Seeing

John Berger

Seeing comes before words. The child looks and recognizes before it can speak. But there is also another sense in which seeing comes before words. It is seeing which establishes our place in the surrounding world; we explain that world with words, but words can never undo the fact that we are surrounded by it. The relation between what we see and what we know is never settled. Each evening we *see* the sun set. We *know* that the earth is turning away from it. Yet the knowledge, the explanation, never quite fits the sight. The Surrealist painter Magritte commented on this always-present gap between words and seeing in a painting called *The Key of Dreams.*

The way we see things is affected by what we know or what we believe. In the Middle Ages when men believed in the physical existence of Hell the sight of fire must have meant something different from what it means today. Nevertheless their idea of Hell owed a lot to the sight of fire consuming and the ashes remaining—as well as to their experience of the pain of burns.

When in love, the sight of the beloved has a completeness which no words and no embrace can match: a completeness which only the act of making love can temporarily accommodate.

Yet this seeing which comes before words, and can never be quite covered by them, is not a question of mechanically reacting to stimuli. (It can only be thought of in this way if one isolates the small part of the process which concerns the eye's retina.) We only see what we look at. To look is an act of choice. As a result of this act, what we see is brought within our reach—though not necessarily within arm's reach. To touch something is to situate oneself in relation to it. (Close your eyes, move round the room and notice how the faculty of touch is like a static, limited form of sight.) We never look at just one thing; we are always looking at the relation between things and ourselves. Our vision is continually active, continually moving, continually holding things in a circle around itself, constituting what is present to us as we are.

Soon after we can see, we are aware that we can also be seen. The eye of the other combines with our own eye to make it fully credible that we are part of the visible world.

If we accept that we can see that hill over there, we propose that from that hill we can be seen. The reciprocal nature of vision is more fundamental than that of spoken dialogue. And often dialogue is an attempt to verbalize this—an attempt to explain how, either metaphorically or literally, "you see things," and an attempt to discover how "he sees things."

In the sense in which we use the word in this book, all images are man-made. An image is a sight which has been recreated or reproduced. It is an appearance, or a set of appearances, which has been detached from the place and time in which it first made its appearance and preserved—for a few moments or a few centuries. Every image embodies a way of seeing. Even a photograph. For photographs are not, as is often assumed, a mechanical record. Every time we look at a photograph, we are aware, however slightly, of the photographer selecting that sight from an infinity of other possible sights. This is true even in the most casual family snapshot. The photographer's way of seeing is reflected in his choice of subject. The painter's way of seeing is reconstituted by the marks he makes on the canvas or paper. Yet, although every image embodies a way of seeing, our perception or appreciation of an image depends also upon our own way of seeing. (It may be, for example, that Sheila is one figure among twenty; but for our own reasons she is the one we have eyes for.)

Images were first made to conjure up the appearances of something that was absent. Gradually it became evident that an image could outlast what it represented; it then showed how something or somebody had once looked—and thus by implication how the subject had once been seen by other people. Later still the specific vision of the image-maker was also recognized as part of the record. An image became a record of how X had seen Y. This was the result of an increasing consciousness of individuality, accompanying an increasing awareness of history. It would be rash to try to date this last development precisely. But certainly in Europe such consciousness has existed since the beginning of the Renaissance.

No other kind of relic or text from the past can offer such a direct testimony about the world which surrounded other people at other times. In this respect images are more precise and richer than literature. To say this is not to deny the expressive or imaginative quality of art, treating it as mere documentary evidence; the more imaginative the work, the more profoundly it allows us to share the artist's experience of the visible.

Yet when an image is presented as a work of art, the way people look at it is affected by a whole series of learnt assumptions about art. Assumptions concerning:

Beauty
Truth
Genius
Civilization
Form
Status
Taste, etc.

Many of these assumptions no longer accord with the world as it is. (The world-as-it-is is more than pure objective fact, it includes consciousness). Out of true with the present, these assumptions obscure the past. They mystify rather than clarify. The past is never there waiting to be discovered, to be recognized for exactly what it is. History always constitutes the relation between a present and its past. Consequently fear of the present leads to mystification of the past. The past is not for living in; it is a well of conclusions from which we draw in order to act. Cultural mystification of the past entails a double loss. Works of art are made unnecessarily remote. And the past offers us fewer conclusions to complete in action.

When we "see" a landscape, we situate ourselves in it. If we "saw" the art of the past, we would situate ourselves in history. When we are prevented from seeing it, we are being deprived of the history which belongs to us. Who benefits from this deprivation? In the end, the art of the past is being mystified because a privileged minority is striving to invent a history which can retrospectively justify the role of the ruling classes, and such a justification can no longer make sense in modern terms. And so, inevitably, it mystifies.

Let us consider a typical example of such mystification. A two-volume study was recently published on Frans Hals.* It is the authoritative work to date on this painter. As a book of specialized art history it is no better and no worse than the average.

The last two great paintings by Frans Hals portray the Governors and the Governesses of an Alms House for old paupers in the Dutch seventeenth-century city of Haarlem. They were officially commissioned portraits. Hals, an old man of over eighty, was destitute. Most of his life he had been in debt. During the winter of 1664, the year he began painting these pictures, he obtained three loads of peat on public charity, otherwise he would have frozen to death. Those who now sat for him were administrators of such public charity.

The author records these facts and then explicitly says that it would be incorrect to read into the paintings any criticism of the sitters. There is no evidence, he says, that Hals painted them in a spirit of bitterness. The

* Seymour Slive, *Frans Hals* (Phaidon, London).

author considers them, however, remarkable works of art and explains why. Here he writes of the Regentesses:

> Each woman speaks to us of the human condition with equal importance. Each woman stands out with equal clarity against the *enormous* dark surface, yet they are linked by a firm rhythmical arrangement and the subdued diagonal pattern formed by their heads and hands. Subtle modulations of the *deep,* glowing blacks contribute to the *harmonious fusion* of the whole and form an *unforgettable contrast* with the *powerful* whites and vivid flesh tones where the detached strokes reach *a peak of breadth and strength.* (our italics)

The compositional unity of a painting contributes fundamentally to the power of its image. It is reasonable to consider a painting's composition. But here the composition is written about as though it were in itself the emotional charge of the painting. Terms like *harmonious fusion, unforgettable contrast,* reaching *a peak of breadth and strength* transfer the emotion provoked by the image from the plane of lived experience, to that of disinterested 'art appreciation'. All conflict disappears. One is left with the unchanging 'human condition', and the painting considered as a marvellously made object.

Very little is known about Hals or the Regents who commissioned him. It is not possible to produce circumstantial evidence to establish what their relations were. But there is the evidence of the paintings themselves: the evidence of a group of men and a group of women as seen by another man, the painter. Study this evidence and judge for yourself.

The art historian fears such direct judgment:

> As in so many other pictures by Hals, the penetrating characterizations almost seduce us into believing that we know the personality traits and even the habits of the men and women portrayed.

What is this "seduction" he writes of? It is nothing less than the paintings working upon us. They work upon us because we accept the way Hals saw his sitters. We do not accept this innocently. We accept it in so far as it corresponds to our own observation of people, gestures, faces, institutions. This is possible because we still live in a society of comparable social relations and moral values. And it is precisely this which gives the paintings their psychological and social urgency. It is this—not the painter's skill as a 'seducer'—which convinces us that we *can* know the people portrayed.

The author continues:

> In the case of some critics the seduction has been a total success. It has, for example, been asserted that the Regent in the tipped slouch hat, which hardly covers any of his long, lank hair, and whose curiously set eyes do not focus, was shown in a drunken state.

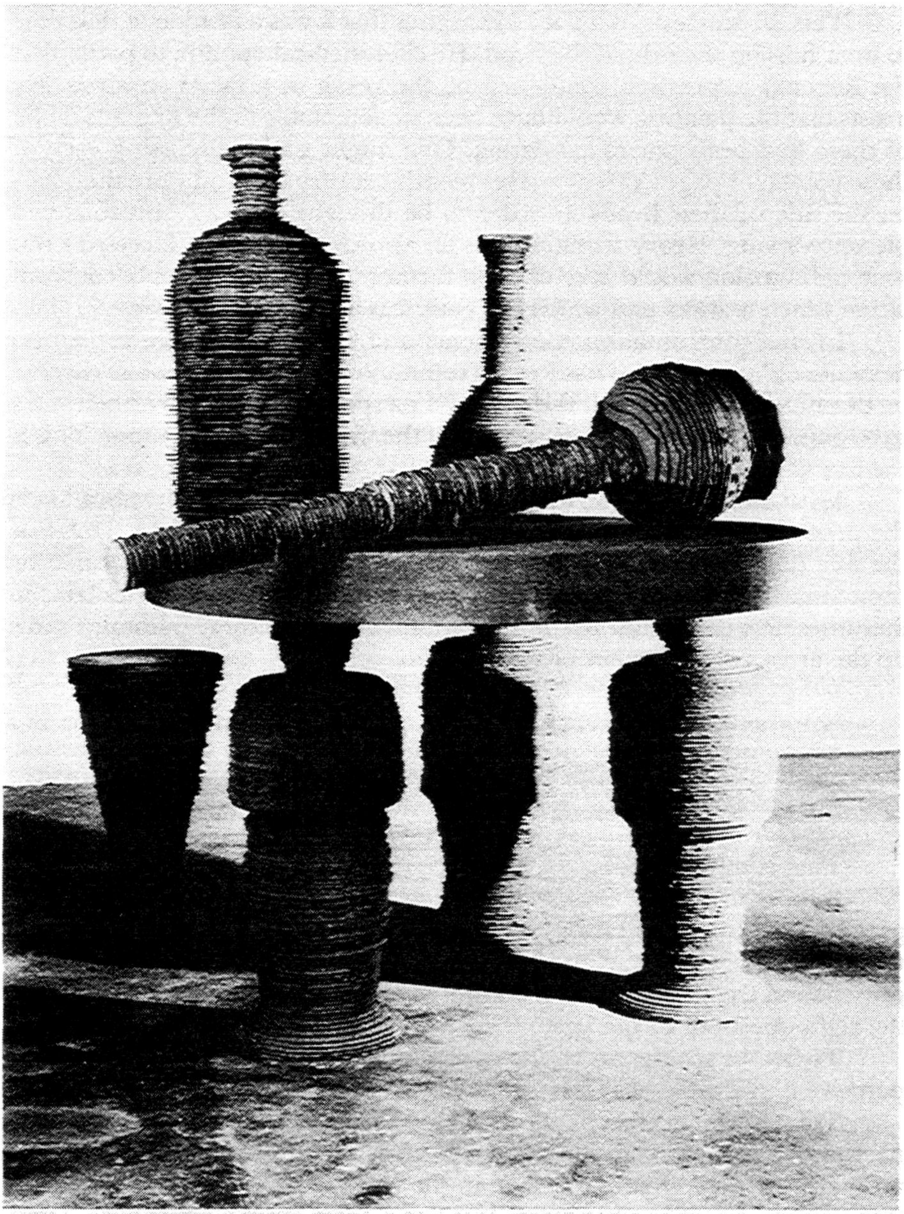

Tony Cragg, *Untitled*, 1988, Sandstone sculpture in eight elements. *Courtesy of Marian Goodman Gallery, New York.*

This, he suggests, is a libel. He argues that it was a fashion at that time to wear hats on the side of the head. He cites medical opinion to prove that the Regent's expression could well be the result of a facial paralysis. He insists that the painting would have been unacceptable to the Regents if one of them had been portrayed drunk. One might go on discussing each of these points for pages. (Men in seventeenth-century Holland wore their hats on the side of their heads in order to be thought of as adventurous and pleasure-loving. Heavy drinking was an approved practice. Etcetera.) But such a discussion would take us even farther away from the only confrontation which matters and which the author is determined to evade.

In this confrontation the Regents and Regentesses stare at Hals, a destitute old painter who has lost his reputation and lives off public charity; he examines them through the eyes of a pauper who must nevertheless try to be objective, i.e., must try to surmount the way he sees as a pauper. This is the drama of these paintings. A drama of an 'unforgettable contrast'.

Mystification has little to do with the vocabulary used. Mystification is the process of explaining away what might otherwise be evident. Hals was the first portraitist to paint the new characters and expressions created by capitalism. He did in pictorial terms what Balzac did two centuries later in literature. Yet the author of the authoritative work on these paintings sums up the artist's achievement by referring to

> Hals's unwavering commitment to his personal vision, which enriches our consciousness of our fellow men and heightens our awe for the ever-increasing power of the mighty impulses that enabled him to give us a close view of life's vital forces.

That is mystification.

In order to avoid mystifying the past (which can equally well suffer pseudo-Marxist mystification) let us now examine the particular relation which now exists, so far as pictorial images are concerned, between the present and the past. If we can see the present clearly enough, we shall ask the right questions of the past.

Today we see the art of the past as nobody saw it before. We actually perceive it in a different way.

This difference can be illustrated in terms of what was thought of as perspective. The convention of perspective, which is unique to European art and which was first established in the early Renaissance, centres everything on the eye of the beholder. It is like a beam from a lighthouse—only instead of light travelling outwards, appearances travel in. The conventions called those appearances *reality*. Perspective makes the single eye the centre of the visible world. Everything converges on to the eye as to the vanishing point of infinity. The visible world is arranged for the spectator as the universe was once thought to be arranged for God.

According to the convention of perspective there is no visual reciprocity. There is no need for God to situate himself in relation to others: he is himself the situation. The inherent contradiction in perspective was that it structured all images of reality to address a single spectator who, unlike God, could only be in one place at a time.

After the invention of the camera this contradiction gradually became apparent.

> I'm an eye. A mechanical eye. I, the machine, show you a world the way only I can see it. I free myself for today and forever from human immobility. I'm in constant movement. I approach and pull away from objects. I creep under them. I move alongside a running horse's mouth. I fall and rise with the falling and rising bodies. This is I, the machine, manoeuvring in the chaotic movements, recording one movement after another in the most complex combinations.
>
> Freed from the boundaries of time and space, I co-ordinate any and all points of the universe, wherever I want them to be. My way leads towards the creation of a fresh perception of the world. Thus I explain in a new way the world unknown to you.*

The camera isolated momentary appearances and in so doing destroyed the idea that images were timeless. Or, to put it another way, the camera showed that the notion of time passing was inseparable from the experience of the visual (except in paintings). What you saw depended upon where you were when. What you saw was relative to your position in time and space. It was no longer possible to imagine everything converging on the human eye as on the vanishing point of infinity.

This is not to say that before the invention of the camera men believed that everyone could see everything. But perspective organized the visual field as though that were indeed the ideal. Every drawing or painting that used perspective proposed to the spectator that he was the unique centre of the world. The camera—and more particularly the movie camera—demonstrated that there was no centre.

The invention of the camera changed the way men saw. The visible came to mean something different to them. This was immediately reflected in painting.

For the Impressionists the visible no longer presented itself to man in order to be seen. On the contrary, the visible, in continual flux, became fugitive. For the Cubists the visible was no longer what confronted the single eye, but the totality of possible views taken from points all round the object (or person) being depicted.

The invention of the camera also changed the way in which men saw

* This quotation is from an article written in 1923 by Dziga Vertov, the revolutionary Soviet film director.

paintings painted long before the camera was invented. Originally paintings were an integral part of the building for which they were designed. Sometimes in an early Renaissance church or chapel one has the feeling that the images on the wall are records of the building's interior life, that together they make up the building's memory—so much are they part of the particularity of the building.

The uniqueness of every painting was once part of the uniqueness of the place where it resided. Sometimes the painting was transportable. But it could never be seen in two places at the same time. When the camera reproduces a painting, it destroys the uniqueness of its image. As a result its meaning changes. Or, more exactly, its meaning multiplies and fragments into many meanings.

This is vividly illustrated by what happens when a painting is shown on a television screen. The painting enters each viewer's house. There it is surrounded by his wallpaper, his furniture, his mementoes. It enters the atmosphere of his family. It becomes their talking point. It lends its meaning to their meaning. At the same time it enters a million other houses and, in each of them, is seen in a different context. Because of the camera, the painting now travels to the spectator rather than the spectator to the painting. In its travels, its meaning is diversified.

John Berger, an English novelist and art critic, was born in London in 1926. Currently Berger lives in a small village in rural France where he is researching and writing about the effects of the Industrial revolution on the lives of nineteenth-century European peasants.

4

Hot Potatoes: Art and Politics in 1980

Lucy Lippard

Every summer I sit down and try again to write about "art and politics." Every summer, the more the possibilities have expanded and the changes have been frustrated, the harder it gets. Despite years of "art activism" the two still crouch in separate corners of my life, teasing, sometimes sparring, coming to grips rarely, uneasily, and without conclusion or issue. Even now, when many more visual artists are informed about radical politics, when "political" or "socially concerned" art has even enjoyed a doubtful chic, artists still tend to think they're above it all and the Left still tends to think art's below it all. Within the feminist art movement as well, polarities reign, although because of its fundamental credo—"the personal is political"—they have different roots, and different blossoms.

I wrote the paragraph above in the summer of 1977, two years before the cusp of 1980, where I stand now. Things haven't changed much. Contrary to the popular image of the wild-eyed radical, artists are usually slow to sense and slower to respond to social currents. Yet perhaps in response to the anti-'60s economic backlash that has only recently reached the art world in the guise of punk and/or "retrochic," it does seem that an increasing number of young artists are becoming concerned with social issues—though often in peculiar and ambivalent ways. I tend to be overoptimistic, and at the moment am obsessed with the need to integrate ivory tower and grass roots, particularly with the "cultural" and "socialist" branches of femi-

This essay was originally published in *Block* no. 4 (1981). Reprinted with permission of the author.

nism. So I could be wrong, as I was when I hoped for too much from the Conceptual third stream around 1970. But first, a little history.

A LITTLE HISTORY

Art and progressive politics as currently defined can't get together in America because they come from opposite sides of the tracks. Art values are seen by the Left as precisely bourgeois, even ruling-class, values, while even the most elitist artists often identify vaguely—very vaguely—with an idealized working class. Or perhaps painter Rudolf Baranik's way of putting it is fairer: "Art both serves and subverts the dominant class of every society. Even the most passive or subservient art is not the precise carrier of ruling class ideas, though in every way the ruling class makes an effort to make it so."[1] Art may feel trapped in the ivory tower, now and then complaining bitterly, now and then slumming for a while, but it lets its hair down selectively so only a chosen few can climb to its chamber. Politics has other things to think about and, aside from occasional attempts to knock down the tower, is little concerned with what goes on inside it. At financial crises, politics may solicit money and propaganda from art's liberal conscience, which also provides benefits, cocktails and imaginative bursts of energy until "too much time is taken away from the studio." Caught in the middle of all this is the socially conscious and sometimes even socially involved artist.

The American art world (aka "the art scene"), where most of these forays take place, is a curious barnacle on capitalist society that imagines itself an esthetic free agent. The art world has been wary of politics since the late '40s, when artists were in danger of being called before the House Un-American Activities Committee if their work was too comprehensibly "humanist." In 1948 a soon-to-be-famous painter and a critic jointly declared that "political commitment in our time means no art, no literature."[2] Variations on this position dominated the next twenty years, only a few holdouts insisting that "painting cannot be the only activity of the mature artist" (though continuing to support the separation between art and politics).[3]

American art subsequently became a world power precisely by severing itself from politics (read Left politics, since the center and Right status quo are just presumed to be "society" or "life"). By the late '50s, the New American Art—abstract and therefore, paradoxically, far more socially manipulable than representation—sidled forth from the tower to issue internationally impressive "breakthroughs." Those who had initially objected to its red range began to like warm colors when these could be paraded as testimony to the glories of esthetic freedom in a democracy. No one seemed to notice until the late '60s that artists had lost control of their art once it left the studio—perhaps because the whole experience was a new one. Some American artists were enjoying for the first time a general prestige. In the process of acknowledging that content in art was inseparable from form, many also fell for the next step (offered by critics who had been "political" themselves in the '40s)—that form alone was the only possible content for "important" or "quality" art. This recipe was swallowed whole in the period between Korea and Vietnam. How, after all, could pure form be political? How indeed. The problem seemed solved as the international Triumph of American Painting paralleled the triumph of American multinationals. Again, in all fairness, it should be noted that the artists themselves were rarely if ever aware of these implications, and when they were, their extraordinary esthetic achievements could be identified, as Irving Sandler has suggested, as a holding action on the threshold of resistance.[4]

All this time there was a good deal of banter about the superior "morality" of American art as compared to European art; yet political morality—ideas affecting culture from the depths rather than on the famous surface and at the famous edges—was all but invisible in the art world. For a while the yacht was too comfortable to rock, even though it was still too small to accommodate the majority of the artist population, not to mention the audience. By the mid-'60s, the small number of highly visible artists who had "made it" offered a false image of the future to all those art students rushing to New York to make their own marks, and to have nervous breakdowns if they didn't get a one-man show within the year (I say one-man advisedly, since the boys suffered more than the girls, who had been led to expect nothing and had to cultivate personal survival powers).

Throughout the '60s a good healthy capitalist dog-eat-dog competition flourished with the free-enterprise esthetic. More-or-less abruptly, at the end of the decade, reaction set in, taking the form of rebellion against the commodity the art object had involuntarily become. Conceptual Art was conceived as a democratic means of making art ideas cheap and accessible by replacing the conventional "precious object" with "everyday" or "worthless" and/or ephemeral mediums such as typed sheets, Xeroxes, snapshots, booklets, streetworks. Conceptualism coincided for obvious reasons with the conscientious downward mobility of the counterculture and the theoretical focus of the often academic New Left. It was crowded in the streets in 1970, what with the Blacks, the students, the antiwar movement, the feminists, the gays. Art felt like one of the gang again, rubbing elbows with the masses, fighting a common enemy. After all, despite the elitist fate of their art, artists can all too easily identify with oppressed minorities whose civil rights are minimal.

But wait. The enemy looks familiar. It is The Hand That Feeds Us. We were picketing the people we drank with and lived off of. We were making art in a buyer's market but not a consumer's market. We were full of "mixed feelings," because we wanted to be considered workers like everyone else and at the same time we weren't happy when we saw our products being treated like everyone else's, because deep down we know as artists we *are* special. What we (artworkers) wanted, and still want, as much as control over our labor power and over the destiny of our products, was *feedback*. Because art is communication, and without contact with its audience it becomes the counterpart of a doorhandle made on a Detroit assembly line. (I have this vision of a '90s artist seeing a film of a SoHo gallery in the '70s and finding herself unable to recognize her own work—just as the factory worker would not be able to distinguish her doorhandle.)

A little dissent goes a long way in the art world. By 1972 the ranks were dissolving back into the white-walled rooms. Pluralism reined and there was more room at the top. For the most part this pluralism was healthy, though attacked from the right as a fall from grace, too democratically open to mediocrity; and from the left as a bribe, too tolerant of anything marketable, a confusion of the issues. Dissent was patronized, patted on its ass and put in its place. Those who were too persistent were ghettoized or, more subtly, discredited on levels they were never concerned with. After a brief flurry of Women's Art and Black Art shows, the institutions subsided to prepare for a backlash campaign, like exhibiting the Rockefeller Collection to commemorate the Bicentennial. Yet one thing that the art activism of the late '60s and the increased (if intermittently applied) theoretical awareness of the '70s did accomplish was a fairly thorough purge of the "my art is my politics" copout, which encouraged Business as Usual and blocked all avenues (or alleys) to change. Many of us were aware by then that every move we made was political in the broad sense, and that our actions and our art were determined by who we were in the society we lived in. (This is not to say that most of us cared to think about these insights.) We were also beginning to realize that Conceptual Art (the so-called movement, not the third-stream medium) had, like the dress and lifestyles of the period, made superficial rather than fundamental changes, in form rather than in content. When we trooped back into the galleries, back to a SoHo already cluttered with boutiques and restaurants its residents couldn't afford (a far cry from the Artists Community envisioned around 1968), we bore this new burden of awareness. We could no longer seriously contend that because art tends to be only indirectly effective, artists should be exempt from all political responsibility and go bumbling on concerned only with their own needs. (Yet again, this is not to say that most of us cared to act on these insights.)

IF MY ART ISN'T MY POLITICS, WHAT IS?

One point at which art and politics meet is in their capacity to move people. Even though communication with nonbuying or nonwriting viewers is an unpopular or unconsidered goal in the high art world, art that has no one to communicate with has no place to go. Contemporary criticism has offered no solid analyses of the artist's exile status, nor any sophisticated notion of art's audience—either present or future/ideal. We might get further faster by asking ourselves as artists and artworkers: Who are we working for? The accepted avant-garde answer has long been "for myself," and "for other artists." These responses reflect the rugged individualist stance demanded of American (male) artists and the fundamental insecurity of an artist's existence in a society that tolerates but does not respect cultural-activities and practically denies the existence of cultural *workers*. Reaching a broader public, aside from its populist correctness *and* aside from the dangers of esthetic imperialism, might revitalize contemporary art by forcing artists to see and think less narrowly and to accept ideological responsibility for their products. By necessity, the feminist art community has made important moves toward a different conception of audience. Perhaps this is what Jack Burnham meant when he saw feminism as offering a potentially "vernacular" art to replace the "historical" art that has dominated modernism.[5] (My dictionary's first definition of *vernacular* gave me pause: "belonging to homeborn slaves.") Although it was still possible in 1977 for *Studio International*'s special issue on "Art and Social Purpose" to ignore feminism, this has been a central concern of the most original feminist artists and writers for some time. Feminist artists are luckier than most in that we have a constant dialogue between a network of intimate art support groups and the rest of the Women's Movement, which is dealing with nonart issues in the real world. (An example is the current campaign in New York of Women Against Pornography.)

Yet the "high" or commercial art world's lack of respect for a less than classy audience whose tastes differ from its own continues to be conveyed through its patronizing (and, alas, matronizing) accusations that any popular work is "rabble-rousing" and "crowd-pleasing." The institutional reception, or lack thereof, given Judy Chicago's monumental and cooperatively executed sculpture *The Dinner Party*, and the overwhelming enthusiasm it has sparked in nonartworld audiences, is a significant case in point, which I've treated at length elsewhere. Suffice it to say that the notion that elitism is necessary to the survival of Quality is tendered by the same liberals who deny all evidence of repression in America and continue to extoll the perfection of a capitalist democracy.

For all the global village internationalism supposedly characterizing the '70s, in 1979 most artists are still working for exactly the same economically provincial audience. "It's a free country." We are supposed to recognize that personal tastes differ. In the high art world, however, Quality *is* the status quo. It is imagined to be permanently defined by those controlling the institutions. While stylistic pluralism had been encouraged in the '70s, deeper divergences from the mainstream are still not tolerated. Given the reigning criteria by which lousy art cast in the proper mold or accompanied by the proper prose is consistently hung, bought, approved by the most knowledgeable professionals, the issue of Quality seems irrelevant. Since Quality comes from art, and not vice versa, the question is: How do we arrive at an art that makes sense and is available to more, and to more varied people, while maintaining esthetic integrity and regaining the power that art must have to provoke, please, and mean something?

For better or for worse, most people go through life without even wanting to reach the inner sanctums where Art coyly lurks. What the ruling class considers "low art" or "bad art" plays a role in the lives of many more people than "high art" does, and it is this need that new art is trying to tap. Right now, only the lucky few get "good art" or are educated to recognize it, or decide what it is. (Recently feminists, Marxists and Third-World artists have been trying to reeducate ourselves in order to avoid seeing with the conditioned eyes of the white capitalist patriarchy.) But are we really so lucky? How much of the avant-garde high art we see gives us profound sensuous or intellectual pleasure? How often do we lie to ourselves about our involvement in the art we have convinced ourselves we should like? How many sensible middle-class people devoted to the survival of "good taste," as intoned by the powers that be, secretly pine for the gaudy flimsiness, the raucous gaiety of "lower-class" culture? Judging from the popularity of such art from other, more "primitive" or ancient cultures, of Pop Art, "camp" and the whole punk or New Wave phenomenon—quite a few.

IS THERE ART POST LIFE?

In the '70s it became critically fashionable to call art "post" anything that peaked in the '60s: "poststudio," "post-Conceptual," "postmodernist," "post-Minimalist," even "postmodern." (Where does *that* leave us?) Maybe in the '80s we'll just find out that "beyond" was nothing but a vacuum. Or a void—as in a *tabula rasa,* which is not a bad thing, especially when things need cleaning up as badly as they do now. For some of us who lived through the '60s and have spent the last ten years waiting for the '70s to stand up and identify itself, the '70s have been the vacuum. It was only in its last three years or so that the decade got it together to pinpoint an esthetic of its own, and this it did with a lot of help from its friends in the rock music scene, not to mention S & M fashion photography, TV and movie culture, *and* a lot of '60s art ideas conveniently forgotten, thus now eligible for parole. As we verge on the '80s, "retrochic"[6]—a reactionary wolf in countercultural sheep's clothing—has caught up with life and focuses increasingly on sexist, heterosexist, classist and racist violence, mirroring, perhaps unwittingly, the national economic backlash.

(Some parenthetical examples of retrochic, in case it hasn't spread as far as I'm afraid it has: An exhibition of abstract drawings by a first-name-only white artist gratuitously titled "The Nigger Drawings" for reasons so "personal" he is as reluctant to murmur them as he is to wear blackface in public; this was studiously defended as a "revolutionary" position by a young Jewish critic who has adopted a pen name associated with Prussian nobility. Or a male Canadian rock group called "Battered Wives," which sings a song called "Housewife"—"She's a housewife/Don't know what to do/So damn stupid/She should be in a zoo." Or a beautifully executed and minutely detailed "photorealist" painting called *The Sewing Room* dedicated to some poor soul named Barbara, which depicts a pretty middle-class sitting room in which a work-clothed man gorily stabs the lady of the house in the neck.)

While most of the hot potatoes seem to have cooled to an acceptable temperature and been made into a nice salad, some still seem to see the retrochic trend as a kind of ecstatic but dangerous drug not everybody has the guts to try. It has been called a "DC current that some people pick up on and others don't," that combats "'60s tokenism" and is "too hot to handle."[7] Some retrograde punk artists share with the Right Wing an enthusiasm for the '50s, which are seen as the Good Old Days. They are either too young, too insensitive or too ill-informed to know that the '50s were in fact Very Bad Old Days for the Left, Blacks, unions, women (viz. the crippling and deforming fashions like stiletto heels, long tight skirts and vampire makeup) and for anyone else McCarthy cast his bleary eye on. The earth-shaking emergence of rock'n'roll notwithstanding, it was also a time of censorship in the arts, of fear and dirty secrets that paved the way for the assassinations, open scandals and quasi revolution of the '60s.

Punk artists—retro and radical—also trace their bloodline back to Pop Art and Warhol (though the latter epitomized the scorned '60s) and to Dada (though it's not fair to blame a partially socialist movement for its primarily reactionary offspring). The real source of retrochic is probably Futurism, which made no bones about its fundamental fascism and disdain for the masses. Violence and bigotry in art are simply violence and bigotry, just as they are in real life. They are socially dangerous, not toys, not neutralized formal devices comparable to the stripe and the cube. So I worry when a young artist whose heart and mind I respect tells me he's beginning to like the reactionary aspects of punk art because he sees them as a kind of catharsis to clear the decks and pave the way for change in the art world. At this point, as in the idealization of the '50s, I become painfully aware of a generation gap. The anticipated catharsis sounds like the one I was hoping for in 1969 from Conceptual Art and in the '70s from feminist art.

I hope retrochic is not the banner of the '80s, but merely the '70s going out on an appropriately ambiguous note, the New Wave rolling on and leaving behind an ooze primed for new emergences. I have nightmares about a dystopian decade dominated by retrograde fascist art which, while claiming on one hand to be "space age social realism"[8] manages on the other

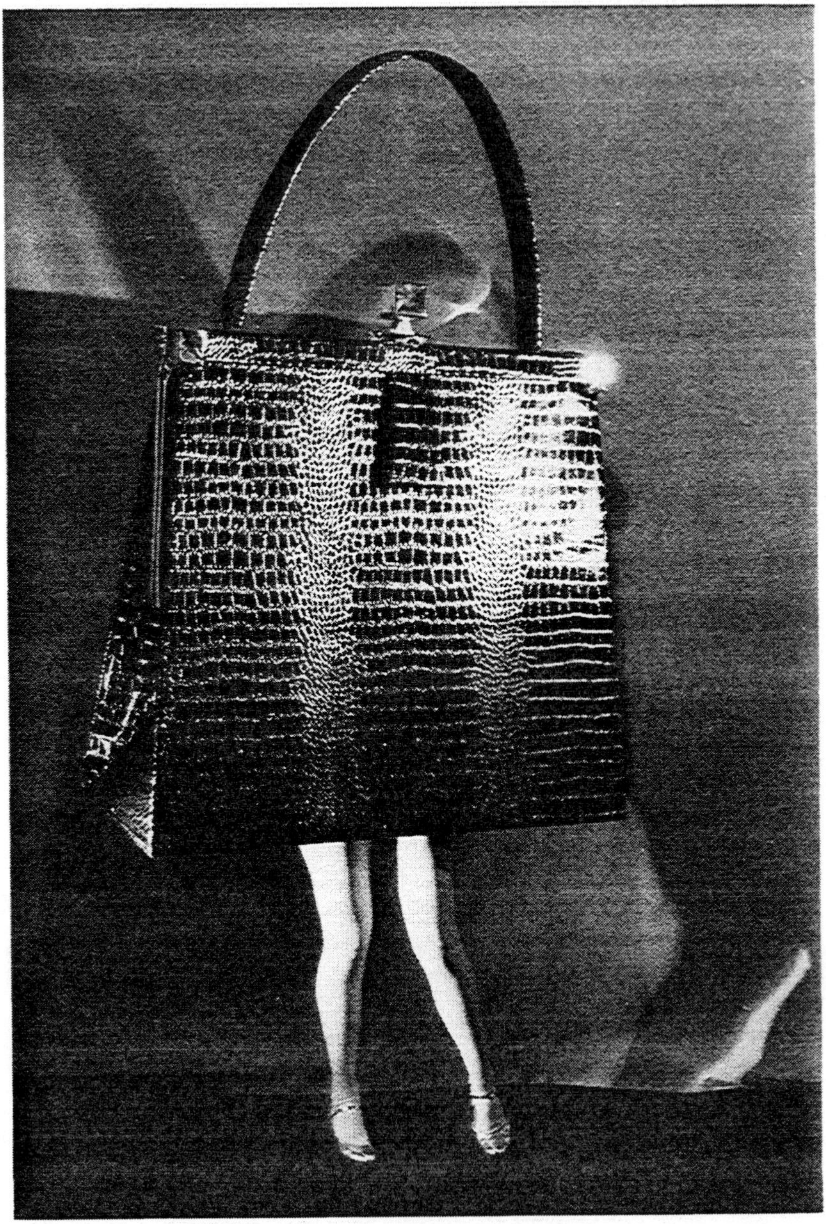

Laurie Simmons, *Walking Purse*, 1989, black and white photograph. *Courtesy of Metro Pictures.*

hand to be just Right for up-and-coming extremists, for those people who simultaneously get off on and morally condemn violence and bigotry. The living rooms of the powerful, however, will not be hung with blurry photos of gum-chewing, sock-hopping terrorists torturing each other. The establishment's taste in politics and art does not coincide any more than does that of the artists themselves. With a nod to upward mobility, one can probably expect to find hanging over these mantels the same good solid bluechip formalism associated with the '50s and '60s, which continued to be successfully promoted and sold throughout the '70s. Inflation encourages such acquisitions, and the SoHo boutique mentally will maintain its strongholds. Or perhaps the art of the '80s will be a hybrid of the '70s progeny: impressive acres of colored canvas and tons of wood and steel functioning as covers for safes full of money and dirty pictures, with giveaway titles like *Snuff, Blowupjob, Monument to a Rapist, Faggot Series, Kike I, Kike II, Kike III,* and so forth—a charming and all-too-familiar blend of the verbally sensational and the visually safe.

There is, I'm glad to report, another, more hopeful side to all of this, which is subtly entwined with the above. The pivot is an ambiguous notion of "distancing." We critics have been talking about "distancing" or "detachment" or good old "objectivity" with admiration since the early '60s, applying it in turn to Pop Art, Minimalism, Conceptual Art, and now to performance, video, photography and film. Irony is usually an ingredient, and if we're seeking a *tabula rasa,* irony is a good abrasive. But irony alone, irony without underlying passion, becomes another empty formal device. Today *distancing* is used two ways, which might be called passive and active. Distinguishing them is perhaps the most puzzling aspect of today's esthetic and moral dilemma.

The passive artists tend toward the retrochic extreme. They are sufficiently "distanced" (or spaced out) to see offensive racist or sexist words and images as a neutralized and harmless outlet for any perverse whim; after all, it's only Art. (They are not usually so far gone, however, as to use such epithets outside of the art context—in the subway, for instance.) These artists would subscribe to the formalist maxim "If you want to send a message, call Western Union," and they tend to have great disdain for old-fashioned radicals (like me) who take such things seriously.

The active artists also use distancing as an esthetic strategy, but to channel social and personal rage, to think about values, to inject art with precisely that belittled didacticism. Instead of calling Western Union, these artists hope that they will be able to put their message across by themselves. They often use understated satire or deadpan black humor to reverse offensive material and give it a new slant. The younger they are, the rougher they get, and sometimes the cycle reverses itself and it's difficult to distinguish earnestness from insanity.

Passive or active, the crux of the matter is how do we know what's intended? We're offended or titillated or outraged; now we have to figure out whether it's satire, protest or bigotry, then whether the intended content has been coopted by its subject matter. These are questions that must be asked about much of the ambiguous new art. These are questions particularly important for feminists working against, say, pornography and the violent objectification of women, and Blacks working against racists in liberal clothing.

For example, when a woman artist satirizes pornography but uses the same grim images, is it still pornography? Is the split beaver just as prurient in a satirical context as it is in its original guise? What about an Aunt Jemima image, or a white artist imitating a Black's violent slurs against honkies?

Answers, though not solutions, have just been proffered by two leading and very different practitioners of social irony. Yvonne Rainer, who works from a Brechtian viewpoint, treated sex and female nudity with humor and "distance" in her films until she realized from audience responses that the strategy wasn't working. At that point she became convinced, according to Ruby Rich, "that no matter what techniques surrounded such a depiction, no matter what contradictions were embedded in the presentation, nothing could ever recoup the image of woman's body or sexuality bared."[9] Similarly, Black stand-up comedian and pop hero Richard Pryor has just vowed publicly to give up a staple of his routines: the word *nigger*. "There was a time," he says, "when black people used it as a term of endearment because the more we said it, the less white people liked it, but now it seems the momentum has changed. . . . There's no way you can call a white person a nigger and make him feel like a black man." Asked why whites are getting so fond of the word, he replied, "I don't think enough of them have gotten punched in the mouth."[10]

Distancing, it seems to me, is effective only if it is one half of a dialectic—the other half being approaching, or intimacy, or optimism. You move away to get a good look but then you move back toward the center where the energy is. This seems to be the position of a number of younger artists whose often para-punk work bears some superficial (and perhaps insidious) resemblance to retrochic. An increasing number are disillusioned with what they have found in art and the art world (including the alternate spaces and the current dissenters): "Embrace fearlessness. Welcome change, the chance for new creation. . . . There is no space for reverence in this post-earthrise age. We are all on the merit system. The responsibility for validity is the individual artist's. The art critic is dead. Long live art."[11] To which I would holler Hallelujah, but not Amen.

Some young artists are working collectively, making art for specific installations, public places, or for their own breezy, often harsh little shows in flaky impermanent spaces (the model for which may have been Stefan Eins' idealistic if not always fascinating 3 Mercer Street Store, and now his more fully developed Fashion Moda in the South Bronx). One of the most talked-about exhibitions last season in New York was "The Manifesto Show," collaboratively organized and open to friends, invitees, and off-the-street participation, through which it organically almost doubled in size. There was no single, recognizable political line, but a "social and philosophical cacophony"[12] of specific statements, rhetoric straight and rhetoric satirized, complaints, fantasies, threats—some more and some less geared to current art attitudes. Distancing techniques were used against themselves in self-referential hooks into content from art, as in Barbara Kruger's contribution, which began: "We are reading this and deciding whether it is irony or passion/We think it is irony/We think it is exercising a distancing mechanism. . . . We are lucky this isn't passion because passion never forgets." There were also the unselfconscious, atypically straightforward works that said what they meant and meant what they said. And there were Jenny Holzer's dangerously conventional collages of contradictory propaganda with lethal reminders built in for anyone who swallows them whole ("REJOICE! OUR TIMES ARE INTOLERABLE. TAKE COURAGE FOR THE WORST IS A HARBINGER OF THE BEST . . . DO NOT SUPPORT PALLIATIVE GESTURES: THEY CONFUSE THE PEOPLE AND DELAY THE INEVITABLE CONFRONTATION. . . . THE RECKONING WILL BE HASTENED BY THE STAGING OF SEED DISTURBANCES. THE APOCALYPSE WILL BLOSSOM"). The message seems to be Think for Yourself.

THIS UP AGAINST THAT

Those invested in a perpetual formal evolution in art protected from the germs of real life won't like my suspicion that the most meaningful work in the '80s may depend heavily on that still pumping heart of twentieth-century art alienation—the collage esthetic, or what Gene Swenson called "The Other Tradition." Perhaps it will be only the alienated and socially conscious minority that will pursue this, and perhaps (this demands insane heights of optimism) the need for collage will be transcended. Obviously I mean collage in the broadest sense, not pasted papers or any particular technique but the "juxtaposition of unlike realities to create a new reality." Collage as dialectic. Collage as revolution. "Collage of Indignation."[13] Collage as words and images exposing the cultural structure of a society in which art has been turned against itself and against the public.

For instance, the media strategies for public performance used by West Coast feminists Suzanne Lacy and Leslie Labowitz (with the "social network" Ariadne) juxtapose two kinds of image within the context of street, shopping mall or press conference.[14] The first is an image of social reality as we all know it through TV and newspapers. The second is that image seen through a feminist consciousness of a different reality—for instance, looking at the media coverage of the Hillside Strangler murders in Los Angeles, analyzing its sensationalism and demeaning accounts of the victims' lives, then offering an alternative in the form of a striking visual event (*In Mourning and in Rage,* see p. 150) and controlling the subsequent media interpretations. The public thus receives, through art, information contrary to that which it sees as "the truth" and receives it in a manner that is sufficiently provocative visually to encourage reconsideration of "the truth." Ariadne's media strategies obviously have limited means at their disposal, but their performances have played to audiences of thousands and have an imaginative impact only professional artists can bring to bear.

The attraction of a collage esthetic is obvious when we realize that most of us, on the most basic level, exist in a downright Surrealist situation.

Consider the position of any artist in a society that perceives art as decoration or status symbol, investment or entertainment.

Consider the position of a visionary artist in a society devoted solely to material well-being.

Consider the position of a person making impermanent objects of no fixed value in a time of inflation and hoarding.

Consider the position of an artist laboring under the delusion that individuality is respected in an age of bland, identical egos and homogenized culture.

Perhaps most Surrealist of all, consider the position of a feminist/socialist/populist artist in a patriarchal capitalist marketplace.

NOW WHAT?

After the pluralism of the '70s, the '80s are going to have to make art that stands out in sharp relief against our society's expectations for art. Artists are just beginning to understand the flood of new mediums available, after a decade of enchantment with their novelty. Comprehension of "the nature of the medium" may sound like an echo of formalist dogma, but if the medium is one whose nature is *communication*—the video, the street performance, posters, comic strips, graffiti, the ecologically functional earthwork, even photography, film and that old but new-for-the visual-artist medium, the book—then such comprehension may have more impact on audience and on art. We are supposed to have grown up absurd already. Yet through the '70s I've asked myself why the hell these new mediums were the vehicle for so little socially concerned art. If there is all this rebelliousness and unease among young artists about how the art world treats art (and there is), why are such appropriately outreaching mediums so little explored and exploited? Why is there such a dearth of meaningful/provocative and/or effective public art? Has distancing gone too far? Have we gotten Carried Away? Space Age objectivity over our heads? Over and out?

I hope we're not just doomed to follow the bouncing ball through endless cycles of romanticism/classicism, subjective/objective, feeling/intellect, etc. If the '60s proved that commitment didn't work, the '70s proved that lack of commitment didn't work either. The '80s decade is coming into a legacy of anxiety, of barely articulated challenges to boringly predictable mainstream art. It is going to have to restore the collective responsibility of the artist and create a new kind of community within, not apart from, the rest of the world. The danger on all esthetic fronts is the kind of factionalism that already divides the politicized minority within the art world. Too many of us spend our time attacking everyone else's attempts at relevance while paranoiacally guarding our own suburban territories. There is an appalling tendency to insist on the need for theoretical understanding of the artist's position in a capitalist society and simultaneously to destroy by "logic" every solution offered. It is all too easy for any intelligent observer to be devastatingly cynical about Marxists making abstractions, artists made vulnerable by working at the same time in communities and in museums, feminists riding the Women's Movement to commercial success and getting off there. The denial of support to an artist or a group who is trying to work out of this dilemma we all share, the kvetching about presentation, form, and motivation when it appears that communication *is* nevertheless taking place—all this merely recapitulates the competition that maintains the Quality-based "high-art" world.

Merely opportunist as some of it may be, art with overtly social content or effect still poses a threat to the status quo. And ironically, no group is so dependent on the status quo as the avant garde, which must have an establishment to attack, reverse, and return to for validation. It is true that most politically aware artists and artworkers would sooner give up politics than give up art. Embedded in the whole question of why more visual artists aren't more committed to combining form and content in more interesting ways is the taboo against "literary" art. Artists emphasizing words and ideas over formal success have been seen since the '60s as traitors to the sacred modernist cause; just as the Dadas and Surrealists are not considered serious contributors to modernism even when their *contributions* are considered serious. This sort of prejudice has been blurred by the mists of pluralism, but it remains as subtle conditioning. Because visual art *is* about *making* things (even if those things have no "pictures"). And this is what visual artists justifiably don't want to give up. In the late '60s we got sidetracked by the object/nonobject controversy. Sheets of paper and videotapes, though cheaper than paintings and sculptures, are still objects. Conceptualism, we know now, is no more *generically* radical than any other ism, but it's no less art.

Another major question we have to ask ourselves as we enter the '80s is: Why is it that culture today is only truly alive for those who make it, or make *something*? Because making Art, or whatever the product is called, is the most satisfying aspect of culture? Its subsequent use or delectation is effective only to the extent that it shares some of that intimacy with its audience? Even as a critic, I find that my own greatest pleasure comes from empathetic or almost kinesthetic insights into how and why a work was made, its *provocative* elements. So the necessary changes must broaden, not merely the audience, but the makers of art (again a fact the feminist art movement has been confronting for some time over the issue of "high," "low," craft and hobby arts). Maybe the ultimate collage is simply the juxtaposition of art and society, artist and audience. Maybe that's what a humanist art is: it comes in all styles and sizes, but it demands response and even imitation. It is alive.

For the vast majority of the audience now, however, culture is something dead. In the '50s the upwardly mobile bourgeois art audience (mostly female) was called the *culture vultures.* They didn't kill art but they eagerly devoured it when they came upon its corpse. As Carl Andre has observed, art is what we do and culture is what is done to us. That fragile lifeline of vitality, the communication to the viewer of the ecstasy of the making process, the motive behind it and reasons for such a commitment, can all too easily be snapped by the circumstances under which most people see art: the stultifying classist atmosphere of most museums and galleries and, in the art world, the personal intimidation resulting from overinflated individual reputations.

What, then, can conscious artists and artworkers do in the coming decade to integrate our goals, to make our political opinions and our destinies fuse with our art? Any new kind of art practice is going to have to take place at least partially outside of the art world. And hard as it is to establish oneself in the art world, less circumscribed territories are all the more fraught with peril. Out there, most artists are neither welcome nor effective, but in here is a potentially suffocating cocoon in which artists are deluded into feeling important for doing only what is expected of them. We continue to talk about "new forms" because the new has been the fertilizing fetish of the avant garde since it detached itself from the infantry. But it may be that these new forms are only to be found buried in social energies not yet recognized as art.

Lucy Lippard is a politically oriented art critic and the author of numerous influential books, including Overlay: Contemporary Art and the Art of Prehistory. *This book explores the conceptual relationships between contemporary concerns in art and some of the earliest forms of art.*

NOTES

1. In conversation with the author. In this and other conversations and writings over the years, Baranik has been a rational/radical voice in my art-and-politics education.
2. ROBERT MOTHERWELL and HAROLD ROSENBERG in *Possibilities,* no. 1 (Winter 1947–1948).
3. AD REINHARDT, *Arts and Architecture* (Jan. 1947). Many of the ideas in this article have their sources in Reinhardt's ideas and personal integrity.
4. IRVING SANDLER, *The Triumph of American Painting* (New York: Praeger, 1970). Max Kozloff, William Hauptman and Eva Cockcroft have illuminated the ways in which Abstract Expressionism was manipulated during the Cold War in *Artforum* (May 1973, Oct. 1973, and June 1974).
5. "Patriarchal Tendencies in the Feminist Art Movement," *The New Art Examiner* (Summer 1977).
6. I don't know who coined the term *retrochic,* but it was used frequently during the controversy over the "Nigger Drawings" show in March–April 1979.
7. DOUGLAS HESSLER, letter to the editor of the *SoHo News* (June 21, 1979) in response to a piece by Shelley Rice (June 7, 1979), which bemoaned the prevalence of "apolitical sophistication."
8. J. HOBERMAN, "No Wavelength: The Para-Punk Underground," *The Village Voice* (May 21, 1979).
9. Quoted in the *New Art Examiner's* special issue on "Sexuality" (Summer 1979).
10. Quoted by Richard Goldstein in *The Village Voice* (July 23, 1979).
11. LAUREN EDMUND, review (in the spirit of) "The Manifesto Show," *East Village Eye* (June 15, 1979).
12. PETER FRANK, "Guerrilla Gallerizing," *The Village Voice* (May 7, 1979), p. 95.
13. "Collage of Indignation" I and II were the titles of two separate antiwar exhibitions in New York, in 1967 and 1970–1971; see p. 29.
14. For more on Ariadne, see *Heresies,* no. 6 (1978), and no. 9 (1980).

5

Towards a Feminist Theory of Art Criticism

Joanna Frueh

Like Marxism and structuralism, which receive due attention, feminism has altered the content and constructs of art history over the past 15 years and continues to do so. However, many art historians, like their compatriots in other academic disciplines, view the adoption of a feminist perspective with suspicion. Simply put, detractors claim that feminist art historians and critics are narrow and self-indulgent and that they distort and polemically misread images and material, thereby undermining art history.

Actually, feminists serve both art and art history: by seeking knowledge about the overlooked meanings of art; by examining our own unacknowledged assumptions and biases and those of previous and contemporary art historians and critics; and by developing ways to write about art that will serve as new models for art critical discourse.

Art history and criticism are frequently divorced: you practice one or the other. Basically, the myth is that art historians aim for objectivity by gathering data that will prove the "truth" about various aspects of an artist's life and career or of a particular period's aesthetic mentality. By keeping their distance, art historians supposedly maintain intellectual neutrality.

Traditionally, art critics, whose function and pleasure is primarily

Reprinted from *Feminist Art Criticism,* copyright © by Arlene Raven, Cassandra L. Langer, and Joanna Ellen Frueh, with permission from UMI Research Press, Ann Arbor, MI.

writing about the art of their own time, also seek "truth." However, many of the best critics have been, and are, highly subjective. For Diderot, the first modern art critic, criticism was an empathetic occupation. In fact, he demanded passion from art so that he could feel it. In 1766 he wrote, "move me, surprise me, rend my heart; make me tremble, weep, shudder, outrage me; delight my eyes afterwards if you can."[1]

Traditional art historical methodology answers certain questions about art: Who made it? When? Where? How? Whys are often unsatisfactorily answered through stylistic analyses or investigations of iconography and patronage.

Whys also demand analyses and interpretations of social and conceptual contexts. Because it involves discernment, criticism is a more inclusive activity than historical study that focuses on the recording, analysis, and interpretation of events. Pursuing old questions in new ways, as feminism does, extends art historical methodology and makes connections between historical context and culture. Such a pursuit turns the historian into a critic.

Feminist art critics join the supposedly incompatible modes of art historical and art critical practice, wedding deep responsiveness to art with factual information, such as biography, sources of an individual artist's work, and stylistic connections with other artists and movements. Many traditionalists find such a marriage wanting in intellectual neutrality, but feminist historian/critics like Arlene Raven believe in intimacy with art. As Raven writes in the first sentence of an essay on Harmony Hammond, "I enter Harmony Hammond's works."[2] Raven is speaking of complete identification: being at one with the art, and through it, the creator, another voman. Thus, subject, Raven, and object, the art works and another human eing, are not detached at all. The object no longer exists. In this kind of riticism, the term art object does not make sense, and a subject to subject elationship replaces the standard subject to object one.

Utter involvement without loss of self is the outcome of this new ritic-to-art connection, which is discourse as intercourse: entry into an-her's body (of art). Feminist criticism of this order belongs to an art iticism of overtly personal engagement, which has waxed and waned in ppeal during the past two centuries. After a period of disfavor, for most of he twentieth century, it is now on the upswing. In a 1979 issue of *Art in nerica,* Nancy Marmer wrote about "the . . . critic's openly subjective nterpretation of art" and stated that "the expressive possibilities of a personalist prose have once again become highly attractive."[3]

Moreover, Marmer noted that "such criticism weaves the fabric of its content out of the critic's subjective, psychological response to the work—thus absorbing the artist into the critic's mental universe."[4] Feminist critics do this and more, for a penetrating study of art, being physical as well as mental, requires that the penetrator, as poet and thinker Robin Morgan has said in *The Anatomy of Freedom,* "feel with the brain and think through the body."[5] Penetration, then, should not be viewed as phallic, an insertion of self into other (subject into object). Rather, penetration may be understood in terms of mutuality, a diffusion of (my)self into (your)self into (my)self. In this way, the study of art becomes even more empathetic than it was for Diderot.

Although it has some exemplary practitioners, such as Carol Duncan, Lucy Lippard, Roszika Parker, Griselda Pollock, and Arlene Raven, feminist art criticism is woefully unevolved. Far more sophisticated than feminist theory and scholarship is feminist literary criticism. Consequently its development in the 1970s and methodology serve as useful models for an understanding of feminist art criticism.

Three "critical" stages exist in recent feminist literary criticism. The first has been a resurrection of lost or ignored women writers and works. Concurrently, feminists in art have been rediscovering women artists and works. H. W. Janson's classic survey text does not mention one woman artist. Therefore, scholars such as Eleanor Tufts, in *Our Hidden Heritage: Five Centuries of Women Artists,* and Linda Nochlin and Ann Sutherland Harris, in *Women Artists 1550–1950,* redress this omission. Also, through such a comparison as Artemisia Gentileschi's and Caravaggio's versions of Judith beheading Holofernes, in which a woman boldly treats the same subject as the man from whom her style of dramatic realism derives, feminist critics can prove that women, unlike what male-engendered myth would have us believe, are fertile and productive in other ways than simply as sexual creatures and mothers.

First-stage scholarship has been important, by showing that women are a part of art history and thereby providing women artists with a sense of belonging. Also, unlike traditional art history, which generally examines "major" monuments by venerated "masters," first-stage feminism shifts the focus of study to "minor" works by artists whose skill has not been deemed consummate. Dealing with "secondary" artists and objects fleshes out the skeletal "truth" of art history, encouraging us to create new bodies of knowledge. Such "bodybuilding" strengthens art history.

Despite the accomplishments of first-stage efforts, they are often reformist rather than truly re-visionist; for they exemplify scholars' interest in new subjects, but with a continuing employment of standard art historical tools. As Roszika Parker and Griselda Pollock write in *Old Mistresses,* the "determination to relocate women in art history on the discipline's own terms" is "subscrib[ing] to a slightly modified, but none the less conventional notion of art history; its system of values and criteria of significance . . . a radical reform, if not a total deconstruction of the present structure of the discipline is needed in order to arrive at a real understanding of the history of women and art."[6]

Second-stage critics have considered the possibility of a women's tradition either counter or related to the male literary tradition. They have examined a "female imagination," their counterparts in art a "female sensibility." When we think of Eva Hesse's and Sol LeWitt's minimalist sculptures, can we say that the pieces reveal the sex of their creators? Is Hesse more involved in a visceral response to materials, indicative of women's perhaps socialized awareness of their bodies, both inside and out? Is LeWitt more concerned with rationalizing the materials, ordering them in an evenly systematic fashion?

These questions and their implicit answers are simplistic. Nonetheless, in the mid-1970s female sensibility was a burning issue, and the following hypothesis, among others, was presented: women's art is obsessive and often characterized by central core imagery. But are Alfred Jensen's works any less obsessive than Joyce Kozloff's? Or are Barnett Newman's voids any less symbolic of a central core (a cunt, a womb) than many of Georgia O'Keeffe's flowers or Judy Chicago's *Dinner Party* plate images?

Despite the superficiality of such hypotheses, they were significant attempts to think about the differences between female and male art. Perhaps Newman sees the central core as a void (as a gross generalization: for the male, the womb is empty, the vagina something to be filled), whereas O'Keeffe and Chicago see the central core as full (for the female, the inside of her body is complete in itself).

Second-stage questioning also revealed the class aspect of art world sexism in the distinction between high (men's) and low (women's) art. Crafts and decorative objects made by women were reconsidered as fine art, proving the absurdity of labeling Mondrian's or Rothko's paintings as high art and, say, a reductively composed and colored Amish quilt as low art, for all are examples of nonobjective design.

However, because the first two existed within the avant-garde, intellectualized framework of modernism and the quilt was created for use in the everyday world, the paintings could be praised for their denial of merely decorative (in other words, frivolous) effects and for their absolute aesthetic integrity. Indeed, it is their "immaculate" conception that assured their value to viewers and critics.

The exposure of classism also opened the way for women and men to make use of pattern and decoration in their art, and Miriam Schapiro's deliberate use of fabric and floral and geometric designs in many works of the late 1970s demonstrates a "low" art, "feminine" aesthetic transferred to a "high" art context; for Schapiro exhibits and is written about in the art world dominated by male-identified authority figures.

Third-stage feminism is more theoretical than the first two and centers on gender analysis of literature or art, and thereby the interconnections among text or object, historical context, and culture. Here, critics reassess the values placed on art in regard to content as well as function. What would previously have been viewed as just "feminine" sentimentality in, for example, the heart motif of some of Schapiro's "femmages," is reinterpreted in several ways: society has relegated women to the degraded sphere of emotion; feeling, however, is powerful and beautiful; sentiment, then, can expose the heart of the matter (of life), which is Love; and Love emerges from and leads to both intellectual and emotional exploration.

Third-stage critics also reappraise men's art, the gender implications of which have been either ignored or considered innocently intentioned because of the creator's supposed pure, serious, commitment to Art. Most art critics and historians, however, fail to discuss the power of images to inform and educate the viewer.

A feminist perspective does not replace traditional art historical methodology. Rather, the new complements and amplifies the old, for fresh analyses and interpretations of style and iconography show that art is not value-free and that previous scholarship has not taken this into consideration.

Feminist art criticism is significant and necessary because it challenges what feminist literary critic Annette Kolodny calls the "dog-eared myth of intellectual neutrality."[7] Such neutrality presupposes the neuter status of the mind; as if gender imbalances did not exist in scholarship. For the most part, male-identified minds study art, and as feminist philosopher Mary Daly understands, the sexist products of such intellects affirm what she terms Methodolatry, which is the worship of method, the devotion and faith in "the rite of right re-search."[8]

I turn again to the model of feminist literary criticism, in Kolodny's article "Dancing through the Minefield: Some Observations on the Theory, Practice and Politics of a Feminist Literary Criticism," for an argument against Methodolatry. Kolodny offers three pertinent propositions. (I have substituted art terms for literary ones): (1) Art history (and with that the historicity of art) is a fiction; (2) insofar as we are taught to see, what we engage are not objects but paradigms; and, finally, (3) that since the grounds upon which we assign aesthetic value to objects are never infallible, unchangeable, or universal, we must reexamine not only our aesthetics but as well, the inherent biases and assumptions informing the critical methods which (in part) shape our aesthetic responses.[9]

Kolodny is proposing what Adrienne Rich calls re-vision; and feminist art critics re-view and re-vise by looking at well-known works in fresh ways and seeing what art historical "authority" has taken for granted or made invisible. Even those mainstays of traditional art history—style, iconography, and patronage—can illuminate a work from a re-visionist perspective.

Embedded in Gustave Courbet's *The Source* (1868), for instance, is the deep-rooted notion that woman is nature. Both the subject—a naked woman at a spring—and the theme—woman as origin of life—are conventional, but Courbet's conflation of woman and nature is unusually deft. A fleshy woman sits by a stream. One hand holds onto a branch, seems almost molded to it, as if she herself were part of the tree; and her contours, from the buttocks up, are eaten by shadows, so that nature absorbs her flesh, is actually one with it. Her lower left leg and right foot are submerged, so that she and the water are also one; more so, because Courbet creates an equivalent sensuousness between her dimpled thighs and the rippling water. Woman and nature literally mirror one another for the material of the female body is the material world.

Not only does this equation cast woman as body, as opposed to man as mind, which, of course, is analogous to culture; but also, because Courbet is a master of making paint read as the texture of whatever it describes, landscape and woman reverberate with one another's physicality. Water feels like flesh, dense, smooth, heavy; and flesh feels like water—surely it would "give" with pressure. Courbet elaborates this bonding in various ways: the spring gushes from the dark vegetation much as the nude emerges from it; the water pours over her left hand, and light dapples skin and liquid; lush greenery reads as a metaphor for the lushness of the body.

All in all, woman symbolizes fecundity and lack of consciousness. But who is this nude? She is the single, anonymous woman who represents all women, not as a social group, but as Woman—Female of the Species in one aspect of the Eternal Feminine: Earth Mother/Mother Earth. This myth of Woman is not necessarily repugnant. However, it is only a fragment of reality, an ideology through which we should not expect to see what any individual woman genuinely is.

Courbet painted *Woman with White Stockings* (1861) for Khalil Bey, a wealthy one-time Ottoman ambassador in St. Petersburg, who settled in Paris. In the painting a seated young woman pulls a stocking over a bare foot balanced on an already stockinged, raised knee. The view, from below, angles up, making her genitals a focal point. Patronage indicates where aesthetic, economic, and political power lies, bluntly, who can "own" people and things. The artist owns the image as a creation, but the buyer owns the art as an object of aesthetic and/or monetary value and the image as an object of desire.

Most likely, Khalil Bey did not want the painting primarily because, as Jack Lindsay writes, "This is a masterpiece in its organization of form, making of the nude a compact unity without parallel."[10] According to Lindsay, Khalil Bey "kept it locked in a sort of tabernacle or cabinet."[11] An image of power resonates: Khalil Bey as purchaser of two "sacred" objects: the painting and the woman, who he "has" (to himself). She, of course, is woman, whose being is locked up in *her* tabernacle, the genitals. Lindsay disengages her from any selfness, for she is only "a brilliantly original piece of patterning, with the body a single solid mass, yet with the limbs clearly articulated in a rhythmic structure balanced on the slit of the genitals."[12] That slit! It is the pivotal point: not only of the composition, but also of the myth that Woman is a cunt and no more.

If feminism is about freedom, then feminist art criticism strives for the accomplishment of mental freedom. I use the word mental rather than intellectual because the latter is generally thought to be the power of rational thought as distinguished from the power to feel or to will, and the former relates to the total emotional and intellectual response of an individual to an environment.

Notions of intellect discount the possibility that knowledge can be gained through the body, the emotions, or wishes. Consequently, intellect, alone, confines the critic by denying not only the usefulness, but also the worth and relevance of his desire to use himself fully. Exclusive emphasis on intellect denies a critic's being, the fact that she lives: on many levels and in many modes, and in an aggregate of social and cultural conditions.

From Duchamp's *Bicycle Wheel* to John's *Painted Bronze (Beer Cans)* to Chicago's *Menstruation Bathroom,* modern and contemporary art have dealt with, to paraphrase Robert Rauschenberg, the gap between art and life. The interplay between the two, demanded by their disparity, involves the feminist critic as much as the artist. It is as a participant in this interplay that she can truly penetrate the art and it her, that she can know it as subject.

I imagined someone writing me a letter after reading a recently published article of mine. "Joanna, your ideas are interesting, and you state them with some passion, but why is the structure so tight, the style so dry? I'm familiar with your criticism, and I've seen it be personal and engaging. I would like more of you and less of the objective observer."

I reply.

Thanks. You caught me in an act of validation through conventional logic. Not long ago, some keepers of the art wor(l)d told me that my thinking was disorganized, my writing pointless. I was hurt and angry. I loved my vagrant mind; but I needed to prove that I could think in a "professional" mode.

I confess, I dislike the airtight cases that the scholar wants to build. They do not let me breathe. Most art history and criticism coming from a so-called feminist perspective are conventionally academic and uninspiring. Inspire derives from the Latin *inspirirare,* to breathe, which is akin to *spiritus,* breath, from which the English "spirit" comes. I've wondered, where's the spirited criticism I expect from feminists in art? Why haven't they incorporated (given body through language to) the work of women who have been joining feminist theory and practice in their writing?

One of the answers is that feminists in art, like feminists in other fields, want to be acceptable. Their choice of scholarly argument says so. "Prove it," demands the logocentric system that the art historian worships. "Prove that you still love me." As writer Marguerite Duras says, "There are many women who write as they think they should write—to imitate men and make a place for themselves in literature."[13] Or art criticism.

So some feminists become feminist thinker Mary Daly's Methodo-

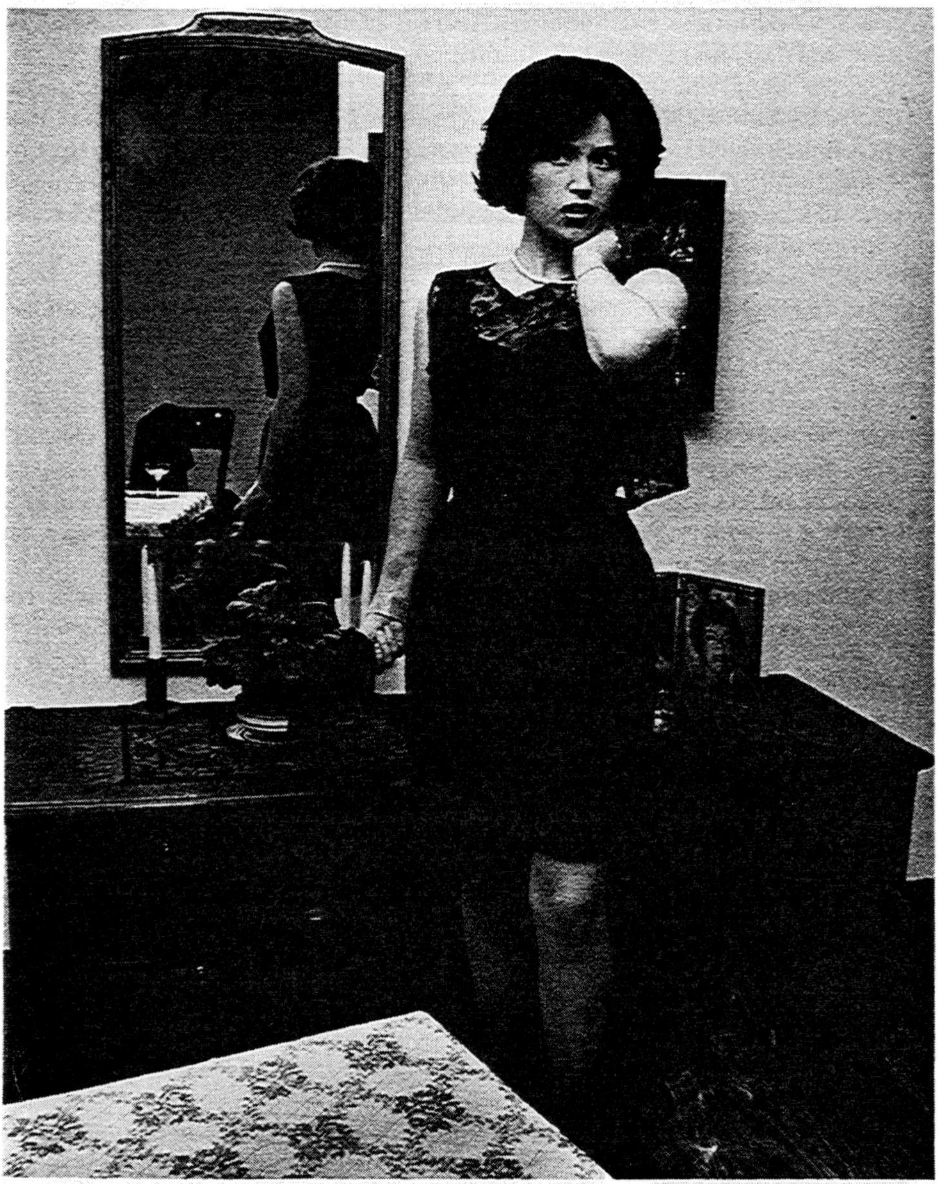

Cindy Sherman, *Untitled Film Still*, 1978, black and white photograph. *Courtesy of Metero Pictures.*

laters, worshipping methodology, fearful of being wrong, of believing in false idols, or, more likely, of desiring no idols at all.

My imagined letter writer has accused me of what French feminist Chantal Chawaf calls "fleshless academicism."[14] However, I am an iconoclast, and, as novelist Monique Wittig writes in *The Lesbian Body,* "m/y heart is in m/y mouth."[15] So I will feel my way through this paper, as I give voice to a body inseparable from a mind. The pulse will be a chorus of possibilities, not a drone of proofs.

> The frightful masculine fashion of speaking always surprises me. Speaking in order to be right—how ridiculous! In fact, to put someone else in the wrong. Speaking to nail the listener's trap shut.
>
> *Xavière Gauthier*[16]

A fellow art historian advised me that revisionists in our field want to convince others of rightness. Daly's "rite of right re-search" came to mind: knowing is being right. I was not interested in this kind of persuasion, an intellectual erection.

An ideal structure for presenting knowledge resembles bricks cemented, row after row, higher and higher. We think this edifice (for edification) has a firm foundation, that it's built to last. Higher and higher, thrusting into the sky, Tower of Babel, ivory towers of babble.

Castles in the air, imagined by minds whose dreams have come true.

> I know I am made from this earth, as my mother's hands were made from this earth, as her dreams came from this earth and all that I know, I know in this earth, the body of the bird, this pen, this paper, these hands, this tongue speaking, all that I know speaks to me through this earth. . . .
>
> *Susan Griffin*[17]

Griffin uses a way of knowing that differs from my colleague who believes that to convince is to arm yourself with reason(s), so that you can win some battle. Knowing-as-defense is a weapon. For Griffin, however, knowing is being, and it exists on and in solid ground, the earth itself, which she equates with the body. Both are matter.

Art criticism, like other disciplines that privilege the intellect, is generally deprived of the spontaneous knowing of intuition—of knowledge derived from the senses, and experience as well as the mind. Nerves connect throughout the body, conduct sensations, bits of knowledge to the brain. Blood pumping to and from the heart flows everywhere inside us. Knowing is being alive, wholly, not just intellectually. It is a recognition of human being, the intelligence of the body. The intellectual may feel enslaved in matter. If only she could escape from the body. But the mind will not fly unless we embrace the body as a path to freedom.

And we learn . . .
that our speech is unholy.

Susan Griffin[18]

"And the Word was made flesh, and dwelt among us. . . ."

God embodied his mind and will in Christ. The Father and Son are holy (words), the Son is a sacred body, of words, a sacred text.

What about mother and daughter? They remain cunts, idolized and idealized, yet unholy holes. The phallic tongue has penetrated the silent vault of the mouth, and many feminists have discussed the idea that women are linguistically colonized. There is no Mother Tongue, only the Word(s) of the Father.

As art critics, we have lost our tongues when we write jargon, words such as great, master, and genius that carry much weight but are simultaneously meaningless through overuse. They have become generic art words, interchangeable and indistinguishable from one another. The solution is not devising some means through which we can give the Word. Rather, a solution is to pass the word that the art gospel need not exist.

Once a woman owns her body, she will speak a different language. When the organ in her mouth belongs to her, we will know that all tongues, all words are flesh.

> Isn't the final goal of writing to articulate the body? For me the sensual juxtaposition of words has one function: to liberate a living paste, to liberate matter. Language through writing has moved away from its original sources: the body and the earth. Too often GOD was written instead of LIFE.

Chantal Chawaf[19]

One of the GODS that has taken the LIFE out of writing is logocentrism. The point is not to set up a countersystem, say, somacentrism, but rather, to pursue the difficult task of inventing, in Hélène Cixous's words "another thinking as yet not thinkable."[20]

> Woman's desire most likely does not speak the same language as man's desire, and it probably has been covered over by the logic that has dominated the West since the Greeks. . . . In this logic, the prevalence of the gaze, discrimination of form, and individualization of form is particularly foreign to female eroticism.

Luce Irigaray[21]

The penis stands out, the vagina does not. The first is proof, the second possibility. Logically, then, that which is evident can be used as evidence of reality. Art historians rely on documents, formalists on what they see; the connoisseur's discriminating eye is valued; and the monograph on a single artist, that individuates him or her from others stylistically, is a standard art historical product. However, that which is "invisible" is unsightly, and for an art critic to write about his feelings or an artist's or about sexual content (when it is not apparent or documented) is suspect.

According to Irigaray and others, language—for the art critic, the way he as the viewer handles the viewed, the way viewer and viewed may unite—bears a strong relationship to erotic impulse. Writing as process and text is pleasure, running the gamut from seduction to orgasm, rather than being persuasion, convincing. Fascinating . . . convince derives from the Latin *convincere,* to conquer. Feminist discourse is not involved in gaining power over others. Rather it is an empowering process, of (be)coming.

> Thought has always worked by opposition,
> Speech/Writing
> High/Low . . .
> And all the couples of oppositions are *couples.* Does this mean something? Is the fact that logocentrism subjects thought—all of the concepts, the codes, the values—to a two-term system, related to "the" couple man/woman?
>
> *Hélène Cixous*[22]

The two-term system is nonprocess oriented, for in it, everything is taken care of. The opposition(s) are in constant struggle, but the conflict is nonetheless always resolved. We have good and bad painting, major and minor works. The battle of the sexes, the battle between the geniuses and the mediocrities. The two-term system, in which one term is usually "better" than the other, promotes hierarchy and conflict while simultaneously keeping the latter in check.

From now on, if anyone asks me why feminists point out the differences between women and men, I will tell her about the two-term system, whose falsifications have already polluted our minds. Feminists try to find a way out of the bind by distinguishing its parts, not be stiffening them further. In Monique Wittig's words, "[M]ay you lose the sense of morning and evening of the stupid duality that flows therefrom."[23]

> Her language does not contain, it carries; it does not hold back, it makes possible.
>
> *Hélène Cixous*[24]

System and hierarchy. They withhold (information). Everything in its place. Discuss an artist's work chronologically. Picasso was more influential than Braque. "Straight" thinking.

Feminist thinking is the curves, bends, angles, and irregularities of thought, departures from prescribed patterns of art historical logic. To be "straight" is to be upright-erect-phallic-virtuous-heterosexual, but feminists turn away from the straight and narrow. Deviants without their heads on straight.

Logocentrism produces closure, tight arguments. It sews up the fabric(ations) of discourse.

Feminists with loose tongues embroider, patch new and worn pieces together, re-fabricate.

> Their distinguishing feature is one of contiguity. They touch (*upon*).
>
> *Luce Irigaray*[25]

Irigaray notes the contiguity of female genitalia and connects it with the contiguity of a woman's language. It comes from feeling as well as thinking and treats its subjects accordingly. It moves from point to point without the rigor (mortis) of logocentric discourse. (Academics praise intellectual rigor.)

Contiguity allows for fragmented structure(lessness), abhorrent to users of logocentric systems. Structure(lessness) may seem to some like nonsense, but it is a new sense; coming to one's senses.

Xavière Gauthier says that "we can *make audible* that which agitates within us, suffers silently in the *holes of discourse*, in the unsaid, or in the non-sense."[26] The holes of discourse are not, as I see it, just a vaginal language of some sort, but rather the voids left by the "sensible" systems of logocentrism, which, according to many feminists, is a product of phallocentrism. A new language of the body will fill in the blanks, do away with the blankness and blandness of logo/phallocentric lingo. Contiguous fragments of discourse form a whole that does not describe or explain, but that is natural, like the earth, like the body.

> The women say that they perceive their bodies in their entirety. They say that they do not favour any of its parts on the grounds that it was formerly a forbidden object. They say that they do not want to become prisoners of their ideology.
>
> *Monique Wittig*[27]

In *The Lesbian Body* Wittig brings the female body back from the dead. The point of focusing on the body, and all of its parts, is to reclaim the whole of a lost and defiled home(land).

> A woman without a body, dumb, blind, can't possibly be a good fighter.
>
> *Hélène Cixous*[28]

Possessing the body empowers us with new sight, speech, and hearing. Moreover, self-possession helps us to shoulder responsibility, stomach criticism, stand on our own two feet, head into the fray.

They say, let those who call for a new language first learn violence.

Monique Wittig[29]

It is necessary to violate the status quo if change is to occur. Challenging language radicalizes thought. Threatening style and structure disrupt outworn ideologies.

So take the blade of your intelligence, and bleed away the lie. Begin with the body.

A gash is a long, deep cut and a slit is a long, narrow one. In slang, you are a gash and a slit because you have a labia and a vagina. Slang suggests that you belong to the walking wounded and that you have been mutilated or punished.

One derivation of gash is the Greek *charassein,*

to sharpen (a gash has wit),
to cut into furrows (a gash knows how to plant her seed),
to engrave (a gash will make the mark she chooses),
to carve (a gash shapes the world).

One derivation of slit is the Lithuanian *skelti,*

to split (a slit breaks the bonds of conventional discourse).

Yoko Ono gave John Lennon a knife to cut away his troubles.

A knife, or athame, is a witch's tool.
Practice magic.

Cut their arguments. Make them so thin that they fade away.

Cut it out. You are the surgeon removing the diseased organs. You are the healer who tells the patient to stop poisoning himself.

You are a cut-up. Enjoy your unruliness.
Cut a swathe. We want to see and hear you.

In fact, why don't you bite, rip, and snarl? Why are you so nice?

Nice derives from the Latin *nescire,* not to know. Choosing to be ignorant is choosing to be nicey-nicey.

The opposite of a nicey-nicey is a bitch, who does bite (take hold of an issue), rip (attack a problem without delay), and snarl (use threatening language).

They say that they foster disorder in all its forms. Confusion troubles violent debates disarray upsets disturbances incoherences irregularities divergences complications disagreements discords clashes polemics discussions contentions brawls disputes conflicts routs débâcles cataclysms disturbances quarrels agitation turbulence conflagrations chaos anarchy.

Monique Wittig[30]

Rupture to achieve rapture.

I drift, I dream, I rave, I lust.

Xavière Gauthier[31]

Gauthier's statement gives an idea of how free writing can be. The self is present, as personality. In logocentrism the I, as excited dreamer, mental vagrant, manic sensualist, is absent. The free writing of feminist criticism is a relationship *with,* not *to,* art. Being with art is like being with a lover, for bodies and minds are pleasurably and demandingly engaged. For the critic Stendhal, the pursuit of both art and love was an ideal, not be to taken on by "moderately passionate people."[32] The feminist art critic assumes the challenge, but in unabashedly showing that she is an "art lover," she risks the charge of intellectual promiscuity; because she supposedly mixes methodologies, ways of writing, and body and mind indiscriminately. Such promiscuity, however, is the mental freedom whose ultimate aim is freedom itself. That goal is so subtle and dramatic, and we are so unfree, that we can barely imagine what freedom is. And yet . . . feminist art criticism is one way to invent that future.

They say, If I take over the world, let it be to dispossess myself of it immediately, let it be to forge new links between myself and the world.

Monique Wittig[33]

Joanna Frueh is an art historian and critic specializing in Feminist issues. In 1988 she co-edited Feminist Art Criticism, *an anthology of essays published by UMI Research Press, Ann Arbor, Michigan.*

NOTES

1. Denis Diderot, quoted in Anita Brookner, *The Genius of the Future: Studies in French Art Criticism; Diderot, Stendhal, Baudelaire, Zola, the Brothers Goncourt, Huysmans* (London: Phaidon, 1971), 21.
2. Arlene Raven, "Harmonies: An Essay on the Work of Harmony Hammond" (Chicago: Klein Gallery, 1982), 1.
3. Nancy Marmer, "The Performing Critic," *Art in American* 67.8 (December 1979): 71.
4. Ibid., 71.
5. Robin Morgan, *The Anatomy of Freedom: Feminism, Physics, and Global Politics* (Garden City: Anchor/Doubleday, 1982), 247.

6. ROSZIKA PARKER and GRISELDA POLLOCK, *Old Mistresses: Women, Art and Ideology* (New York: Pantheon, 1981), 46, 47–48.
7. ANNETTE KOLODNY, "Dancing through the Minefield: Some Observations on the Theory and Practice of a Feminist Literary Criticism," *Feminist Studies* 6.1 (Spring 1980): 21.
8. MARY DALY, *Beyond God the Father: Toward a Philosophy of Women's Liberation* (Boston: Beacon, 1973), 11; and Mary Daly, *Gyn/Ecology: The Metaethics of Radical Feminism* (Boston: Beacon, 1978), 23.
9. KOLODNY, 8.
10. JACK LINDSAY, *Gustave Courbet: His Life and Art* (New York: Harper & Row, 1973), 217.
11. Ibid., 217.
12. Ibid., 217.
13. MARGUERITE DURAS, "From an Interview," trans. Susan Husserl-Kapit, *New French Feminisms,* ed. Elaine Marks and Isabelle de Courtivron (New York: Schocken, 1981), 174.
14. CHANTAL CHAWAF, "Linguistic Flesh," trans. Yvonne Rochette-Ozzello, Marks and de Courtivron, 178.
15. MONIQUE WITTIG, *The Lesbian Body,* trans. David Le Vay (New York: Avon, 1976), 35.
16. XAVIÈRE GAUTHIER, "Why Witches?," trans. Erica M. Eisinger, Marks and de Courtivron, 200.
17. SUSAN GRIFFIN, *Woman and Nature: The Roaring Inside Her* (New York: Harper & Row, 1978), 227.
18. Ibid., 19.
19. CHAWAF, 177.
20. HÉLÈNE CIXOUS, "Sorties," trans. Ann Liddle, Marks and de Courtivron, 93.
21. LUCE IRIGARAY, "This Sex Which Is Not One," trans. Claudia Reeder, Marks and de Courtivron, 101.
22. CIXOUS, "Sorties," 90, 91.
23. WITTIG, *The Lesbian Body,* 143.
24. HÉLÈNE CIXOUS, "The Laugh of the Medusa," trans. Keith Cohen and Paula Cohen, Marks and de Courtivron, 260.
25. IRIGARAY, 103.
26. XAVIÈRE GAUTHIER, "Is There Such a Thing as Women's Writing?" trans. Marilyn A. August, Marks and de Courtivron, 163.
27. MONIQUE WITTIG, *Les Guérrillères,* trans. David Le Vay (New York: Avon, 1973), 57.
28. CIXOUS, "The Laugh of the Medusa," 250.
29. WITTIG, *Les Guérrillères,* 85.
30. Ibid., 93.
31. GAUTHIER, "Why Witches?," 203.
32. Quoted in Brookner, 54.
33. WITTIG, *Les Guérrillères,* 107.

6

Second-Generation Art Criticism and Methodology

Thalia Gouma-Peterson &
Patricia Mathews

A more consistently radical critique of traditional methodologies exists among second-generation feminist art critics than among art historians. Critics have been quick to adopt new approaches. This may be the result of the lack of a strong tradition in art criticism that would foster integration of new ideas rather than a radical appropriation of a totally new methodology. In art history, such traditions sometimes result in a resistance to new ideas. In feminist literary theory and criticism, on the other hand, the reception of deconstructive and psychoanalytic methodologies has been tempered by their preexisting tradition and thus more fully incorporated into earlier studies of female experience and sensibility in literature.

Two basic positions coexist in feminist art criticism today, each with a number of variations. One has existed from the beginning of the women's movement in art, while the other is not yet a decade old. The transformations in both critical and artistic concerns between first- and second-generation feminism are not necessarily to be distinguished qualitatively.

These two positions in other disciplines are described in the anthology,

Reprinted from the *Art Bulletin,* vol. LXIX, no. 3, by permission of the College of Art Administration, Inc. This section is excerpted from a much longer article titled "The Feminist Critique of Art History."

The Future of Difference: "early states of feminist thought" emphasized the "condition and experience of being female," and attempted to "diminish and minimize the importance of differences" because "difference from men meant inequality and continued oppression." Women thus "set out to document the worlds of women" and their experience, previously excluded from analysis. The "shift in emphasis" for second-generation feminists has been not to "minimize difference" but to "assert its importance as a crucial focus of study.[1]

Lippard designates the polarities in these positions in art as cultural versus socialist feminism.[2] The terms are articulated through the notions of the category "Woman." The first position, sometimes termed essentialist, conceives of woman as a fixed category determined through societal and cultural institutions, and less often through the concept of an inherent and biological female nature. Its advocates often attempt to characterize or celebrate specifically female attributes, within a separatist mode, or to reveal the history and the nature of the repressions of woman within those categories. The second sees woman as an unfixed category, constantly in process, examined through her representations and ideological constructions within a male system. Rather than a definition of gender per se, of woman, the issue becomes, as Tickner puts it, "the problematic of culture itself, in which definitions of femininity are produced and contested and in which cultural practices cannot be derived from or mapped directly onto a biological gender." Second-generation artists and critics are concerned rather with "an interrogation of an unfixed femininity produced in *specific systems of signification.*" The work of such artists as Mary Kelly, Yve Lomax, and Marie Yates, which Tickner discusses in her article for the exhibition "Difference: On Representation and Sexuality" at the New Museum of Contemporary Art in New York (1985), are concerned, as she says, with "sexuality in process which Luce Irigaray described as 'woman as the not-yet'—a continued countering of cultural hegemony in its ceaseless and otherwise unquestioned production of meanings and of subject positions for those meanings."

> The most important contribution of the feminism under consideration here is the recognition of the relations between representation and sexed subjectivity *in process,* and of the need to intervene productively within them. The artists considered here hold the common aim of "unfixing" the feminine, unmasking the relations of specularity that determine its appearance in representation, and undoing its position as a "marked term" which ensures the category of the masculine as something central and secure.

Tickner links the development of the later position to the understanding of the "psycho-social construction of sexual difference."

> The result was a shift in emphasis from equal rights struggles in the sexual division of labor and a cultural feminism founded on the revaluation of an

> existing biological or social femininity to a recognition of the processes of sexual *differentiation,* the instability of gender positions, and the hopelessness of excavating a free or original femininity beneath the layers of patriarchal oppression.[3]

Exemplifying these two positions, *The Post-Partum Document, 1973–79* by Mary Kelly, an American artist living in London, might profitably be compared to Judy Chicago's *Birth Project,* 1985, since both are concerned with the female experience of giving birth and child-rearing. Beyond the obvious differences of emphasis, one on birth and the other on the mother/child relationship, the two approach their subjects from totally opposite viewpoints. Kelly's work is theoretical and ideologically oriented, based on the concept of a socially constructed motherhood and including a psychoanalytic perspective, while Chicago's is mythical, historical, and experiential, based on a celebration of the female.[4]

A debate concerning methodology has recently erupted in art-critical circles between these two groups, which further illustrates their different positions. Unfortunately, it has been antagonistically conceived and simplistically distorted from both sides. Deborah Cherry, clearly a second-generation feminist, in her review of Pollock and Parker's *Old Mistresses,* counsels against "perpetuating unificatory stereotypes" such as the "isolated, frozen category" of "Woman."[5] She further pushes first-generation feminists into a biologically deterministic camp, which they by no means all occupy, by defining sex as a reference to biological differences and gender as a matter of culture, and by assuming that all artists and critics who are not concerned with "gender" adhere to an essentialist, unchanging view of woman throughout history. On the contrary, although first-generation feminists often investigate specific traits that belong to the female, such traits are generally seen as culturally determined and changing through history as those determinants change. This group of feminists looks at both the continuities and the changes, through the "fixed *signs* of femininity," as in work such as Chicago's *Dinner Party,* whose "political/aesthetic strategy" is based "on the same terms in which 'difference' has already been laid down." Second-generation feminists seek to "unfix" the feminine rather than reveal its determinants based in male institutions and structures.[6]

Concerns of first-generation feminist artists have been more specifically criticized by the filmmaker and film critic Jane Weinstock. She characterizes much first-generation feminist art, in particular that of Nancy Spero, as the "celebration of Otherness." Like many other Postmodern feminists, she disdains the "celebration of difference" and the "myth of Otherness," and prefers artists who, she says, "expose myths rather than create them," such as Ilona Granet, Jenny Holzer, Mary Kelly, and Barbara Kruger.[7] Those artists analyze "how meaning is produced and organized" and therefore undermine "the structures of domination."[8] This attitude expresses the shift that has occurred in feminist art and criticism over the last decade.

Nancy Spero responds to this criticism[9] by citing Simone de Beauvoir: "Otherness is a fundamental category of human thought. . . . If the woman question seems trivial, it is because masculine arrogance has made of it a 'quarrel'" (*The Second Sex*). Spero condemns this second generation of feminist criticism as it is manifested in Weinstock's article as "a new wave of phallocentrism, under the guise of 'difference.'" She aggressively defends the legitimacy of art such as her own "*Let the Priests tremble* . . ." as a "new representation on the subject of sexuality, on being female," and she insinuates that the alternative chosen by Weinstock and others amounts only to "playing pet or merely 'subversive' to male symmetries and privilege." She cites Hélène Cixous to support her interest in female sexuality as opposed to male, just as Weinstock cited the same writer to refute "traditional male/female opposition" as she sees it in the art of Spero.[10]

Weinstock's response to Spero's letter is to question what she calls Spero's "search for a female essence," once again distorting the notion of representation of sexuality into essentialism. Many feminists of Spero's camp consider that very sexuality to be socially constructed. The difference between Spero and Weinstock, as representatives of the two concomitant phases of feminist thought on art, reduces to the difference between the understanding of the female as somehow existent, fixed, and thus excavatable, at least within a moment in history, synchronically, and the alternative investigation of the unstable process of gender construction. Although sexuality may not exist except as a construction, women do have common shared experiences, and the constructs of gender themselves result from repeated experiences, whether one takes Spero's view of sexuality or Mary Kelly's. Spero grounds her work in the condition of being female, in what woman is in relation to herself, and to other women, while Kelly considers how that self is constructed in relation to social, ideological, and psychological structures. Spero wants to take a moment of that fixed position and examine and/or celebrate it; Weinstock and others want to unfix the position entirely. They are mutually exclusive concepts, yet both are operable. The level at which constructions are encoded is the level of common, shared experiences. One reveals the continuities between, the other exposes the discontinuities and disjunctions within.

Tickner does not see the two generations in such negative, dichotomous terms. Not only has she written some of the most trenchant and penetrating analyses of second-generation concerns, but she is also sympathetic to first-generation feminist art as an ongoing project, as can be seen in her recent article on Nancy Spero. Tickner disagrees with Weinstock that Spero is celebrating "difference," and claims instead that her intent is to create "la peinture féminine" related to "l'écriture féminine" of which the French feminist theorists speak.[11] In her article, Tickner offers not only a substantial model of scholarship and methodology for feminist criticism, but she also rescues first-generation art from exile and re-establishes it as a viable enterprise.

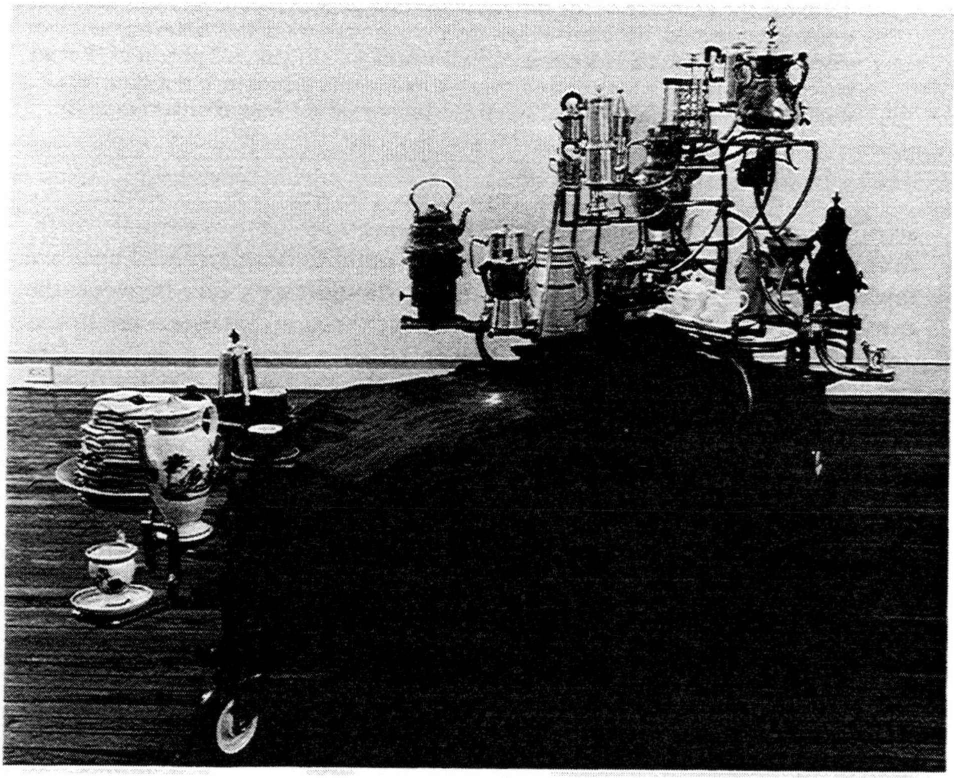

Joel Otterson, *The Coffeetable Museum*, 1989, Mixed Media. *Courtesy of Jay Gorney Modern Art, N.Y.*

Lippard also has refused to give up the one position in her move towards the more deconstructive one. In the debate between "socialist feminism and radical or cultural feminism," she takes both sides. She included both Mary Kelly and Nancy Spero in her exhibition in London at the Institute of Contemporary Arts (1980), "Issue: Social Strategies by Women Artists." Lippard observes:

> Some of the artists in "Issue" . . . refuse to separate their social activism and their involvement in the myths and energies of women's distant histories and earth connections
>
> It seems to me that to reject all of these aspects of women's experience as dangerous stereotypes often means simultaneous rejection of some of the more valuable aspects of our female identities. Though used against us now, their final disappearance would serve the dominant culture all too well.[12]

Griselda Pollock also assumes a more encompassing perspective:

> To avoid the embrace of the feminine stereotype which homogenizes women's work determined by natural gender, we must stress the heterogeneity of women's art work, the specificity of individual producers and products. Yet we have to recognize what women share—as a result of nurture not nature, i.e., the historically variable social systems which produce sexual differentiation.[13]

This exchange effectively represents the different ideological positions of the two feminist groups. Both positions have potential worth, despite the fact that it is in the nature of the committed to deny it. (The move toward revisionist psychoanalytic feminist thought as a link between the constructed self and the constructed category "Woman" makes sense in this impasse.) The recent art of May Stevens, for example, has managed to negotiate both positions, through her Postmodern vocabulary of disjunction and fragment, which both critiques patriarchal institutions and addresses specifically female concerns.[14] Weinstock's accusation that Cherry's definition of "sex" difference is *only* biological, that it posits a "female essence," and many other such implications in recent feminist literature are in danger of simplistically "colonizing" first-generation feminism into an essentialist camp. Such categorical closure is certainly in opposition to the proclaimed aims of a dismantling and deconstructing Postmodern feminism.[15]

Contemporary art critics among this second generation bring a feminist perspective to their use of new Postmodern methodologies of poststructuralism, semiotics, and psychoanalytic criticism. Such critics are growing in number and include Craig Owens, particularly with his essay, "The Discourse of Others: Feminists and Postmodernism,"[16] and a number of women, often artist themselves, such as Martha Rosler, Silvia Kolbowski, Jane Weinstock, Kate Linker, Tickner, and Abigail Solomon-Godeau, among many others. Feminist Postmodern criticism has even entered the mainstream art magazines, although it is still under-represented.[17] Such criticism generally deals with a particular artistic content that, not surprisingly, is concerned with political, Postmodern theoretical issues, such as political deconstructive tactics, or psychoanalytically structured works that are concerned with desire, and the way women are imaged and ideologically constructed. Such art is quite prevalent and growing at a rapid pace, as is its criticism. The situation at the moment seems to favor the new methodological criticism and thus the art it supports, while leaving a whole range of art by active first-generation feminist artists working in a different though still important arena of feminism without enough solid criticism. It thus falls on critics who, from the beginning, dealt with women's art in its social contexts to carry the entire burden of all other criticism of women's art.

The exhibition at the New Museum of Contemporary Art in New York, "Difference: On Representation and Sexuality," exemplifies many of the new tendencies in methodology and art. Since it was curated by both an art critic, Kate Linker, and a film critic, Jane Weinstock, it included film and video along with more "traditional" art; such a breakdown of categories is characteristic of current tendencies. Through both the art works and the catalogue, the exhibition represented poststructuralist, psychoanalytically informed thinking on both art and film.[18] Catalogue essays were written by members of the same "radical establishment," including Owens and Tickner. As its title asserts, the exhibition was concerned with sexuality and representation, emphasizing the female gender. The show was composed mostly of feminist artists and critics, including deconstructionist artists such as Barbara Kruger, Martha Rosler, Sherrie Levine, Silvia Kolbowski, and Hans Haacke from America, and Mary Kelly, Yve Lomax, Marie Yates, and Victor Burgin, residents of Great Britain. Typical of the new methodological focus of feminism on difference and gender rather than the female *per se,* the exhibition was not separatist. Not only were both male artists and critics represented, but Tickner, among others, brought a discussion of male sexuality into her feminist discourse on representation and sexuality.[19]

Despite its rising influence, a critique of these new methodologies in relation to feminism has been undertaken, although it is still inadequately developed. In his assessment of them, Owens first noted a point of conjunction between "the feminist critique of patriarchy and the postmodernist critique of representation," that in both reject a totalizing theoretical construct. However, as Owens observed, it is not "theory *per se* that women repudiate, nor simply, as Lyotard has suggested, the priority men have granted to it. . . . Rather . . ., they challenge . . . the distance it maintains between itself and its objects—a distance that objectifies and masters." Indeed, Postmodern and poststructuralist methodologies often refer to feminism and the female in their rejection of an authoritarian discourse of mastery. Despite the importance of the "feminist voice" as a model for breaking down a discourse of mastery in Postmodern culture, theories of it have "tended either to neglect or to repress that voice," as Owens said. He suggested, therefore, that "Postmodernism may be another masculine invention engineered to exclude women."[20]

Tickner questions the very use of "feminine metaphors" to refer to the Postmodern refusal of authority and "master discourses" by writers such as Jameson and Derrida. She asks if this is not just another cliché of the female.

> Are these intellectual abdications on one level the flirtation of male philosophers with the place of the Other . . . ? . . . Is the embrace of the feminine a fashionable flirtation which avoids the consequences of psychoanalytic and feminist theories of subjectivity for men? . . . When the masters who are demonstrating their ultimate mastery by refusing the discourse of mastery . . . make fashionable reference to feminism it remains a *lumpen* category without reference to names, dates or texts to be argued with.[21]

In such discourse, there is the danger that women will once again be positioned as the weaker, essentialist voice of "nature" and "experience" in opposition to culture, theory, and intellect.

In spite of such dangers, the feminist Postmodern engagement with theory has been quite rich and fruitful. If, as Tickner believes, "feminism is a politics, not a methodology,"[22] it is legitimate to utilize and transform whatever methodological tools are available, including "male" theory. Unfortunately, such feminist, Postmodern positioning can often take the form of authoritarianism itself.

Thalia Gouma-Peterson is active in two scholarly fields: Byzantine icons and frescos, and contemporary art. Currently she teaches in the Department of Art, the College of Wooster, OH.

Patricia Mathews studies the relationships between art, theory, and criticism. She is on the faculty of Oberlin College and has written criticism on artists May Stevens and Joyce Kozloff.

NOTES

1. See Hester Eisenstein, "Introduction," *The Future of Difference,* ed. Hester Eisenstein and Alice Jardine, New Brunswick, NJ, xvi–xviii.
2. LUCY LIPPARD, "Issue and Taboo," *Get the Message?* (as in n. 31), 147; also see Tickner, "Sexuality" (as in n. 67), 19, 28–29; the debate between Spero and Weinstock discussed below; and Elaine Showalter, "Feminist Criticism in the Wilderness," *The New Feminist Criticism* (as in n. 59), 255. She notes that these different approaches produce "the tensions in the women's movement." Showalter describes two similar groups of feminists in the women's movement generally: "Those who would stay outside the academic establishments and the institutions of criticism and those who would enter and even conquer them."
3. TICKNER, "Sexuality and/in Representation: Five British Artists," 28, 19.
4. These differences also relate to the difference between British and American feminism. In fact, both British and French thought has had an enormous influence on the second group of American feminists (see the discussion below).
5. CHERRY (as in n. 19), 502, citing Sheila Rowbotham. Cherry also points to the "appropriation" of psychoanalytic theory by feminists, especially of the French psychoanalyst Jacques Lacan, in order to "understand how femininity is socially constructed." For feminist interpretations of psychoanalytic theory, see Juliet Mitchell, *Psychoanalysis and Feminism,* New York, 1974; Juliet Mitchell and Jacqueline Rose, eds., *Feminine Sexuality: Jacques Lacan and the école freudienne,* London, 1982; and Jane Gallop, *The Daughter's Seduction, Feminism and Psychoanalysis,* Ithaca, 1982. Also see Jane Gallop, "Psychoanalytic Criticism: Some Intimate Questions," *Art in America,* Nov., 1984, 9–15.

   For a similar debate with a different slant, see Carol Ockman's response (*Art in America,* Dec., 1986, 11) to Anne M. Wagner's review of *The Female Body in Western Culture: Contemporary Perspectives.* ed. Susan Rubin Suleiman (*Art in America,* Oct., 1986, 17, 19), and Wagner's reply, 11, 13.

   Lucy Lippard, too, moved away from a biological investigation of female sensibility in her later work. She says in the catalogue essay, "Issue and Taboo" (in *Get the Message?*, as in n. 31), 125–26, that "I still hold the opinion that women's art differs from that of men, but I have moved away from my earlier attempt to analyze these differences in formal terms alone."

6. TICKNER, "Sexuality" (as in n. 3), 29. The legitimation of craft through its integration into "high" art as the celebration of the female sensibility might also be seen as concerned with the "fixed" signs of the feminine. Such celebration has been called "the singing of the slaves." However, it is important to note that oppressed peoples, and "outsiders" generally, have a special vantage point that makes their voices worth hearing.
7. JANE WEINSTOCK, "A Lass, A Laugh and a Lad," *Art in America*, Summer, 1983, 7–10.
8. Cited by Weinstock, *ibid.*, 8, from Jo-Anna Isaak's essay on the exhibition, "The Revolutionary Power of Women's Laughter," at Protetch McNeil Gallery, New York, 1983. Weinstock's essay is a critique of the exhibition. Citing Lyotard in support of her statement, Weinstock says that the "Goddess" and the "Body," both exalted by many feminist artists, "have become victims of the capital letter" (p. 7). In opposition to Weinstock, Donald Kuspit claims that Spero "demythologizes" woman as passive victim, rather than creating myths. See his essay, "Symptoms of Critique: Nancy Spero and Francesc Torres," *Art and Ideology*, exh. cat., The New Museum of Contemporary Art, New York, 1984, 21–22.
9. In a letter to *Art in America*, Nov., 1983, 7.
10. WEINSTOCK (as in n. 170), 7.
11. TICKNER, "Nancy Spero: Images and *la peinture féminine*" (in press). Her art-historical work also employs new methodologies in its attempt to situate women within their own space. See her work on the suffragists (also in press).
12. "Issue and Taboo" (in *Get the Message?*, as in n. 31), 147.
13. GRISELDA POLLOCK, "Modernity and the Spaces of Femininity," was presented at the meetings of the British Association of Art Historians held at Brighton Polytechnic, April, 1986, and will appear this year in her collected essays. Also see the intelligent and sensitive study by Albert Boime, "The Case of Rosa Bonheur: Why Should a Woman Want to be More Like a Man?" *Art History*, iv. 1981, 384–409, who discusses the importance of gender construction (or, in his words, "sex typing") for Rosa Bonheur in major decisions she made both about her life and her art.
14. See especially the large paintings from her work, *Ordinary/Extraordinary*, 1977–1986, reproduced in the catalogue *May Stevens: Ordinary/Extraordinary: A Summation, 1977–1984*, Boston University Gallery, 1984. For a discussion of these aspects of the work, see Patricia Mathews, "A Dialogue of Silence: May Stevens's *Ordinary/Extraordinary*, 1977–1986," forthcoming in *Art Criticism*.
15. In her introduction to the *Difference* catalogue, Kate Linker once again points to a distinction between "sexuality as a cultural construction" and the "opposing . . . perspective based on a natural or biological 'truth'" (p. 5). The latter may refer to the 19th-century concept of inherent femininity, but certainly also refers to the dichotomy within feminism today that writers take advantage of to infer a totally new perspective. First-generation feminism is not so simply categorized, and the differences are more subtle and more important. This antagonistic position is not the only position taken by second-generation feminists, of course.
16. Published in the widely read anthology of Postmodern thought, *The Anti-Aesthetic: Essays on Postmodern Culture*, ed. Hal Foster, Port Townsend, WA, 1983, 57–82.
17. For several among many examples, see the feminist critiques of the collaboration of the photographer Robert Mapplethorpe and the bodybuilder and artist Lisa Lyons by the artist Silvia Kolbowski, "Covering Mapplethorpe's 'Lady,'" *Art in America*, Summer, 1983, 10–11; of the collaboration of David Salle and Karole Armitage, by Jill Johnston, "The Punk Princess and the Postmodern Prince," *Art in America*, Oct., 1986, 23–25; and a critique of art and the media's depiction of violence against women, by Leslie Labowitz and Suzanne Lacy, "Mass Media, Popular Culture, and Fine Art," *Social Works*, exh. cat., Los Angeles Institute of Contemporary Art, 1979, repr. in Richard Hertz, *Theories of Contemporary Art*, Englewood Cliffs, NJ, 1985, 171–78.
18. Feminist film theory and criticism is highly developed, especially in its use of psychoanalytic theory, as seen in the work of Laura Mulvey, "Visual Pleasure and Narrative Cinema," *Screen*, xvi, Autumn, 1975, 6–18 (repr. in Wallis, as in n. 68, 361–73); Annette Kuhn, *Women's Pictures, Feminism and Cinema*, London, Boston, Melbourne, and Henley, 1982, and *The Power of the Image: Essays on Representation and Sexuality*, London, Boston, Melbourne, and Henley, 1985; and E. Ann Kaplan, *Women and Film: Both Sides of the*

Camera, New York, 1983, among many others. Photography criticism, too, incorporates a sophisticated feminist perspective. For example, see the writings of the British artist Victor Burgin, such as *Thinking Photography,* London, 1982. Several magazines support such research, and publish a number of feminist analyses of film and photography, including *Screen* and *Afterimage.*

19. TICKNER, "Sexuality" (as in n. 3), 24ff. For a critique of this show, see Paul Smith, "Difference in America," *Art in America,* Apr., 1985, 190–99. Although he generally praises the exhibition, he also criticizes its "theoretical passivity" (p. 194).
20. "Discourse" in *The Anti-Aesthetic: Essays on Postmodern Culture,* ed. Hal Foster, Port Townsend, WA, 1983.
21. From "Feminism and Art History," a paper given in April, 1986, at the meetings of the British Art Association of Art Historians, held at Brighton Polytechnic.
22. *Ibid*

7

Psychoanalytic Criticism: Some Intimate Questions

Jane Gallop

I may say at once that I am no connoisseur in art, but simply a layman. I have often observed that the subject matter of works of art has a stronger attraction for me than their formal and technical qualities, though to the artist their value lies first and foremost in these latter.

These lines could easily be mine: I am no connoisseur in art and am usually embarrassed to find that what interests me most is certain subject matter, rather than the more artistic values of form and technique. But these sentences are not mine; they are the opening lines from one of the first pieces of psychoanalytic art criticism ever written, Freud's short article "The Moses of Michelangelo."

Those opening lines inaugurate a new genre, and from the very beginning of the genre, Freud sets out one of the major problems of psychoanalytic art criticism: it reduces art to its subject matter; it interprets away specificities of form or technique or medium to get at psychological themes.

But Freud also begins the genre by stating its illegitimacy. He says "at once" that he is no connoisseur. "Connoisseur" from the French *connaitre,* connoting a certain kind of knowledge, knowledge you cannot just learn by rote or schooling, but which gives its possessor, the connoisseur, a certain

This essay originally appeared in *Art in America,* November 1984. Reprinted with permission of the author and publisher.

aura. The verb *connaitre,* as distinguished from the verb *savoir,* is most often used for knowing people, not knowing the facts about them, but being familiar with them. When used about things, it suggests that one knows them like one knows people, suggests familiarity with and understanding through familiarity and interaction. Perhaps this sort of knowing, connoisseurship, is not so very far from the kind of empathic knowledge we tend to ascribe to psychoanalysts. Even when we have every reason (experience, for example) to know better, we tend to think that psychoanalysts have the power to read into the hearts of men and women and discern their secret wishes.

Although I am not an art critic, recently I was invited to speak on psychoanalytic criticism and feminism at a symposium on art criticism. I decided to read the Freud quotation as my opening line, decided in fact, if only for a moment, to impersonate Freud, in order to calm my own sense of illegitimacy by grounding it in an identification with Freud, legitimating, as it were, my illegitimacy. In fact, every psychoanalytic critic writes in an identification with Freud, whether or not she chooses, as I did, to actually speak his words as if they were her own. To face a work of art, or any other sort of object, with the identity of psychoanalytic critic, is to offset one's sense of uncertainty, ignorance and insufficient understanding with the authority of a body of knowledge, a history of connoisseurship that traces back to Freud's knowledge.

But when I decided to speak Freud's words as if my own, one of those words, only one, gave me pause. There was one word which made my acted-out identification uncomfortable, and that was the word "layman." Feminism had made me uncomfortable with those supposedly neuter and universal words which actually presume that the universal human being is male. But it seems somehow awkward to say "laywoman," and I would not want to use "layperson"; such uses of "person" seem to deny sexual difference, whereas the point of my feminism is to challenge the coverup of sexual difference in relations of power and knowledge. For better or for worse, I can no longer not hear the masculine-sexed being in "layman," and it made my identification an obvious transvestism; the very device that was supposed to assure my legitimacy manifested illegitimacy. To my mind, when I spoke the word "layman" it would give away that these were not my words and spoil the impersonation. But what would be my word if I wanted to declare, "at once," as Freud did, that I was what he calls a "layman"?

I looked up the adjective "lay" in my dictionary, and found that the second definition—after its first meaning, in opposition—is "practicing psychoanalysis but not having a medical degree," which the dictionary follows by the phrase "lay analyst." Psychoanalysis has added its own meaning to "lay." I was thus speaking not only as a layman, or rather, more awkwardly, a laywoman, but as a lay analyst, one who practices psychoanalysis without degree, without medical authority. In general, the American psychoanalytic establishment is opposed to lay analysis, in favor of wedding psychoanalysis to the power and prestige of the American Medical Association and the intimidating authority of the Doctor's knowledge. But even though Freud was a physician, he came out in favor of lay analysis when the International Psychoanalytic Association was debating the question. If Freud, although a doctor, explicitly writes art criticism as a layman he is perhaps calling into question a certain kind of authoritative and authorized knowledge, the sort exemplified by the AMA, but present in any organized, legitimated professional identity. Feminists have been foremost among those challenging the intimidation and mystification of medical authority and even authoritative knowledge in general. My feminism makes me feel great solidarity with the idea of lay opinion and lay analysis, but at the same time it makes me take exception to the word "layman."

It might also be said, of course, that there is a great deal of pride behind Freud's assertion of his lay status. He is challenging established authority and clearly feels he has something to contribute to the understanding of art, something that the "connoisseurs" have not been able to come up with. If he unabashedly proclaims that his is a lay opinion, it is because he considers it an excellent opinion. He is not just any old layman; he prides himself on being a good lay. . . .

Now, everyone knows that psychoanalysis is about sex, that it makes latent sexuality manifest. Psycho-analytic art criticism reveals hidden sexual content—the infamous phallic symbols are the most blatant example. When I told a friend of mine that I was reading Freud's essay on Michelangelo's Moses, he quipped: "Oh, Moses jerking off into his beard!" Certainly more irreverent than Freud's style, but is this not what we would expect Freud to say about that sculpture, with the left hand on the crotch meeting the beard that hangs down into his lap? Would we not expect Freud to uncover some sexual subject matter latent in the sculpture?

Freud, however, does not talk about sex in his interpretation of the sculpture. Yet sex is nonetheless present in that short article, in unexpected places. For example, in the quote with which I began, Freud says that "the subject matter of works of art has a *stronger attraction* for me than their formal and technical qualities, though to the artist their value lies . . . in these latter." Freud has a strong attraction to subject matter, and that attraction is in some way forbidden and embarrassing. It is what marks him as a lay rather than a connoisseur. Freud finds himself attracted not to what the artist values but to something else, like when you find yourself strongly attracted to a man's body, even when you are supposed to value him for his mind.

Our education, our culture, teaches us esthetic values. The proper way to appreciate art, we learn, is to enjoy its formal and technical qualities. But something resists that civilizing education; something continues to respond to subject matter. That attraction becomes, for many of us who have a stake in our cultural sophistication, stupid, naive, unmentionable. How can we admit our resemblance to the 12-year-old girl who simply loves all pictures of horses, regardless of their formal and technical qualities? Because the attraction to subject matter is in some way forbidden by civilization, that attraction is charged and ambivalent. The common expectation is that in looking at art psychoanalysis finds sexual subject matter, but I would say rather that the psychoanalytic critic finds subject matter sexual. Subject matter is sexual not because it is *about* some experience of sexuality, but because we experience the relation to subject matter in art as forbidden, powerful, desiring and embarrassing.

If the psychoanalytic critic is he who finds himself attracted to subject matter even though such an attraction is not really proper, then we are all, more or less, but nonetheless unavoidably, psychoanalytic critics. And if it is worth talking about psychoanalytic criticism, it is not because it is a superior or even perhaps an appropriate way of looking at art, but because no one can help being to some extent, at least unwittingly, a psychoanalytic critic, no matter how illegitimate we think such a relation to be.

I am trying to suggest here that there are two different ways in which psychoanalytic criticism can be linked to sex. The more familiar and the least interesting concerns latent subject matter, but the criticism which interests me, which may in fact be one that barely exists at all, is concerned with something we might call the erotics of engagement, a sexuality that is not in the object, however deeply hidden, but in the encounter. In 1905, Freud wrote a short important book called *Three Essays on the Theory of Sexuality* where he called into question reigning notions of sexuality. One of the principal assumptions he challenged there was the idea that sexual attraction was immanent in the object. This idea is still powerfully present—particularly in the notion that sexiness resides in the woman's body. The viewer looks at provocative images of women and locates the attraction she feels in the represented object: the object not the experience is considered to be sexy.

Perhaps one of the reasons I wanted to bring up the idea of the "good lay" is that these two alternative definitions of sexuality are deeply intricated in that slang expression. When one says that someone is a good lay it implies that person has in him, intrinsically, what it takes to produce a highly satisfying sexual encounter regardless of whom the encounter is with. Yet as we all know, even though we cannot quite ever remember it enough, a good lay is something that happens between people and cannot simply be attributed to an individual's anatomical configuration or technical know-how.

The psychoanalytic criticism which uncovers sexual content in the object without ever considering the dynamic of encounter with that object shares the mistaken assumption which Freud was challenging when he began his theory of sexuality. Which is not to say that he was immune to such an illusion. It seems to be one that inheres in desire—a wish to locate the arousal, the erotics, in some object rather than in an intersubjective dynamic. Most psychoanalytic criticism, like most sexuality, has been prey to this illusion. But the psychoanalytic criticism which interests me, which may not yet exist, would not be simply an interpretation of the object's sexuality but would be attuned to what in psychoanalysis is called transference, the dialectical situation in which that interpretation is produced.

In "The Moses of Michelangelo," Freud says something quite telling about his drive to interpret the work of art: "Some rationalistic, or perhaps analytic, turn of mind in me rebels against being moved by a thing without knowing why I am thus affected and what it is that affects me. This has brought me to recognize the apparently paradoxical fact that precisely some of the grandest and most overwhelming creations of art are still unsolved riddles to our understanding."

Something in Freud "rebels against being moved by a thing without knowing why." "Rebels against" is a particularly strong expression, connoting both violence and a challenge to authority. The critic experiences the work of art as "overwhelming," it moves him, has a tremendous power over him, and he rebels against the power. The image of rebellion suggests that Freud's gesture is one of overturning a power hierarchy.

Psychoanalysis, we might say, is the science that aims to understand why we are moved and what moves us precisely when we do not know why we are moved. It is the study of the unconscious causes of our actions and reactions as well as the study of what is most irrational in our sexuality. Freud sets out—a bold and enormous enterprise—to understand that which moves us unbeknownst to us. His enterprise of understanding is, as we see here, the result of a rebellion. Because he cannot tolerate being moved without understanding why, he invents psychoanalysis. When he mentions that some of the grandest works of art are riddles, we can recall that he refers to the dream as a rebus—a kind of riddle—and that he set out to make sense of dreams, to understand why we dream what we dream. The psychoanalytic critic is she who cannot bear to be moved without knowing why, cannot bear to be overwhelmed, and would counter the object's power with her understanding.

Yet Freud in this article manages to move quickly from a position of powerlessness to one of a certain superiority over the work of art. The rebellion, like most successful ones, not only overturns a hierarchy but reverses it. Less than a page later, he writes: "But why should the artist's intention not be capable of being communicated and comprehended in words like any other fact of mental life? Perhaps where great works of art are concerned this would never be possible without the application of psychoanalysis. . . . It is possible, therefore, that a work of art of this kind needs interpretation." The "great work of art" is in some way inadequate, insufficient; it needs psychoanalysis. The great work of art cannot communicate its intentions without the psychoanalytic critic. Freud's rebellion succeeds, and he claims a triumph. No longer overwhelmed, the psychoanalytic critic now presumes a position of superiority.

If we pursue our analogy of art appreciation and sexual relations, this "rebellion" has some interesting resonances. For Freud, sexual arousal is a state of tension, a disequilibrium in the psyche which generates a drive to reduce that tension. The subject is moved, overwhelmed, experiences something very powerful. He is not in control of the situation because he does not comprehend it. His gesture is to possess the disturbing object so as to reassert command of the situation. The mysterious, desirable woman becomes the poor thing who cannot get along without you. The solution to the experience of desire in which the subject feels he is out of control is to possess the object physically, or legally, or through understanding, and reduce it to dependency through a view of its inadequacy. You marry the enigmatic woman, make her your own, see her not as excruciatingly desirable but as dependent upon you for her place in the world. In Freud's story of the child, the infant first experiences the mother as overwhelming, as powerfully moving in a way that underlines the child's powerlessness, but that child, according to Freud, comes to "perceive" that the mother is "castrated," not powerful but lacking, like the work which is not in itself sufficient and needs the psychoanalytic interpreter to fill in its lack.

Which is not to say that we should give up the rebellion. Anti-intellectual gestures, those that would forgo understanding, are simply another ruse of power, another attempt at control. The appreciator who pretends she has no need to understand is denying what is overwhelming, frighteningly powerful in what moves her. The naked aggression of Freud's phrase "rebels against" also constitutes a recognition of the force of the work of art: a force that no one can bear simply to submit to. The problem with psychoanalytic criticism is not Freud's rebellion, not the violence or the desire to possess, but that all too often we see only the aftermath of the rebellion, when the critic is instated in his superiority over the needy work of art. In this article Freud calls that moment "interpretation." This is the psychoanalytic critical gesture with which we are most familiar. But what has been forgotten, what has been covered over, is that the interpretive gesture with its assumption of superiority over a mute object is always based upon a prior rebellion against the object's power. It is the aggression and the desire in that rebellion which constitute the most authentic encounter with the object's power, where we experience not only the object's force but equally our own powerful drive to understand, to possess, that which moves us so intensely.

Psychoanalytic criticism necessarily repeats that revolt over and over again, but too often the revolt is covered over, the strong ambivalent attraction is unmentionable. Usually, by the time the critic speaks or writes the rebellion has "succeeded" and the object been reduced to the position of powerlessness where it needs the critic. When the rebellion has succeeded,

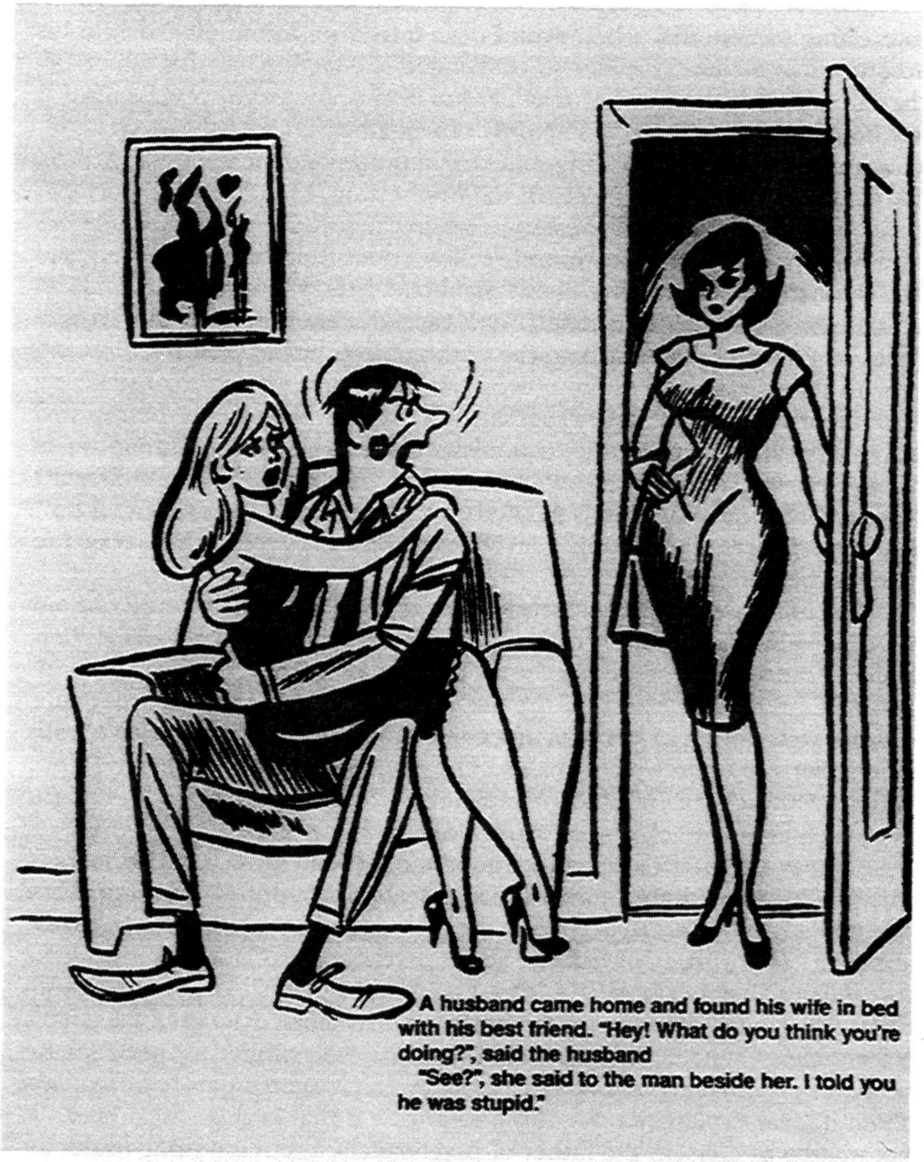

Richard Prince, *Two Husbands and a Wife*, 1989, Acrylic and silkscreen on canvas. *Courtesy Barbara Gladstone Gallery. Photo: Larry Lame.*

everything has been lost. The critic has become a connoisseur; he knows what the work of art is about, and once a connoisseur, he is no longer quite so good a lay.

Earlier, through my own identification, I connected Freud's assertion that he is not a connoisseur with a certain legitimation of illegitimacy. It is interesting to note that when Freud does introduce a connoisseur into his account, it is a connoisseur who challenged the legitimacy, the "name-of-the-father," of various works of art. Freud begins this text by proclaiming "I am no connoisseur in art." The only other appearance of the word "connoisseur" occurs in the opening sentence of the second section of the article, the central section of the piece. In the first section, Freud carefully reviews other people's opinions of the *Moses,* but in the second section he launches into his own analysis. That second section opens thus: "Long before I had any opportunity of hearing about psychoanalysis, I learnt that a Russian art-connoisseur, Ivan Lermolieff, had caused a revolution in the art galleries of Europe by questioning the authorship of many pictures, showing how to distinguish copies from originals with certainty, and constructing hypothetical artists for those works of art whose former authorship had been discredited." Freud is no connoisseur; Lermolieff is. Yet Freud introduces Lermolieff into this essay so as to comment that the art-connoisseur's "method of inquiry is closely related to the technique of psychoanalysis." Having established a kinship with the connoisseur, Freud can proceed to analyze the sculpture.

Freud, as we have seen, "rebels against being moved by a thing without knowing why"; his analysis of art works is motivated by a rebellion. Lermolieff "caused a revolution in the art galleries of Europe." Freud's description of Lermolieff's effect on the authorizing institutions of art resonates with his description of his own attitude in considering a work of art: both descriptions connote violent challenges to the legitimacy of authority. Now, of course, these two revolts are completely different, yet in both cases might we not say that a rebellion has broken out in the art gallery?

It may have struck the reader as odd that Freud introduces Lermolieff with the phrase, "long before I had any opportunity of hearing about psychoanalysis." What does it mean for the founder of psychoanalysis to talk about an "opportunity of hearing about psychoanalysis"? A footnote to the text tells us that Lermolieff's "first essays were published in German between 1874 and 1876." Freud did not invent psychoanalysis until the 1890s. Nonetheless Freud is, in fact, the only person who cannot properly say he heard of psychoanalysis, since that implies that it existed before he learned about it. The explanation for this odd phrase is that in this article Freud is not writing as himself, the father of psychoanalysis, but is writing under an assumed identity, writing as somebody else, somebody who could have heard of psychoanalysis.

This article was originally published anonymously in *Imago,* an official psychoanalytic journal, in 1914, where it was prefaced by the following editorial note: "Although this paper does not, strictly speaking, conform to the conditions under which contributions are accepted for publication in this journal, the editors have decided to print it, since the author, who is personally known to them, belongs to psychoanalytical circles, and since his mode of thought has in point of fact a certain resemblance to the methodology of psychoanalysis."

This article, perhaps the first piece of psychoanalytic art criticism ever written, and which therefore in some way serves to define the genre, is shadowed by an insistent suggestion of illegitimacy. The author is no connoisseur in art. The article "does not conform to the conditions under which contributions are accepted for publication in this journal." The author does not even present himself as Freud, the legitimate connoisseur of psychoanalysis, but as an anonymous layman. The illegitimacy of the author's position is perhaps even more likely to alienate the reader because the latter is told that the article was published only because the author was "personally known to the editors."

As puzzling as Freud's adoption of anonymity might be, what is perhaps most odd to read is that "his mode of thought has in point of fact a certain resemblance to the methodology of psychoanalysis." "A certain resemblance" reads as uncanny understatement when we know the author is in fact Freud, whose mode of thought might be said to *be* the methodology of psychoanalysis. But this editorial footnote becomes otherwise suggestive when brought into conjunction with the later statement about Lermolieff, whose "method of inquiry is closed related to the technique of psychoanalysis."

"The Moses of Michelangelo" is not a proper psychoanalytic article, but it can be published because of "a certain resemblance." The psychoanalytic critic is no connoisseur of art, but what he has to say may be worthwhile because there is a close relation between psychoanalysis and the method of the great art-connoisseur. A certain legitimacy by association pervades this article, which is neither legitimately psychoanalytic nor art criticism, but resembles both. At the same time that association is accompanied by an oddly militant illegitimacy and a puzzling question about authorship. The art-connoisseur caused a revolution by questioning authorship. The founder of psychoanalytic art criticism disguises his authorship, rendering it questionable, as if there were some profound intrication between psychoanalytic art criticism and a radical question about legitimate author-ity.

As we have seen, Freud introduces the connoisseur thus: "Long before I had any opportunity of hearing about psychoanalysis, I learnt that a Russian art-connoisseur, Ivan Lermolieff, had caused a revolution in the art galleries of Europe by questioning the authorship of many pictures." Freud then describes Lermolieff's method, after which he tells us: "I was then greatly interested to learn that the Russian pseudonym concealed the identify of an Italian physician called Morelli who died in 1891 with the rank of Senator of the Kingdom of Italy." Freud inscribes his account of the connoisseur in narrative sequence: "Long ago I learnt . . . I was then greatly interested to learn." The narrative sequence preserves for the reader a surprise. First we are told of the Russian named Ivan Lermolieff and are, at that time, given no reason to be suspicious of his identity. Then we are surprised, or at least, "greatly interested to learn" that the Russian is actually an Italian named Morelli.

Freud wrote his piece of art criticism as an anonymous layman, concealing his identity as physician and connoisseur of the psyche. Morelli, who is also a physician, likewise disguises his identity, publishing his essays on art not anonymously but under a pseudonym. Having concealed his identity (and his country of origin), he proceeded to call into question the identity of the authors of various works of art. Morelli's assumed identity also disguises his profession of physician and protects the man who will become a senator, a man who will have political power. That powerful man is thus not involved in the "revolution in the art galleries."

Why did Morelli hide his identity as a physician in order to be an art connoisseur? Why did Freud conceal his identity in order to write art criticism? I do not pretend to have the answers to these questions, but do want to suggest that these two puzzles seem to be related. Did Freud, for example, disguise his identity in order to identify with the art-connoisseur? In any case, I would suggest that we have here a congruence of questionable identities, identifications, concealed authorships and blatant illegitimacy right at the origin of psychoanalytic art criticism, which serves both to call into question from the beginning any effort at a psychoanalytic interpretation of a work of art, and at the same time to legitimate such questionable effort.

This is probably psychoanalytic criticism at its best, this suspect tradition in which an exacerbated illegitimacy militantly proclaims itself. It is in this tradition that the critic feels her identity radically questionable; that very doubt throws her into an identification with some knowledge, some *connaissance* of the frightening erotic force of art, of the desire for and the resistance to meaning. When the identity gels and forgets its dubious founding identification, its imposture, its originary pseudonym, then the psychoanalytic critic who is now secure in her knowledge becomes truly illegitimate, for knowledge that has lost the truth of its roots in desire and aggression is in its very objectivity a lie.

If the psychoanalytic art critic cannot help but write, think, perceive in an identification with Freud, let it not be an identification with Freud's knowledge, with Freud's connoisseurship, with the position that the French psychoanalyst Jacques Lacan terms "the subject presumed to know." Lacan criticizes "the subject presumed to know" as the analysand's illusory attribution of knowledge to the analyst which is an effect of transference. Lacan warns analysts not to fall prey themselves to this illusion, not to believe they are in fact "the subject presumed to know." "The subject presumed to know" would be powerfully superior to the work of art, would have the ability to divine and analyze that which the art work is not able to express.

Let the critic's identification with Freud be rather with Freud's lay status, with his questionable identity, and with his own desiring, symptomatic identification with the Russian art-connoisseur who turned out to be an Italian physician. If we willfully identify with Freud in order to triumph in our rebellion against the art work's power, let us remember in our triumph that we are identifying not with legitimate authority but with another rebel, another layman, who felt his own authority shaky, who in his own rebellion felt the need to ally himself with yet another rebel whose connoisseurship might be certain but whose authority is rendered dubious by his assumption of an alias. If there is a rebellion here, an aggression against authority, there is also a crime. We do not presume to know what the crime is, but it has left its trace in this trail of concealed identities. What is so shameful about psychoanalytic art criticism that it must be perpetrated under an assumed identity?

Right after Freud says "I was then greatly interested to learn that the Russian pseudonym concealed the identity of an Italian physician called Morelli," he remarks: "It seems to me that his method of inquiry is closely related to the technique of psychoanalysis." That is, right after Freud discloses the art-connoisseur's disguise, he asserts the close kinship between Lermolieff's method and psychoanalysis's (that is, Freud's) technique, which he then proceeds to characterize: "It, too, is accustomed to divine secret and concealed things from unconsidered and unnoticed details, from the rubbish-heap, as it were, of our observations." The technique of psychoanalysis, which it shares with Morelli's method, is to "divine secret and concealed things." Like the "concealed identity of an Italian physician," perhaps. Yet what I am suggesting here is not only that psychoanalysis's technique is involved with uncovering what is secret, but that it is also, at least in its approach to art, involved with concealing, like the disguise of Freud's identity. Both Lermolieff and Freud divine secret and concealed things; but both Morelli and Freud also conceal things, like their identities.

The technique of connoisseurship, whether of art or of the psyche, involves considering and noticing details which are normally unconsidered and unnoticed, retrieving them from the "rubbish-heap." This is, then, the great tradition of psychoanalytic criticism, the attention to the "insignificant" detail, to what is not "worthy of notice," to trash. There are two things most everybody knows about psychoanalysis: the phallic symbol and the Freudian slip. The latter corresponds to the technique Freud is outlining here. The Freudian slip is some small oddity at the margins of expression that ought to go unnoticed, but which Freud retrieved from the "rubbish-heap" by insisting that it carried meaning. While the phallic symbol represents the worst, most reductive, oppressive sort of knowing psychoanalytic interpretation, the Freudian slip must always be interpreted in context and is not allied to any eternal, archetypal meanings.

The phallic symbol might itself symbolize a certain dominant, reductive form of sexuality—phallocentrism. Freud theorized that children went through a phallic phase of sexuality, a period in which they recognized only the phallic organ and did not know anything about the vagina. That phase may be used to symbolize phallocentrism, a refusal to recognize the force, or the sexuality, of anything outside one's own penetrating desire. The object, in the phallic phase, is simply castrated, lacking. But the "rubbish-heap," the appropriate place for the unconsidered detail, reminds us of another infantile sexual notion: the cloaca. Freud says that because children (in the phallic phase) do not know about, do not notice the vagina, they imagine a "cloaca" (that is, a sewer) which is both the anus and where babies come from. Thus the overwhelming force of the object (the mother, for example) is relegated to a cloaca, which is beneath our consideration or notice. Female sexuality, or rather the erotic force and power of the object, is not recognized but rather consigned to the cloaca.

Now I am not trying to assert that the "rubbish-heap" is the vagina. That sort of interpretation, which knows where sexuality is located, is always a denial by the knowing subject of her own erotic and aggressive engagement. After all, one always presumes that there is some female equivalent to the phallic symbol, circles, holes, containers or some such. Yet Freud discovered a sexuality that is not genital, or rather is not where we would have it be, is not confined to its place, just as trash should be confined to the "rubbish-heap" and not lifted out for consideration.

Freud says that Lermolieff (a.k.a. Morelli) "insist[ed] that attention should be diverted from the general impression and main features of a picture, and he laid stress on the significance of minor details, of things like the drawing of finger-nails . . . and such unconsidered trifles." Freud's account of Lermolieff's technique, the consideration of normally unconsidered fingernails, finds an interesting echo in a recent piece of art criticism. In *The Sexuality of Christ in Renaissance Art and in Modern Oblivion,* Leo Steinberg writes: "We have to consider that Renaissance artists, committed for the first time since the birth of Christianity to naturalistic modes of representation, were the only group within Christendom whose métier required them to plot every inch of Christ's body. They asked intimate questions that do not well translate into words, at least not without disrespect; whether, for instance, Christ clipped his nails short, or let them grow past the fingertips. The irreverent triviality of such inquisition verges on blasphemy."

Steinberg's wonderful book concerns the representation of Christ's genitals in Renaissance art, a representation that has been covered over, either literally or by inattention and denial in modern times. Yet what Steinberg makes clear is that we would be gravely mistaken if we understood Christ's penis to be in any simple way a phallic symbol. Christ's penis is precisely not a symbol of sexuality. But something else, not explicitly sexual but forbidden, resurfaces in Steinberg's account, not in the genitals, where we would expect forbidden sexuality, but somewhere else, in the fingernails, the same anatomical extremities that were important for Lermolieff's revolutionary technique.

To consider Christ's fingernails is to indulge in "irreverent triviality" which "verges on blasphemy." Such attention to the trivial, to the insignificant parts of the body, to what Steinberg calls "intimate [if not explicitly sexual] questions" certainly takes on, in Steinberg's language, an air of forbidden, somewhat culpable intimacy. Yet that disrespect, verging on sin, is not exactly immanent in the paintings but happens when we "translate" the artists' intimate questions "into words."

What then is the art critic but he who "translates such intimate questions into words"? That was precisely how Freud saw the task of the psychoanalytic art critic: "But why should the artist's intention not be capable of being *communicated* and comprehended *in words* like any other fact of mental life? Perhaps where great works of art are concerned this would never be possible without the application of psychoanalysis." This translation into words is what Freud calls "interpretation." The work of art needs the psychoanalytic critic so that it can be translated into words. But that translation is precisely what, in Steinberg's view, runs the risk of being disrespectful, irreverent, sinfully intimate. Perhaps this is one of the crimes of the psychoanalytic critic: blasphemy. Blasphemy, not only in a Christian context, but in a larger context where it means putting into words something terribly powerful that is demeaned and reduced by being spoken.

Now, let me be clear, I am not arguing for a respectful silence in face of the ineffable nature of art. I am, in fact, not at all opposed to irreverence, disrespect, even blasphemy. But I am trying to point in the direction of what may be an original sin of psychoanalytic criticism, which may have some connection to why the psychoanalytic art critic works under an alias.

Leo Steinberg is not performing psychoanalytic criticism, not at least as we usually think of it. He is not identifying with Freud's knowledge. At the end of the work he specifically says, "It will not have escaped the reader that my discussion has left out of account all psychological considerations." He is in fact writing against the broad tradition I here call "psychoanalytic," one that presumes to see sexual themes in the work of art. That tradition not only includes the interpreters of Christ's penis as phallic symbol but all those who would cover over that same penis, furious to deny Christ's sexuality because they presume to know what that penis means. Yet in another sense Steinberg's method of inquiry resembles the technique of psychoanalysis (Freud, Lermolieff). He is giving consideration to that which has been deemed unworthy of consideration. He is putting into words "intimate questions," giving attention not to the phallic symbol but to "the rubbish-heap of our observations."

The point is not to claim Steinberg as a psychoanalytic critic, but to argue that the best psychoanalysis has to offer art would attend, erotically and forcefully, not to the genitals (except where they have been overlooked, denied, made marginal) but to something as blasphemous as the fingernails. Not to where we presume sexuality to be, but to peripheral, insignificant trivia where it might appear in a way that surprises, embarrasses and overwhelms the observer. For the potential critic—and everyone who looks at a work of art is potentially a critic—the richest legacy of Freud is not the psychosexual catalogue from which the interpreter supplies meaning to the work of art. Freud's best legacy is his record of the struggle to understand what moves him, a struggle which attests to the critic's violent desire and the object's power, a struggle in which the subject is impelled by a drive that cannot afford to be respectful since the questions raised are disturbingly intimate.

Jane Gallop currently teaches in the Humanities Department of Rice University, Houston. She is the author of The Daughter's Seduction: Feminism and Psychoanalysis *as well as the forthcoming study of the* Ecrits of Jacque Lacan.

8

Artist Envy

Donald Kuspit

There is no denying psychoanalysis' fascination with the artist as a "special case." As the psychoanalyst John Gedo has shown, by now the "artist type" has been put through every conceptual and theoretical apparatus invented by psychoanalysis.[1] Typically, these studies reflect more about the character of psychoanalysis, and about its attitude to the artist and by implication to art, than they tell us about the nature of making art, or about the psychological reasons for making art rather than doing something else. And when they do engage works of art they have almost always regarded them as self-reflexive, symbolic acts of the artist's psyche rather than as possessing, despite their case-historical dimension, a creative integrity of their own.

For someone in whose life the arts play a serious part—without necessarily being fetishized or overidealized—the whole psychoanalytic understanding of art seems far removed from the experience of it. For example, although that experience is not exclusively aesthetic, and certainly has a strong psychological dimension, over and beyond that dimension is a sense of creative reconstruction and reconsideration of reality that is often missed from the psychoanalytic viewpoint. Because of this felt discrepancy between the psychoanalytic approach to art and art's self-understanding, many artists have been reluctant to accept the psychoanalytic gambit toward art as even minimally heuristic. This is more than the common resistance to analytic understanding, more than the patient's repression of his or her inner life. It is a defense of art against what seems to be a misunderstanding of it committed by people with no real conviction in it. To the artist, the psychoanalyst adds a twist to the conventional, vulgar attitude to art, the view of art as at best a fortuitous pleasure and more often as the symptom of a maladaptation to reality. Thus it makes sense for the artist to resist psychoanalysis as a threat to his or her very existence: if art is a symptom, surely the cure would mean the elimination of art. This is the artist's understandable anxiety, but clearly there are many misunderstandings between the two fields, and many points to the paradoxical story.

Successful psychoanalysis really wants to liberate psychic energy, which is essentially creative, from its bondage in symptoms. It has no intention of hindering the artist from making his or her art, but rather recognizes that art is a major indicator of creativity, and thus of health. It respects art as a civilized and civilizing source. It sees that if the artist does not live up to his or her own artistic potential, that may be because of commonplace or specific psychic dysfunctions, and it seeks to free the artist—and the art—from those dysfunctions. As Susan Deri remarks, though psychoanalysis "can elicit patients' authentic form-creative potentials and liberate them from functioning under the auspices of a 'false self' and from repetitious fixation on the traumatizing aspects of the past," it "cannot produce artists."[2] The good psychoanalyst recognizes this, and deals with the artist's person, and, no doubt, with the meaning to that person of being an artist. Sometimes, during the analytic process, people whose calling is not art may indeed opt not to be artists. In fact, psychoanalysis may strengthen the commitment of convinced artists to their art in the face of "realistic" odds, and it may help them understand more clearly the goals of their art.

In general, however, both psychoanalysts and artists, each in their different ways, have repeated W. B. Yeats's idea that perfection of the life or of the work is possible, but not both. As Ellen Handler Spitz has pointed out, psychoanalysis generally follows Plato in believing that the artist's psychopathology, or "madness," is intense and intractable, "inspiring" him or her to art yet making for a damaged life.[3] But psychoanalysis is not alone here; many people follow Plato in this view. This preconception has led to the psychoanalytic correlation of art and madness, a correlation with profound implications yet also a great potential for shallow misuse. Psychoanalysis often seems to suggest that art does not so much overcome madness as intricately reflect it, and that the artist has a more intimate, aware experience of madness than any other human type, apart from the outright mad.

The considerations stretched out so far here on the relations of art and psychoanalysis could take off in a seemingly infinite number of possible examinations of this intricate theme. One could, for example, examine why psychoanalysts seem more attracted to grand literary figures such as Sophocles, Shakespeare, and Goethe than to visual artists, despite the fact that the most influential psychoanalytic theorizing on art is to be found in Freud's essays on Leonardo and Michelangelo. For Freud, despite his extensive citation of literary artists, visual artists seemed ultimately more interesting, because the visual medium resembles the dream more than the literary narrative does. One could also write about why certain artists hold a special interest for psychoanalysts—why in visual art, for example, expressive, angst-driven work tends to attract more analysis than the Duchampian "art about art" tradition. Or one could proceed through the vast jungle of psychoanalytic literature on art, acknowledging its brilliantly ingenious interpretations here, its peculiar insensitivity to art and artists there. A number of extraordinary examinations of particular artists have been written, such as that of Goethe by Kurt Eissler, of Michelangelo by Robert Liebert, and Freud's own on Leonardo. A number of writers have in fact worked their way critically through this literature; among the most interesting recent discussions are those by Gedo, Spitz, and Elizabeth Wright.[4] These are all important topics. They are not, however, the raison d'etre of this essay.

Since its birth, psychoanalysis as a branch of knowledge has been fascinated with the figure of the artist. And basically for just as long, paradoxes have pervaded its discourse on artists. On the one hand the artist has been the model, as it were, for the healthy human being, the person whose mysterious ability to create is made concrete and actual. But the artist has also been seen as more fixated on infantile or primitive processes, in effect more traumatized, than other people. The paradox echoes the psychoanalyst's ambivalence toward the artist, and ambivalence is the tip of the iceberg.

Freud's term for his inquiry of 1910 into the unconscious of Leonardo was "pathography," and as Spitz points out, "pathography implies writing about suffering, illness, or feeling, with important overtones of empathic response on the part of the author for this subject."[5] While Freud never claimed psychoanalysis could "give an account of the way in which artistic activity derives from the primal instincts of the mind," and asserted that "pathography does not in the least aim at making the great man's achievements intelligible,"[6] the fact is that pathography was the jumping-off point for the development of a theory of artistic creation. Moreover, by reason of its empathic character, pathography implies the special energy—the energy of identification—with which psychoanalysts have pursued artists.

This relationship has many levels. It began in the early days of psychoanalysis, and its roots are partly historical. Psychoanalysis then was deeply suspect intellectually, and unacceptable socially, while art, even if often controversial, was an ingrained, time-honored part of culture. Psychoanalysts saw artists as more socially acceptable than they themselves, yet they also recognized artists as outsiders like themselves. Psychoanalysts also defined themselves as a kind of artist, masters of the "art of interpretation," as Freud called it.[7] The identification persists today, though the social condition of psychoanalysis has changed. Like most identifications, this one involves admiration, empathy, and envy, both the desire to incorporate in oneself a quality one is drawn to in someone else and an uneasy, often unconscious feeling of one's own lack of that quality. At the same time, such "artist envy" is balanced by the most ordinary psychoanalyst's unconscious feeling of superiority to the greatest artist, for psychoanalysts see themselves as using the art of interpretation to apply a scientific understanding of the psyche—see themselves as scientists as well as artists. To scientists, after all, art is a way not so much of gaining new knowledge as of expressing in socially novel ways the already known; it is science that they believe to be the field of true discovery. Thus to the psychoanalyst's artist envy is added the scientist's implicit contempt for the arts, going back at least to Plato's banishment of poets from the Republic and his degradation of art as inferior knowledge—an illusion of knowledge hardly worthy of the name.

Freud praised Michelangelo as an "artist in whose works there is so much thought striving for expression," an artist who "has often enough gone to the utmost limit of what is expressible in art." Yet Freud's talk of "the obscurity which surrounds his work" cannot help but imply that Michelangelo has not expressed enough.[8] And this extends to the idea that he has not understood enough: how could he have, when obscurity is endemic to his art, and to art in general. The implication is that Michelangelo's art does not express as much as artful yet scientific psychoanalytic interpretation, which is devoted to eliminating the obscurity surrounding the workings of the human psyche.

Freud admired the playwright and novelist Arthur Schnitzler, who seemed to Freud to intuit truths about the psyche that he himself only discovered through laborious scientific work with patients. Similarly, in his essay "Fear of Breakdown" D. W. Winnicott writes, "Naturally, if what I say has truth in it, this will already have been dealt with by the world's poets [artists], but the flashes of insight that come in poetry [art] cannot absolve us from our painful task of getting step by step away from ignorance toward our goal."[9] Psychoanalysis, then, has to struggle for its revelations, while art, whatever the inadequacy of its expression, achieves its understanding spontaneously, at least in this view. (It is, however, referred to as just a "flash," and in practical opposition to the idea of actually getting away from ignorance.) This supposed disparity is one source of the psychoanalyst's envy of the artist, but an even more crucial issue than that of intuition is relevant here. In a letter to Oskar Pfister, a pastor and psychoanalyst, Freud took his correspondent to task "for being 'overdecent' and insufficiently ruthless to his patient," and advised him "to behave like the artist who steals his wife's household money to buy paint and burns the furniture to warm the room for his model."[10] It is revealing here that Freud justifies the necessary "coldness in feeling in the analyst"[11] that he recommends elsewhere by allusion to the artist, and the artist's hypothetical criminality. An apocryphal story—told by an anonymous psychoanalyst—illustrates this supposed criminal coldness: the sculptor Benvenuto Cellini, casting a statue, is said to have needed some calcium for the bronze alloy, and, finding none in the studio, to have thrown a little boy into the pot for the calcium in his bones. "What was the life of a little boy to the claim of art?"[12]

On more or less the same subject, in a telling passage on the artist in his article "Psycho-Analysis and the Sense of Guilt" (1958), Winnicott writes,

> It is interesting to note that the creative artist is able to reach to a kind of socialization which obviates the need for guilt-feeling and the associated reparative and restitutive activity that forms the basis for ordinary constructive work. The creative artist or thinker may, in fact, fail to understand, or even may despise, the feelings of concern that motivate a less creative person; and of artists it may be said that some have no capacity for guilt and yet achieve a socialization through their exceptional talent. Ordinary guilt-ridden people find this bewildering; yet they have a sneaking regard for ruthlessness that does in fact, in such circumstances, achieve more than guilt-driven labor.[13]

The tough-minded, amoral attitude that Winnicott finds in the artist is found professionally essential and admirable in psychoanalysis. It is the attitude that the psychoanalyst must maintain in his or her practice, an attitude that Freud, in a famous metaphor, compared to that of a surgeon.[14] Guiltless ruthlessness is often presented in the service of a higher cause (perhaps its quintessential sign), whether for art or for psychoanalysis. But psychoanalysts usually imagine that through their silence and science they outdo the artist in coldness, raising themselves over the artist, just as the artist, in this view, is assumed to be higher than the ordinary, less creative person. The psychoanalyst, I would argue, is envious of the artist—for reasons inherent to the nature of psychoanalysis and art—and this envy informs the psychoanalytic understanding of the artist.

In her brilliant analysis of envy, Melanie Klein describes it as "the angry feeling that another person possesses and enjoys something desirable—the envious impulse being to take it away or to spoil it."[15] Furthermore, as Klein points out, envy tends to feed on itself, to increase by its own momentum; and so, as the artist becomes more envied, he or she becomes at once more begrudged. The psychoanalyst envies the artist's guiltless ruthlessness, and at the same time wants to spoil it by analyzing it as a defect in humanity. (In doing so, of course, the analyst, who sees in the artist's supposed ruthlessness his or her own, raises the question of his or her own defectiveness—another troubling unconscious recognition.) Part of that spoiling is to conceive the artist as amoral. Excessive envy is especially pernicious, for it tends to devalue what it envies. As Klein says,

> The fact that envy spoils the capacity for enjoyment explains to some extent why envy is so persistent. For it is *enjoyment* and the *gratitude* to which it gives rise that mitigate destructive impulses, envy, and greed. To look at it from another angle: greed, envy, and persecutory anxiety, which are bound up with each other, inevitably increase each other. The feeling of the harm done by

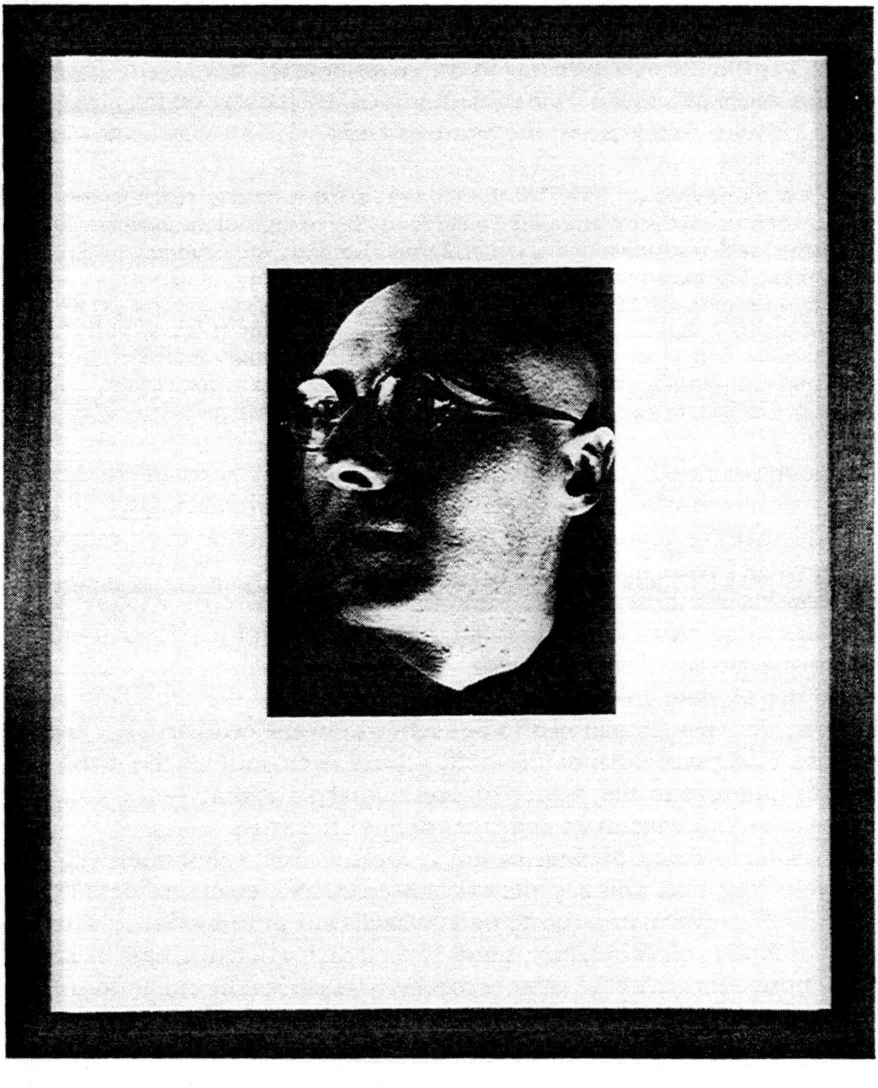

Sherrie Levine, *Untitled (After Alexander Rodechenko: 11)*, 1987, black and white photograph.
Courtesy of Mary Boone Gallery, N.Y.

envy, the great anxiety that stems from this, and the resulting uncertainty about the goodness of the object, have the effect of increasing greed and destructive impulses.[16]

The envy of psychoanalysts for artists has often led them toward skepticism of art, an eternal nagging doubt that it can ever really be wholly authentic as an endeavor. Their skepticism is mitigated by their appreciation of art's power to describe human beings and human ideas and emotions, and to convince society of the validity of its descriptions, but their ambivalence toward art makes their appreciation of it more disturbing rather than less. Their position resembles, in Klein's words, the criticism of "the envious patient [who] grudges the analyst the success of his work," and who even comes to doubt the validity of the analytic enterprise as such.[17] Psychoanalysis can devalue the artist's work the way this kind of patient's criticism can devalue the psychoanalyst's work. As Klein says, "There are very pertinent psychological reasons why envy ranks among the seven 'deadly sins.'"[18]

The psychoanalyst claims a power of resurrection greater than that of the artist, far greater, in fact, since from the psychoanalytic perspective the resurrection offered by art, however ecstatic, is a deceptive, transient high, the fraudulent illusion of healing rather than its reality. Envy of the artist's guiltless ruthlessness is only a part of the psychoanalyst's anxious, envious "understanding" of the artist. The analyst cannot help but envy the artist, who supposedly lets his or her sense of omnipotence run loose, and may even use it as the emotional basis of creativity. The psychoanalyst has to confront his or her own sense of omnipotence—or, as Winnicott calls it, the "area of omnipotent control"[19]—since it may threaten the patient, whose feeling of vulnerability is a sine qua non of psychoanalyst's work. As Freud wrote in *Totem and Taboo* (1912), in a chapter entitled "Animism, Magic and the Omnipotence of Thoughts,"

> In only a single field of our civilization has the omnipotence of thoughts been retained, and that is in the field of art. Only in art does it still happen that a man who is consumed by desires performs something resembling the accomplishment of those desires and that what he does in play produces emotional effects—thanks to artistic illusion—just as though it were something real. People speak with justice of the "magic of art" and compare artists to magicians. But the comparison is perhaps more significant than it claims to be. There can be no doubt that art did not begin as art for art's sake. It worked originally in the service of impulses which are for the most part extinct today. And among them we may suspect the presence of many magical purposes.[20]

What astonishes Freud is the way the artist can be socially operational and successful yet retain intact the anti-social narcissistic principle of omnipotence of thought. But the artist, of course, is not entirely narcissistic. Works of art, Freud writes, "differed from the asocial, narcissistic products of dreaming in that they were calculated to arouse interest in other people and were able to evoke and to gratify the same unconscious wishes in them [as in the artist] too." While "the artist, like the neurotic, had withdrawn from an unsatisfying reality into [the] world of imagination . . . unlike the neurotic, he knew how to find a way back from it and once more to get a firm foothold in reality."[21] In the end, however, Freud must repudiate art in the name of science, and he does so in the last chapter of the *New Introductory Lectures of Psycho-Analysis* (1933). Here, declaring "religion alone" as science's "really serious enemy," he dismisses art as "almost always harmless and beneficent, [for] it does not seek to be anything else but an illusion. Save in the case of a few people who are, one might say, obsessed by Art, it never dares to make any attacks on the realm of reality."[22] (Freud's description of such an art-obsessed person is worth quoting in this context: "A clever young philosopher, with leanings towards aesthetic exquisiteness, hastens to twitch the crease in his trousers into place before lying down [on the couch] for the first sitting; he reveals himself as an erstwhile coprophiliac of the highest refinement, as was to be expected of the developed aesthete.")[23]

Behind psychoanalysis' envy of art lies the fact that the psychoanalyst is afraid of becoming the same kind of dealer in illusion—"confidence man"—that he or she believes the artist to exemplify. Psychoanalysis is haunted by the thought that it may be inauthentic science (as, in fact, has been cogently argued).[24] As long as this suspicion remains, psychoanalysts cannot help but unconsciously fear that they are illusionists like artists. To psychoanalysts, art's magical illusions have their value, but they are a form of subjective expression, no doubt with piecemeal insights but lacking genuine, scientific validity. (Since Freud, psychoanalysis has of course been reconceived by philosophers as a hermeneutics and phenomenology of the dialectics of feeling, its "scientism" supposedly being self-misunderstanding. This view aims to overcome the idea that the only legitimate kind of science is modeled on one kind of supposedly solid knowledge. At the same time, it tilts psychoanalysis toward art, which, like psychoanalysis, can be regarded as an interpreter of the illusions inherent in life, if by way of the creation of "counter-illusions.") However, psychoanalysis, while wanting to free itself and us of illusions, knows that the life-world is pervaded by them; understands that because we are always in a condition of projecting our unconscious expectations on the world we are always in a condition of illusion; knows that they must be perpetually worked through. Authentic psychoanalysis, like authentic avant-garde art, is premised on enormous dissatisfaction with, even disbelief in, existing psychosocial illusions; but it is aware that the truth with which it replaces them is another kind of illusion that is also all too artistic. Thus, for all its disdain of illusion, and its fear of being regarded as merely art, psychoanalysis in effect finds itself in a kind of dependent relationship with art. It knows it needs knowledge of illusions in all their various cultural manifestations.

This awareness is implicit in Freud's avant-garde proposal that in "a college of psychoanalysis, . . . analytic instruction would include branches of knowledge which are remote from medicine and which the doctor does not come across in his practice: the history of civilization, mythology, the psychology of religion and the science of literature. Unless he is well at home in these subjects, an analyst can make nothing of a large amount of his material."[25] Freud implies an essential relationship between psychoanalysis and art, one that gives psychoanalysis access to art's insights—licenses psychoanalysis to bring up from the artistic netherworld such ideas as those embodied in the very name of its perhaps most salient discovery, the Oedipus complex.

A major formulation of this "dependent" relationship between art and psychoanalysis is Heinz Kohut's "hypothesis of artistic anticipation," which gives the "great artist" credit for being "ahead of his time in focusing on the nuclear psychological problems of his era,"[26] but argues that "the investigative efforts of the scientific psychologist"[27] comprehensively and coherently realize the goal of understanding that the artist recognizes only intuitively. Winnicott says something similar when he remarks that "the intuitive flashes of the great, . . . and even the elaborate constructs of poets and philosophers, are lacking in clinical applicability," and that psychoanalysis makes scientifically and usefully available—clinically operational—"much that was previously locked up" in such intuitive flashes.[28] In the very act of praising artists for their intuitions, Kohut and Winnicott dismiss them by regarding them as "anticipatory" but inoperational in the actual circumstances of life or therapy. They credit the artist, the object of envy, who is acknowledged as offering the seminal intuitive flashes that start thought moving, but they also claim that these insights are impractical in the end, remaining merely "artistic."

One last word about the psychoanalyst's envy of the artist, particularly the visual artist. For Freud, visual art is necessarily more erotic than literary art, since after touch the visual is the major medium of communication of sexual excitement and ideas.[29] For the psychoanalyst, the visual in general is more primitive than the verbal, particularly because it implies "the earliest closeness with the mother in the preverbal state," the "understanding [that] needs no words to express it."[30] Thus more sexual pleasure lies in the visual artist's work than in that of the psychoanalyst, who works in words, and is a kind of literary artist. To the analyst, the visual artist seems closer to the source of primal enjoyment than the literary artist. This is another reason for the psychoanalyst's confused attraction to the artist: the analyst suspects that it is in the very nature of art's effort that it can establish an enviable state of preverbal closeness with the viewer. The analyst desires this state, for preverbal closeness is the optimum condition toward which the relationship between patient and analyst drifts, a regressive condition reparative of the damage each does to the other by reason of each's unconscious envy of the other. As in Kafka's *A Country Doctor*, the psychoanalyst in effect must empathetically lie on the couch with the patient. Without that empathy, the analyst will not be cured of his or her delusion of omnipotence. (Empathy takes one out of that delusion.) Nor will the patient be cured, since he or she needs the analyst as a part of him or herself. Perhaps the final reason for the psychoanalyst's envy of the artist is that the artist seems spontaneously to have this empathy or unconscious closeness with his or her public, or at least creates the illusion of having it. Just as psychoanalysis has worked woman's "penis envy" into the ground, up pops its own artist envy.

Donald Kuspit is a critic and professor at the State University of New York, Stony Brook Campus. He is the author of numerous monographs of contemporary artists. One of his most recent projects is a catalogue raisonne of the paintings of Charles Hinman from 1964 to the present.

NOTES

1. JOHN E. GEDO, *Portraits of the Artist* (New York Guilford Press, 1983): section 1, pp. 1–40.
2. SUSAN K. DERI, *Symbolization and Creativity* (New York: International Universities Press, 1984), p. 346.
3. ELLEN HANDLER SPITZ, *Art and Psyche* (New Haven: Yale University Press, 1985), p. 28.
4. GEDO and SPITZ are cited above; Wright is Elizabeth Wright, *Psychoanalytic Criticism: Theory in Practice* (London and New York: Methuen, 1984).
5. SPITZ, *Art and Psyche,* p. 28
6. Quoted in ibid.
7. Among other places, Freud alludes to the "art of interpretation" in "Further Recommendations in the Technique of Psychoanalysis" (1914), collected in Philip Rieff, ed., *Freud: Therapy and Technique* (New York: Macmillan Publishing Co., Inc., Collier Books, 1963), p. 158.
8. SIGMUND FREUD, "The Moses of Michelangelo" (1914), collected in Rieff, ed., *Freud: Character and Culture* (New York: Collier Books, 1963), p. 106.
9. Quoted in Murray Cox, *Structuring the Therapeutic Process: Compromise with Chaos* (Oxford, England: Pergamon Press, 1978), pp. 280–81.
10. Quoted in Janet Malcolm, *Psychoanalysis: The Impossible Profession* (New York: Aflred A. Knopf, Borzoi Books, 1982), p. 80.
11. FREUD, "Recommendations for Physicians on the Psychoanalytic Method of Treatment" (1912), in Rieff, *Freud: Therapy and Technique,* p. 80.
12. MALCOLM, *Psychoanalysis,* p. 80.
13. D. W. WINNICOTT, "Psycho-Analysis and the Sense of Guilt" (1958), *The Maturational Processes and the Facilitating Environment* (New York: International Universities Press, 1965), p. 26.
14. FREUD, "Recommendations for Physicians on the Psychoanalytic Method of Treatment," p. 121. Freud wrote: "I cannot recommend my colleagues emphatically enough to take as a model in psychoanalytic treatment the surgeon who puts aside all his own feelings, including that of human sympathy, and concentrates his mind on one single purpose, that of performing the operation as skillfully as possible." Such "coldness in feeling," he said, "is the condition which brings the greatest advantage to both persons involved, ensuring a needful protection for the physician's emotional life and the greatest measure of aid for the patient that is possible at the present time." That is, "coldness" represses the psychoanalyst's own psychopathology so that he or she can fully attend to the patient's.
15. MELANIE KLEIN, "Envy and Gratitude" (1957), *Envy and Gratitude and Other Works 1946–1963* (New York: Macmillan Publishing Co., Inc., Free Press, 1984), p. 181.
16. Ibid., pp. 186–87.
17. Ibid., p. 184.
18. Ibid., 189.

19. Quoted in Arnold H. Modell, "Object Relations Theory," in Arnold Rothstein, ed., *Models of the Mind: Their Relationships to Clinical Work* (New York: International Universities Press, 1985), p. 97.
20. FREUD, *Totem and Taboo* (New York: W. W. Norton & Company, Norton Library, 1950), p. 90.
21. FREUD, *An Autobiographical Study* (New York: W. W. Norton & Company, Norton Library, 1963), pp. 122–23.
22. FREUD, *New Introductory Lectures on Psycho-Analysis* (New York: W. W. Norton & Company, 1933), p. 219.
23. FREUD, "Further Recommendations in the Technique of Psychoanalysis," p. 151.
24. See Adolf Grünbaum, *The Foundations of Psychoanalysis, A Philosophical Critique* (Berkeley: University of California Press, paperback edition, 1985).
25. Quoted in Peter Loewenberg, "Why Psychoanalysis Needs the Social Scientist and the Historian," in Geoffrey Cocks and Travis L. Crosby, eds., *Psycho/History: Readings in the Method of Psychology, Psychoanalysis, and History* (New Haven: Yale University Press, 1987), p. 30. More recently, Richard Chessick has made a somewhat similar recommendation; see his "Education of the Psychotherapist," *Why Psychotherapists Fail* (New York: Science House, 1971), pp. 35–49.
26. HEINZ KOHUT, *The Restoration of the Self* (New York: International Universities Press, 1977), p. 285.
27. Ibid., p. 296.
28. WINNICOTT, "Psycho-Analysis," p. 15.
29. FREUD, "Three Essays on the Theory of Sexuality" (1905) *Standard Edition,* vol. 7, p. 156.
30. KLEIN, "Envy and Gratitude," p. 188.

9

Simulacra and Simulations

Jean Baudrillard

The simulacrum is never that which conceals the truth—it is the truth which conceals that there is none.
The simulacrum is true.

Ecclesiastes

If we were able to take as the finest allegory of simulation the Borges tale where the cartographers of the Empire draw up a map so detailed that it ends up exactly covering the territory (but where, with the decline of the Empire this map becomes frayed and finally ruined, a few shreds still discernible in the deserts—the metaphysical beauty of this ruined abstraction, bearing witness to an imperial pride and rotting like a carcass, returning to the substance of the soil, rather as an aging double ends up being confused with the real thing), this fable would then have come full circle for us, and now has nothing but the discrete charm of second-order simulacra.[1]

Abstraction today is no longer that of the map, the double, the mirror or the concept. Simulation is no longer that of a territory, a referential being or a substance. It is the generation by models of a real without origin or reality: a hyperreal. The territory no longer precedes the map, nor survives it. Henceforth, it is the map that precedes the territory—*precession of simulacra*—it is the map that engenders the territory and if we were to revive the fable today, it would be the territory whose shreds are slowly rotting across the map. It is the real, and not the map, whose vestiges subsist here

Reprinted from Jean Baudrillard, *Simulations* (New York: Semiotext(e), 1983). This section is excerpted from a longer essay.

and there, in the deserts which are no longer those of the Empire, but our own. *The desert of the real itself.*

In fact, even inverted, the fable is useless. Perhaps only the allegory of the Empire remains. For it is with the same imperialism that present-day simulators try to make the real, all the real, coincide with their simulation models. But it is no longer a question of either maps or territory. Something has disappeared: the sovereign difference between them that was the abstraction's charm. For it is the difference which forms the poetry of the map and the charm of the territory, the magic of the concept and the charm of the real. This representational imaginary, which both culminates in and is engulfed by the cartographer's mad project of an ideal coextensivity between the map and the territory, disappears with simulation, whose operation is nuclear and genetic, and no longer specular and discursive. With it goes all of metaphysics. No more mirror of being and appearances, of the real and its concept; no more imaginary coextensivity: rather, genetic miniaturization is the dimension of simulation. The real is produced from miniaturized units, from matrices, memory banks and command models—and with these it can be reproduced an indefinite number of times. It no longer has to be rational, since it is no longer measured against some ideal or negative instance. It is nothing more than operational. In fact, since it is no longer enveloped by an imaginary, it is no longer real at all. It is a hyperreal: the product of an irradiating synthesis of combinatory models in a hyperspace without atmosphere.

In this passage to a space whose curvature is no longer that of the real, nor of truth, the age of simulation thus begins with a liquidation of all referentials—worse: by their artificial resurrection in systems of signs, which are more ductile material than meaning, in that they lend themselves to all systems of equivalence, all binary oppositions and all combinatory algebra. It is no longer a question of imitation, nor of reduplication, nor even of parody. It is rather a question of substituting signs of the real for the real itself; that is, an operation to deter every real process by its operational double, a metastable, programmatic, perfect descriptive machine which provides all the signs of the real and short-circuits all its vicissitudes. Never again will the real have to be produced: this is the vital function of the model in a system of death, or rather of anticipated resurrection which no longer leaves any chance even in the event of death. A hyperreal henceforth sheltered from the imaginary, and from any distinction between the real and the imaginary, leaving room only for the orbital recurrence of models and the simulated generation of difference.

THE DIVINE IRREFERENCE OF IMAGES

To dissimulate is to feign not to have what one has. To simulate is to feign to have what one hasn't. One implies a presence, the other an absence. But the matter is more complicated, since to simulate is not simply to feign: "Someone who feigns an illness can simply go to bed and pretend he is ill. Someone who simulates an illness produces in himself some of the symptoms" (Littre). Thus, feigning or dissimulating leaves the reality principle intact: the difference is always clear, it is only masked; whereas simulation threatens the difference between "true" and "false", between "real" and "imaginary". Since the simulator produces "true" symptoms, is he or she ill or not? The simulator cannot be treated objectively either as ill, or as not ill. Psychology and medicine stop at this point, before a thereafter undiscoverable truth of the illness. For if any symptom can be "produced," and can no longer be accepted as a fact of nature, then every illness may be considered as simulatable and simulated, and medicine loses its meaning since it only knows how to treat "true" illnesses by their objective causes. Psychosomatics evolves in a dubious way on the edge of the illness principle. As for psychoanalysis, it transfers the symptom from the organic to the unconscious order: once again, the latter is held to be real, more real than the former; but why should simulation stop at the portals of the unconscious? Why couldn't the "work" of the unconscious be "produced" in the same way as any other symptom in classical medicine? Dreams already are.

The alienist, of course, claims that "for each form of the mental alienation there is a particular order in the succession of symptoms, of which the simulator is unaware and in the absence of which the alienist is unlikely to be deceived." This (which dates from 1865) in order to save at all cost the truth principle, and to escape the specter raised by simulation: namely that truth, reference and objective causes have ceased to exist. What can medicine do with something which floats on either side of illness, on either side of health, or with the reduplication of illness in a discourse that is no longer true or false? What can psychoanalysis do with the reduplication of the discourse of the unconscious in a discourse of simulation that can never be unmasked, since it isn't false either?[2]

What can the army do with simulators? Traditionally, following a direct principle of identification, it unmasks and punishes them. Today, it can reform an excellent simulator as though he were equivalent to a "real" homosexual, heart-case or lunatic. Even military psychology retreats from the Cartesian clarities and hesitates to draw the distinction between true and false, between the "produced" symptom and the authentic symptom. "If he acts crazy so well, then he must be mad." Nor is it mistaken: in the sense that all lunatics are simulators, and this lack of distinction is the worst form of subversion. Against it, classical reason armed itself with all its categories. But it is this today which again outflanks them, submerging the truth principle.

Outside of medicine and the army, favored terrains of simulation, the affair goes back to religion and the simulacrum of divinity: "I forbade any simulacrum in the temples because the divinity that breathes life into nature cannot be represented." Indeed it can. But what becomes of the divinity when it reveals itself in icons, when it is multiplied in simulacra? Does it remain the supreme authority, simply incarnated in images as a visible theology? Or is it volatilized into simulacra which alone deploy their pomp and power of fascination—the visible machinery of icons being substituted for the pure and intelligible Idea of God? This is precisely what was feared by the Iconoclasts, whose millennial quarrel is still with us today.[3] Their rage to destroy images rose precisely because they sensed this omnipotence of simulacra, this facility they have of erasing God from the consciousnesses of people, and the overwhelming, destructive truth which they suggest: that ultimately there has never been any God; that only simulacra exist; indeed that God himself has only ever been his own simulacrum. Had they been able to believe that images only occulted or masked the Platonic idea of God, there would have been no reason to destroy them. One can live with the idea of a distorted truth. But their metaphysical despair came from the idea that the images concealed nothing at all, and that in fact they were not images, such as the original model would have made them, but actually perfect simulacra forever radiant with their own fascination. But this death of the divine referential has to be exorcised at all cost.

It can be seen that the iconoclasts, who are often accused of despising and denying images, were in fact the ones who accorded them their actual worth, unlike the iconolaters, who saw in them only reflections and were content to venerate God at one remove. But the converse can also be said, namely that the iconolaters possessed the most modern and adventurous minds, since, underneath the idea of the apparition of God in the mirror of images, they already enacted his death and his disappearance in the epiphany of his representations (which they perhaps knew no longer represented anything, and that they were purely a game, but that this was precisely the greatest game—knowing also that it is dangerous to unmask images, since they dissimulate the fact that there is nothing behind them).

This was the approach of the Jesuits, who based their politics on the virtual disappearance of God and on the worldly and spectacular manipulation of consciences—the evanescence of God in the epiphany of power—the end of transcendence, which no longer serves as alibi for a strategy completely free of influences and signs. Behind the baroque of images hides the grey eminence of politics.

Thus perhaps at stake has always been the murderous capacity of images: murderers of the real; murderers of their own model as the Byzantine icons could murder the divine identity. To this murderous capacity is opposed the dialectical capacity of representations as a visible and intelligible mediation of the real. All of Western faith and good faith was engaged in this wager on representation: that a sign could refer to the depth of meaning, that a sign could *exchange* for meaning and that something could guarantee this exchange—God, of course. But what if God himself can be simulated, that is to say, reduced to the signs which attest his existence?

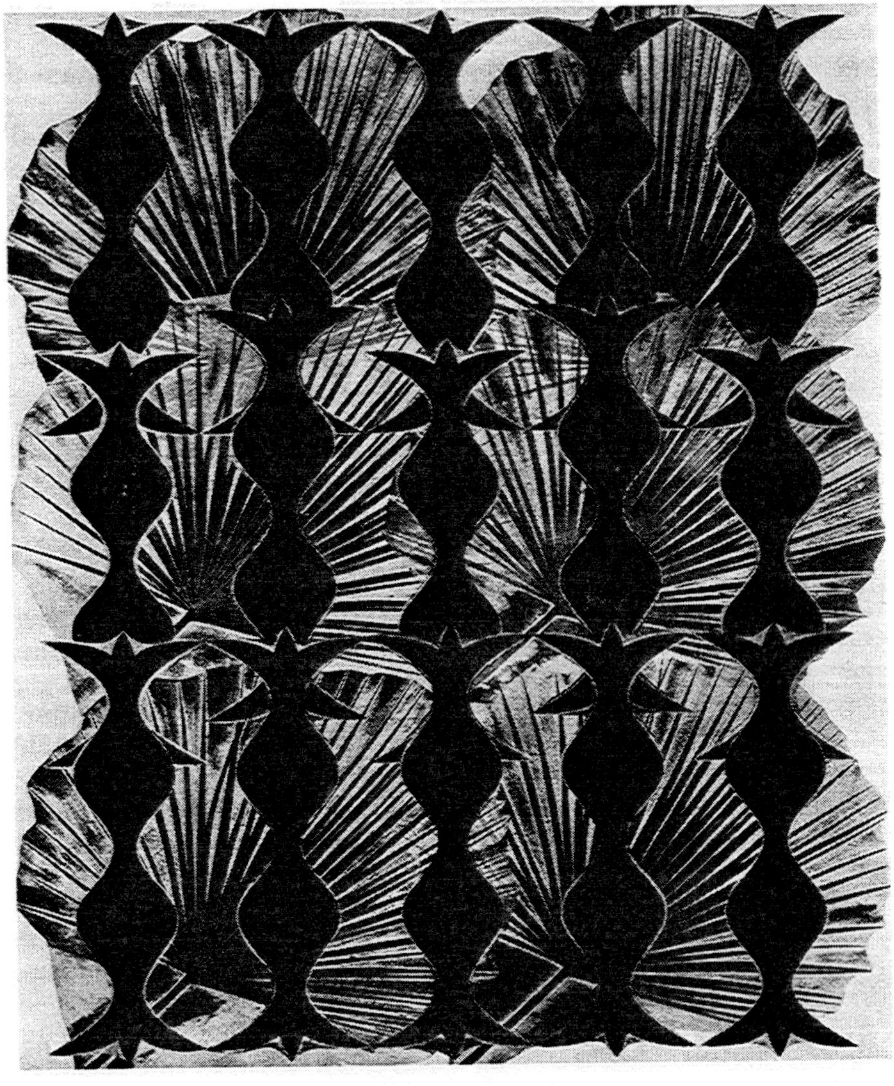

Philip Taaffe, *The Crown of Martyrdom*, 1989, monoprint collage, ink, acrylic on linen. *Collection: Norton Gallery of Art, West Palm Beach, Florida.*

Then the whole system becomes weightless; it is no longer anything but a gigantic simulacrum: not unreal, but a simulacrum, never again exchanging for what is real, but exchanging in itself, in an uninterrupted circuit without reference or circumference.

So it is with simulation, insofar as it is opposed to representation. Representation starts from the principle that the sign and the real are equivalent (even if this equivalence is Utopian, it is a fundamental axiom).

Conversely, simulation starts from the Utopia of this principle of equivalence, *from the radical negation of the sign as value,* from the sign as reversion and death sentence of every reference. Whereas representation tries to absorb simulation by interpreting it as false representation, simulation envelops the whole edifice of representation as itself a simulacrum.

These would be the successive phases of the image:

1. It is the reflection of a basic reality.
2. It masks and perverts a basic reality.
3. It masks the *absence* of a basic reality.
4. It bears no relation to any reality whatever: it is its own pure simulacrum.

In the first case, the image is a *good* appearance: the representation is of the order of sacrament. In the second, it is an *evil* appearance: of the order of malefice. In the third, it *plays at being* an appearance: it is of the order of sorcery. In the fourth, it is no longer in the order of appearance at all, but of simulation.

The transition from signs which dissimulate something to signs which dissimulate that there is nothing, marks the decisive turning point. The first implies a theology of truth and secrecy (to which the notion of ideology still belongs). The second inaugurates an age of simulacra and simulation, in which there is no longer any God to recognize his own, nor any last judgement to separate truth from false, the real from its artificial resurrection, since everything is already dead and risen in advance.

When the real is no longer what it used to be, nostalgia assumes its full meaning. There is a proliferation of myths of origin and signs of reality; of second-hand truth, objectivity and authenticity. There is an escalation of the true, of the lived experience; a resurrection of the figurative where the object and substance have disappeared. And there is a panic-stricken production of the real and the referrential, above and parallel to the panic of material production. This is how simulation appears in the phase that concerns us: a strategy of the real, neo-real and hyperreal, whose universal double is a strategy of deterrence.

HYPERREAL AND IMAGINARY

Disneyland is a perfect model of all the entangled orders of simulation. To begin with it is a play of illusions and phantasms: pirates, the frontier, future world, etc. This imaginary world is supposed to be what makes the operation successful. But, what draws the crowds is undoubtedly much more the social microcosm, the miniaturized and *religious* revelling in real America, in its delights and drawbacks. You park outside, queue up inside, and are totally abandoned at the exit. In this imaginary world the only phantasmagoria is the inherent warmth and affection of the crowd, and in that sufficiently excessive number of gadgets used there to specifically maintain the multitudinous affect. The contrast with the absolute solitude of the parking lot—a veritable concentration camp—is total. Or rather: inside, a whole range of gadgets magnetize the crowd into direct flows; outside, solitude is directed onto a single gadget: the automobile. By an extraordinary coincidence (one that undoubtedly belongs to the peculiar enchantment of this universe), this deep-frozen infantile world happens to have been conceived and realized by a man who is himself now cryogenized; Walt Disney, who awaits his resurrection at minus 180 degrees centigrade.

The objective profile of the United States, then, may be traced throughout Disneyland, even down to the morphology of individuals and the crowd. All its values are exalted here, in miniature and comic-strip form. Embalmed and pacified. Whence the possibility of an ideological analysis of Disneyland (L. Marin does it well in *Utopies, jeux d'espaces*): digest of the American way of life, panegyric to American values, idealized transposition of a contradictory reality. To be sure. But this conceals something else, and that "ideological" blanket exactly serves to cover over a *third-order simulation:* Disneyland is there to conceal the fact that it is the "real" country, all of "real" America, which *is* Disneyland (just as prisons are there to conceal the fact that it is the social in its entirety, in its banal omnipresence, which is carceral). Disneyland is presented as imaginary in order to make us believe that the rest is real, when in fact all of Los Angeles and the America surrounding it are no longer real, but of the order of the hyperreal and of simulation. It is no longer a question of a false representation of reality (ideology), but of concealing the fact that the real is no longer real, and thus of saving the reality principle.

The Disneyland imaginary is neither true nor false: it is a deterrence machine set up in order to rejuvenate in reverse the fiction of the real. Whence the debility, the infantile degeneration of this imaginary. It is meant to be an infantile world, in order to make us believe that the adults are elsewhere, in the "real" world, and to conceal the fact that real childishness is everywhere, particularly among those adults who go there to act the child in order to foster illusions of their real childishness.

Moreover, Disneyland is not the only one. Enchanted Village, Magic Mountain, Marine World: Los Angeles is encircled by these "imaginary stations" which feed reality, reality-energy, to a town whose mystery is precisely that it is nothing more than a network of endless, unreal circulation: a town of fabulous proportions, but without space or dimensions. As much as electrical and nuclear power stations, as much as film studios, this town, which is nothing more than an immense script and a perpetual motion picture, needs this old imaginary made up of childhood signals and faked phantasms for its sympathetic nervous system.

Jean Baudrillard, a sociologist by training, is one of the leading French cultural theorists and writers about the effects of mass communication and consumerism in contemporary Western society.

NOTES

1. Counterfeit and reproduction imply always an anguish, a disquieting foreignness: the uneasiness before the photograph, considered like a witch's trick—and more generally before any technical apparatus, which is always an apparatus of reproduction, is related by Benjamin to the uneasiness before the mirror-image. There is already sorcery at work in the mirror. But how much more so when this image can be detached from the mirror and be transported, stocked, reproduced at will (cf. *The Student of Prague,* where the devil detaches the image of the student from the mirror and harrasses him to death by the intermediary of this image). All reproduction implies therefore a kind of black magic, from the fact of being seduced by one's own image in the water, like Narcissus, to being haunted by the double and, who knows, to the mortal turning back of this vast technical apparatus secreted today by man as his own image (the narcissistic mirage of technique, McLuhan) and that returns to him, cancelled and distorted—endless reproduction of himself and his power to the limits of the world. Reproduction is diabolical in its very essence; it makes something fundamental vacillate. This has hardly changed for us: simulation (that we describe here as the operation of the code) is still and always the place of a gigantic enterprise of manipulation, of control and of death, just like the imitative object (primitive statuette, image of photo) always had as objective an operation of black image.
2. There is furthermore in Monod's book a flagrant contradiction, which reflects the ambiguity of all current science. His discourse concerns the code, that is the third-order simulacra, but it does so still according to "scientific" schemes of the second-order—objectiveness, "scientific" ethic of knowledge, science's principle of truth and transcendence. All things incompatible with the indeterminable models of the third-order.
3. "It's the feeble 'definition' of TV which condemns its spectator to rearranging the few points retained into a kind of *abstract work.* He participates suddenly in the creation of a reality that was only just presented to him in dots: the television watcher is in the position of an individual who is asked to project his own fantasies on inkblots that are not supposed to represent anything." TV as perpetual Rorshach test. And furthermore: "The TV image requires each instant that we 'close' the spaces in the mesh by a convulsive sensuous participation that is profoundly kinetic and tactile."

10

From Imitation to the Copy to Just Effect: On Reading Jean Baudrillard

Kate Linker

The 20th century has observed a striking reduction in the notion of the imagination. What was once the shaping power of thought, the purveyor of meaning, has become a kind of cybernetic machine, its overloaded circuits programmed to spew out scintillating visual forms. "Sheer" images, "pure" surfaces emanate from the image mechanism, only to slither in the glamor of the void that constitutes consumer society, their external enchantments compensating for the loss of substantive matter. These seductive, inherently spectacular forms are not, as before, glosses of meaning; they do not hint at inner depths, silhouetting intent. As phantasmatic phenomena, dispersed throughout contemporary culture and defining its allures, they suggest similarities to the shimmering masks of absence that go by the name of simulacra.

From their conceptual origins, simulacra were instruments of illusion. Although the simulacrum's dictionary definition stays constant as a "mere image, a specious imitation or likeness,"[1] the concept has shifted through time according to social relations and systems of power, and the signifying practices they imply. In the most extensive treatment of the subject to date, Jean Baudrillard distinguishes three orders of simulacra.[2] The first, he writes, that of the counterfeit, was born with the Renaissance in a sign finding value in emulation of nature, posing the metaphysical question of reality against appearance. Based on imitation, it was structured on the natural law of value; with industrial development, it receded before the productivist order, patterned on market law. In this second order, corresponding to the modern period, signs no longer refer to nature but to human production; its models are the machine, energy, and the system of labor itself. The avatar is not the crafted analogue of nature, singular in form, but the plural, reproducible forms of series—forms reflecting the growing importance of technique. The industrial simulacrum, however, diminishes on entry to our period, the postindustrial period, characterized by "simulacra of simulation" dominated by the code, the model, and the operational practices of the cybernetic world.

As Baudrillard indicates, this shift from the stucco angel to computer graphics and synthetic hues is not fortuitous: it is historically determined, reflecting changes whose impact is felt in culture, politics, and economics. Most importantly, however, these changes mirror mutations in the structure of representation, which register the gradual loss of the real or objective world and with it of the notion of reference. Thus the Renaissance counterfeit invoked the terms of the philosophy of representation, of the original, of *ressemblance* and faithful imitation. Its structure corresponded to the classic sign, composed of signifier and signified, repeating its doubled arrangement in the substitution of reality's image for the real. Nature underlies this configuration as the ultimate referent, and it was the aim of creating a parallel universe, echoing the natural world, that haunted the period, inspiring the great theatrical interiors and other examples of trompe l'oeil. The emblem of *ressemblance* was the automaton, conceived as the mechanical counterpart, the ideal figure, the "perfect double" of man.

To the automaton the second order opposed the robot, a figure whose emergence is more than the signal of industrial connotations. For the robot is regulated not by likeness but by equivalence; it is not man's analogue, conceived in his image, but his functional or "operative" adjunct. The equivocations between truth and falsity or reality and appearance that had sustained the preindustrial simulacrum are absorbed by the liquidation of reality through the system of production, and with it, of reproduction. For the industrial simulacrum is not a counterfeit, but a product—since the image is fabricated, it has no referent in the world. With this period, signs no longer refer to specific objects, but to the meanings with which they are invested, resulting in the "arbitrariness" or "abstraction" that was cited by Ferdinand de Saussure. Furthermore, the period also marks the beginning of serial production, for the absorption of the question of origin opens the possibility of a potentially infinite number of identical objects—objects that are equivalent and interchangeable in market terms. The process witnesses the sign's devaluation from conformity to natural law to the market law of value, the system of exchange: "Only the extinction of the original reference permits the generalized law of equivalence, meaning the *possibility of production*."[3]

This shift in representation is evident in the visual arts in the Modernist suspension of the referent so as to stress the purity of the visual signifier, or rather, in the substitution of function and modes of facture as the meanings of cultural modernity. The sense of form as content—or of formal principles as artistic significance—pervades the period within the framework of the productivist esthetic; we find the equivalent of the labor theory of value in the concept of form produced either through manufacture (as in painting, modeling, welding, or carving) or, in the case of Minimalism, through industrial labor. But it is in the photograph that pure serial production finds its apogee; Walter Benjamin's noted axiom that "to ask for the 'authentic' print makes no sense"[4] would phrase the photograph as the very "type" of industrial simulacrum, as one in an endless number of identical copies. Indeed, the increasing circulation of such simulacra in society testifies to reproduction's role as the core of industrial capital. As Baudrillard observes of the decisive shift inaugurated by technique, "We know today that it is on the level of reproduction—fashion, media, publicity, information, and communications networks—on the level of what Marx negligently called the false cost of capital . . . meaning, in the sphere of simulacra and code, that the total processes of capital are knit together."[5] But as he notes, this stage of serial reproduction is short-lived, receding before a third stage corresponding to postindustrial development, and to its rampant technology. In this stage, which represents the autonomy of the system, mutations in the signifiers come to serve as the regulating principle, repeating a logic immanent to the structure, and liquidating the final vestiges of reference. In this third stage, the signifier becomes detached from the signified, estranged from its "natural" pretension to meaning. Reality is now subservient to the signifier: it is produced by the latter, or rather, by the varied modes of signification. In such self-regulating systems, the signifiers are related "digitally," by distinctive oppositions: they no longer reflect "the law of equivalence, but the commutation of terms—no longer market law, but the structural law of value."[6] With these structures of coded oppositions we pass into a world of forces and tensions, moving far from the provisions of natural law and from the representational structure of the classic sign. We move away from the society of production into that of consumption. And we arrive at the regulating power of the signifier, and at the recognition of its tyranny, as the latter motivates contemporary epistemology and, in particular, that branch of reflection characterized as postmodern thought.

Within this universe in which the simulacrum precedes reality, the double the original, the robot's analogue is the computer, a machine programmed to produce reality according to its codes. As with the paradigm of the modern period, such regulation is all-pervasive, establishing correspondences between production, language, and the other structuring instances of society. Its radicality can be grasped by comparison with the earlier model, based on production and labor, which permeates the early and high capitalist period and finds its climax in the Bauhaus. The structuring of modern society corresponds to a utilitarian paradigm: to each thing, a use; to each form, a meaning. To the extent that functionalism imposes itself as "the *dominant rationality*, susceptible to giving an account of everything and to directing all process," function serves as the "transcendental 'signified'" of signs.[7] In each case, the coherence of two elements insures the structure of meaning, binding form to content, object to use, and ending to motive force. This sense of "objective determination"[8] informs the functionalism of period architecture, the notion of style, and the ideology of progress. And it finds expression in the teleological structure of Modernism, by which the

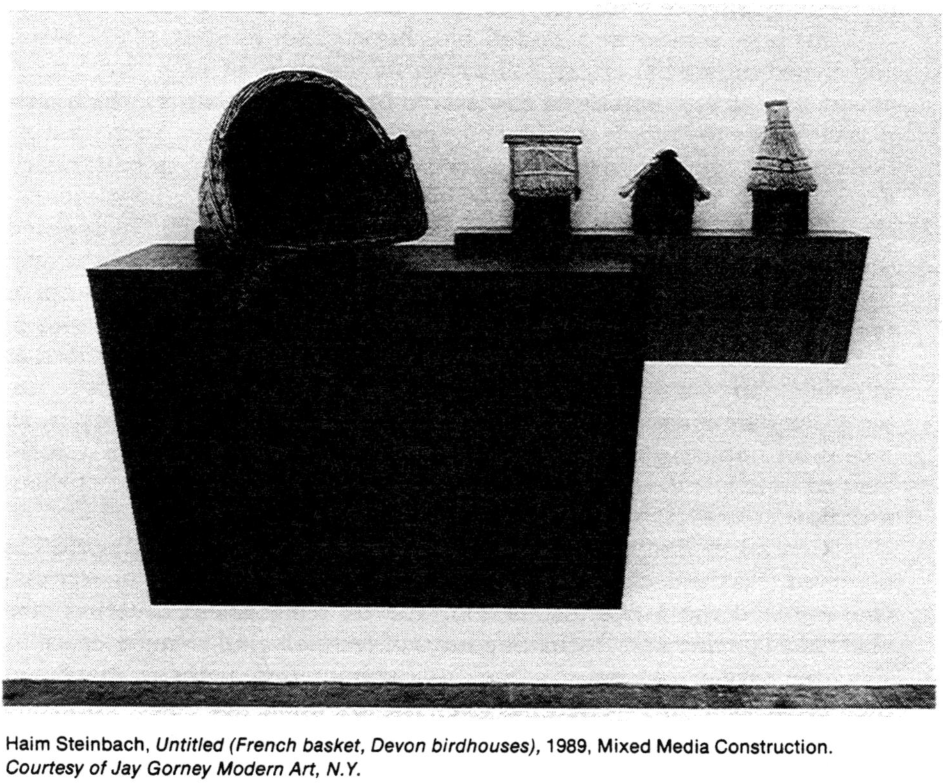

Haim Steinbach, *Untitled (French basket, Devon birdhouses)*, 1989, Mixed Media Construction. *Courtesy of Jay Gorney Modern Art, N.Y.*

totality of art is directed toward an encompassing ending, toward fulfillment of an inner logic.

To this vertical paradigm of interiority recent theory has responded with a horizontal model, based on the lateral play of signifiers. This is a historical mutation which Baudrillard has described in a simple structural opposition, invoking a clear inversion of terms. The 19th century, he writes,[9] was characterized by the destruction of appearances to the profit of meaning, by a general activity, dispersed through criticism, representation, and history, of the world's "disenchantment" by interpretation. However, the 20th-century postmodern period has witnessed the destruction of meaning and the hollowing-out of criticism, the elevation of system, structure, and surface. Gone is the aim of hermeneutics: signs no longer refer to a "subjective or objective 'reality,'"[10] but to themselves, and to the reticulation of their networks. The signifier becomes its own referent, in a tautological repetition of itself. And gone are the illusions of utilitarianism, for rationality is transferred to the system's own self-defining closure. Within such contemporary production, the signs for reality come to replace reality, registering the eclipse of reference: these "simulated" forms generate an unreal real, a real without origin, foregrounding their superficial, supplementary, surface status.

Artificial sunsets and Technicolor hues, glossy finishes, plastic wood and hyped-up special effects fall within the compass of such "hyperreal" production, to say nothing of Disneyland or Great Adventure, which purports to evoke the jungle consigned by civilization to the past. Such production does not conform to the structure of representation for, as Baudrillard notes, there is no reality left to re-present. Unlike "true" or "classic" simulacra, simulated forms do not imitate reality in an illusory manner; as opposed to the copy, the double, or the mirror, they precede and formulate the real. They register that irony of contemporary existence—that what we accept as reality is already simulated, a massive fabrication of effects which stands in for reality's absence. And although such hyperreality has been described as attesting to the "falsification of social life,"[11] the grounds for objective truth have been annihilated with the destruction of reference and, with it, all means for imputing the "false." What simulation discloses, then, is a world beyond truth, reference, and causality, an artificial universe without meaning.

Central to the productions of this period, as Frederic Jameson has observed,[12] is the decline of *affect,* the passionate investment of anxiety that characterized the Modernist period, and its replacement by effect, the alternately jarring and fascinating lures of technological incandescence. A sheer pleasure in surfaces, in a "look"—in shimmering synthetics that flaunt their artificial origins—effect has given rise to a whole new object world and to a distinctive cultural style. It is a style determined by and reflective of the complexity of new technology, which has moved beyond simple serial repetition to dazzling virtuoso effects. As Jameson notes, this phenomenon is a historical one, a function of a specific moment in late capitalism when "it is very precisely those older vehicles of production which have been subsumed under the radically different industrial dynamic of the computer, of nuclear energy and of the media."[13] Yet it is also a style with moral and epistemological implications: much as the discourse of interiority would abolish appearances, so this empty discourse of surfaces, in its annihilation of meaning, leads to the erosion of all coordinates of value, resulting in the equivalence of images experienced in the media's cool, dispassionate regime. "The era of simulation," Baudrillard writes,

> begins with the commutability of terms that were once contradictory or dialectically opposed. . . . In politics, of the left and the right; in the media, of true and false; in objects, of utility and uselessness, and of nature and culture on every level of signification. All the great humanist criteria . . . have been effaced in our system of images and signs. Everything becomes undecidable—this is the characteristic effect of domination by the code, which rests on a principle of neutralization and indifference.[14]

Within such "decentered" production, it is no longer possible to envision an expressive self as referent for a private, personal style. Nor is it possible to entertain once-elemental distinctions between authentic and inauthentic, original and copy.[15] "Reality" is constructed by the codes of society, by the "already written," by the received languages and conventions that assume the subject's place.

The framework of social construction established by the rule of simulated forms accents the mechanisms of control ever-increasing in contemporary society—mechanisms that are not simple seductions but manipulative, repressive powers. Within this programmatic ambience, reality is subservient to the seemingly represented, and events appear to be produced in advance, as spectacles to be re-enacted. We find examples of this circularity in statistics, where the real is confused with the model, or in television, where it is mistaken for the medium. However, simulation also embraces the poses, gestures, and models of behavior that both direct and determine behavior, just as it includes the many received images and recycled clichés whose ready availability cues use. And it registers the styles or manners, divorced from referents, that provide interchangeable surrogates for a self now eclipsed by the demise of interiority.

Our period has been described as one of frantic production of the effects of reality—effects that cover and, in so doing, attempt to compensate for reality's loss. The process is evident, for example, in the rhetoric of advertising, which masks its artifice through the contrived appeal of naturalism, and in the synthetic creation, in consumer products, of natural-seeming works. But this side of simulation is clearest in nostalgia, which consists of the reinvention of events as fiction, of the celebration of the imaginary style of a past.[16] The current return to history, manifest throughout the range of culture, indicates a desire to rehabilitate the referential through its artificial resurrection; to revive, through signs, what has vanished with the industrial period. Retro fashion, fascist style, the "remake" or historical film are its avatars; the license to play with inherited images develops from this very distance from that past. What we witness is the fetishism of lost objects; a return to the figurative is evident, Baudrillard argues, precisely when object and substance have disappeared.[17] But we also find such nostalgia in the simulation of prior modes of production: in mannerist and "Expressionist" painting, which would emulate the values of the premodern and modern eras; in cast bronze or hand-carved sculpture; or in the cult of sheer photographic replication, a relic of the industrial period. In each case it is the neutralization of content that lends efficacy to the medium, conveying its ability to seduce through fascination, through thrill, through the suasion of surface allures.

Baudrillard's concept of simulation, then, is one of remarkable capacity, indicating the void at the core of contemporary society as it manifests itself in consumerism, economics, and culture. Such regulation by the code describes what Jameson has called the systematization of postcapitalist life, an organization that is "*unrepresentable* and detectable only in its affects like an absent cause" (italics mine).[18] Its compass, however, also indicates the need for a mode of thought that, as Michel Foucault has written,[19] would register the vital consequences of absence, countering a Western conceptual apparatus (and Modernist esthetic) founded on presence. Such a "philosophy of the phantasm," as opposed to representation, would delineate the play of the missing event, whose origin is not measurable against reality and whose impact is diffused through the social sphere. It would inscribe the repercussions exerted by the demise of essences and by the reign of appearances. And it might explain something of the seduction of the brilliant surfaces, of vertiginous and near-impossible exactitude, that surround us, testifying to the dissolution of the real—empty forms, effects of the model.

Kate Linker is a free-lance critic living in New York City. Her most recent book, published in 1990 by Abrams, is on Barbara Kruger titled Love for Sale.

NOTES

1. *The Shorter Oxford English Dictionary*, London, Oxford University Press, 1973.
2. JEAN BAUDRILLARD, *L'Echange symbolique et la mort*, Paris: Editions Gallimard, 1976, pp. 75–117. The other Baudrillard texts under discussion here are *For a Critique of the Political Economy of the Sign*, Charles Levin, trans., St. Louis: Telos Press, 1981, and *Simulacres et Simulation*, Paris: Editions Galilée, 1981. Translations from the French, unless otherwise noted, are by the author. For further discussion of simulation see my

"On Artificiality," *Flash Art,* March 1983, pp. 3–35, and "On Richard Prince's Photographs," *Arts,* November 1982, pp. 120–22.

3. *L'Echange symbolique et la mort,* p. 85.
4. WALTER BENJAMIN, "The Work of Art in the Age of Mechanical Reproduction," as quoted in Christopher Phillips, "The Judgement Seat of Photography," *October 22* (Fall 1982). See discussion of photography as simulation model, p. 27.
5. BAUDRILLARD, *op. cit.,* p. 86.
6. Ibid., p. 87.
7. "Design and Environment," in *For a Critique of the Political Economy of the Sign,* p. 192.
8. Ibid., pp. 185–203, passim.
9. BAUDRILLARD, *Simulacres et simulation,* pp. 231–32.
10. BAUDRILLARD, as quoted in Mark Poster, introduction to Jean Baudrillard, *The Mirror of Production,* St. Louis: Telos Press, 1975, p. 7.
11. GUY DEBORD, *La Société du spectacle,* Paris: Editions Champ Libre, 1971, p. 43.
12. FREDERIC JAMESON, "On 'Diva'", *Social Text,* Fall 1982, pp. 117–18.
13. Ibid., pp. 118.
14. BAUDRILLARD, *L'Echange symbolique et la mort,* pp. 20–21 as translated by Craig Owens in *Art in America,* September 1982, p. 191.
15. For a discussion of these points see Mario Perniola, "Time and Time Again," *Artforum,* April 1983, pp. 54–55; see also Craig Owens, "The Discourse of Others," in Hal Foster, ed., *The Anti-Aesthetic: Essays on Postmodern Culture,* Port Townsend, Wash.: Bay Press, 1983, p. 85.
16. For a discussion of nostalgia in culture in general and cinema in particular, see Jameson, "The Shining," *Social Text,* Fall 1981, as well as the central source for this section, Baudrillard, *Simulacres et simulation,* passim.
17. BAUDRILLARD, ibid., p. 17.
18. JAMESON, "On Diva," p. 118.
19. MICHEL FOUCAULT, "Theatrum Philosophicum," in Donald F. Bouchard, ed., *Language, Counter-Memory, Practice,* Ithaca, N.Y.: Cornell University Press, 1977, pp. 165–96.

11

Nature and Culture

Peter Halley

Just a decade ago, having "soul" was said to be the cure for the alienation with which consciousness in the industrialized world was plagued. In the mechanized, repressed bourgeois world, it was argued, people had been stripped of their vitality, their spontaneity, their emotionality. Thus, an utterance that had "soul," that was endowed with spirituality, could be said to play a role in returning to humankind its oneness with nature, its "essence."

Today, however, thinking about these issues has changed, at least in the art world. The concepts of "soul" and spirituality are viewed by many as a means by which bourgeois culture has consolidated its position by denying its historicity. To say that a work of art is spiritual is to attribute to it universal, timeless value, and to suggest that the society which encourages and validates works with such attributes is itself timelessly and universally valid.

That opinion could be so radically transformed in so short a period provokes examination, for such transformed judgments are the result of a tidal wave of intellectual change that has washed over the art world in the present decade and has seen the practice of art which had been dominant since the Second World War completely swept away and replaced by another.

The practice of art from World War II to the end of the last decade was dominated by ideas derived from phenomenology, existentialism, and Jungian transcendentalism. This period attributed to modernism a vanguard, heroic role, not in the political sense, but in the sense that it claimed

This essay originally appeared in Arts Magazine, September 1983. Reprinted with permission of the author and publisher.

that art at times was capable of reuniting humans with some lost essence and that at other times art was able to release hidden, heretofore unaccomplished potentialities in the human being.

A history of art was written by this consciousness. It confirmed transhistorically the validity of the work of "masters" from other cultures and other historical periods, not simply to confirm a standard of formal values, but because formal quality was the sign by which the transcendental character of the individual master's consciousness could be apprehended. And around this search, which was also for integrity and wholeness, a second canon of modern masters was fashioned. Matisse and Brancusi were upheld for the magician-like quality of their subjective gestures and their embodiment of the role of the patient, transcendent craftsman; Mondrian was revered for the purity of his phenomenological investigation; Klee for the sincerity and ingenuousness of his personal vision-quest.

Along with the search for the integrated and spiritual in the traditional arts and crafts of Indo-European culture, a canon of the primitive was continued from European modernism, furthering the belief that in the cultures of tribal peoples could be located evidence of the possibility of the occurrence of a situation in which the whole human being was integrated with nature.

This first occurred in Abstract Expressionism, in Newman's appreciation of the terror of the primitive and in the influence that indigenous American cultures had on Still and Pollock. Then, in Pollock there is the suggestion of the artifact replaced by action in "real time," a suggestion that would be taken up a decade later in the work of an entire generation of conceptual, performance, and process artists who believed that the tribal experience of real-time art was the key to overcoming the deadening effected by the bourgeois art object.

This was a period of an art of nature—a period in which the artist sought unification with some lost or undiscovered absolute, whether achieved through meditative serenity, the probing of the Jungian universal unconscious, or acts of reunification with the earth itself.

It is a period of landscape, from the landscape-derived imagery of Abstract Expressionism, which was continued in the work of the color-field artists (Caro, Noland, Olitski, etc.), to its final culmination in the earth art movement which sought to literally return consciousness to its primordial mother, earth.

Even manifestations that at first seem to contradict this reading of the period on closer examination can be seen to continue it. Pop art, which had the potential to radically alter the course of this history, was contained by the simple strategy of dismissing it as fun. Within this epoch the Pop artists were isolated and without successors. (Only now has Pop art become an influence on another generation of artists.) The efforts of the formalist artists were likewise misinterpreted because of the dominant needs of the era. To the work of artists like Stella and Judd was attributed "presence," which thereby transcendentalized it, while so many other so-called formalist artists were influenced at least as much by Eastern mysticism as by formalist ideas.

Reigning over this entire era, one finds the philosophical tenets of phenomenology and existentialism. The art of this period is overwhelmingly concerned with the situation of the individual as perceiving and deciding entity. But before one can dismiss the production of this epoch as merely a typical manifestation of late industrialism concerned with preserving the mythic importance of the individual and of some absolute nature upon which the individual can act, one must remember that this ethos was formed and determined by another historical event, an event whose influence must be considered separately from the smooth progression of the stages of the development of capital.

If the art of this period can be seen as positing a relationship between the individual and nature, it is perhaps because World War II constituted an event that acted upon those who experienced it as nature. This mammoth event, although certainly caused by social forces, eventually gathered, for a considerable portion of the world's people, into a phenomenon not very different from a devastating flood or fire. World War II constituted a "natural disaster" insofar as it tore asunder the seamless web of signs that constitutes modern civilization. It left countless persons in a situation in which they were faced not with the codes that their societies had invented for them but rather with a hole in the "empire of signs," an accidental nature.

One has only to look at the tenets of Sartrean existentialism which advocates so many of the same values as Abstract Expressionism, to realize to what extent the experience of the Second World War influenced the era. For Sartre, as for the Abstract Expressionists, responsibility, action, "good faith," and the problem of inventing meaning and morality are the basic issues. It is as if to say that in the codeless world that war on such a scale had created, a world in which the usual laws of market and class—the mechanics of the bourgeois universe as it should be—were in abeyance, philosophy and art should be simply about the possible actions and decisions that a human being who has been stripped of his social role can undertake.

Why then, at the end of the '70s, did this transcendentalist phenomenologically oriented approach which was dominant for thirty years abruptly disappear to be replaced by a new practice that looks exclusively to the mass media for its repertory of images, that rejects the phenomenology of art-making as pretentious and mandarin, that interprets language as a closed sign without reference to any extra-human reality, a new practice that substitutes for phenomenological study a fascination with sociological and political reality, rejects the positivism of both the physical and social sciences, and replaces the cult of originality with myriad variations on the theme of repetition?

And how and why, around 1980, did a group of French texts loosely referred to as post-structuralist or structuralist, which includes works written from ten to twenty years earlier by Barthes, Foucault, Derrida, and Baudrillard, suddenly gain favor in the intellectual climate of the art world, influencing both artists and theorists and at the same time heralding and effecting the sudden vanquishing of nature from this world of culture in the name of culture?

To start with, it is impossible not to recognize that the generation of artists responsible for this upheaval is the first to be born after World War II and, conversely, that gradually the significant figures whose work was formed by the experience of the war have disappeared. Consequently the

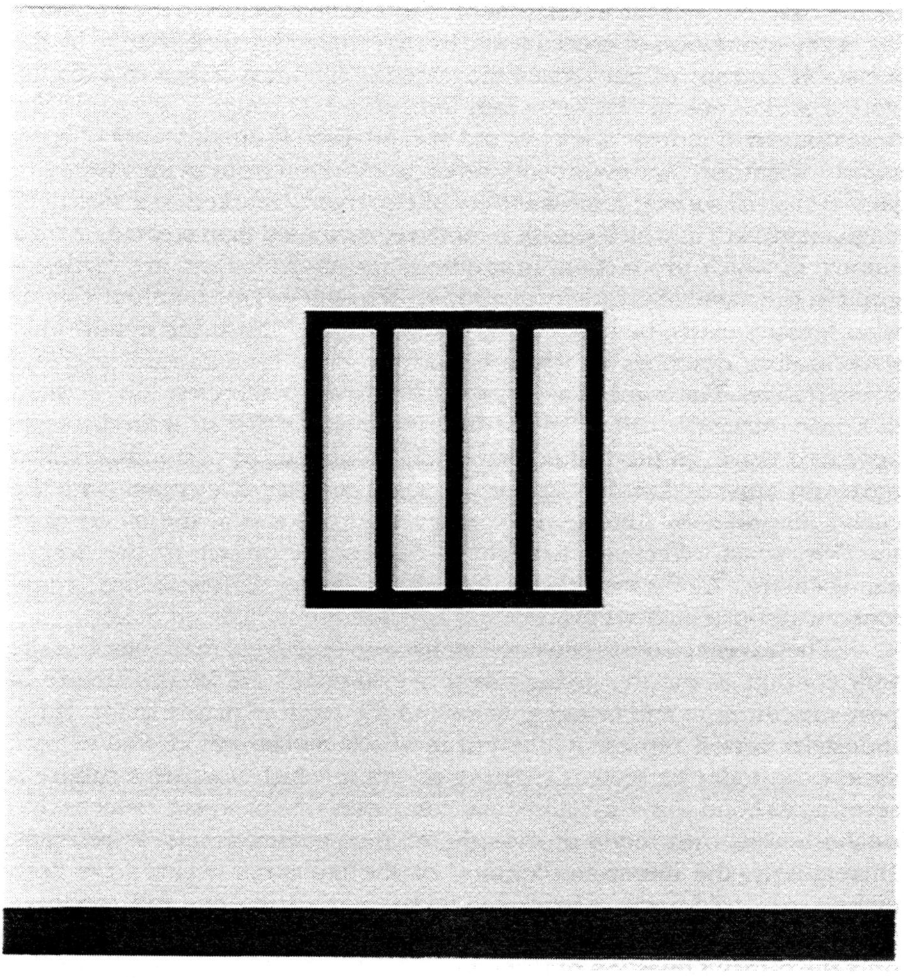

Peter Halley, *Prison*, 1987, Vacuum-formed relief print. *Courtesy of Editions Ilene Kurtz.*

existentialist values of the World War II generation have faded away, while the younger generation which (in the Western world, at least) has never experienced such a situation, in which all the rules are found inapplicable, has become fixated on rules, that is, on language.

This reading would perhaps indicate that Europe, which was far more devastated by the war than the United States, should remain intellectually affected by it longer, whereas not a decade after the war ended the structuralist movement was already underway there. This perhaps only indicates how strong an intellectual force Marxism was in Europe that structuralism, which is so much a Marxian way of thinking, could so quickly evolve in the wake of the war experience.

Or perhaps, unless one would seek an explanation in a formalist theory that connects the development of intellectual trends to the necessary lag in the translation of crucial texts, or that explains artistic change by the inevitable entropy of intellectual movements, one must return to a discussion of socioeconomic factors which links cultural change to events in the development of industrial society and of capitalism. From this point of view, structuralism and the new art both reflect a transition from an industrial to a post-industrial society; from a society of expanding markets to a society of stagnant growth in which wealth is more redistributed than created; from a culture in which production, innovation, and individualism are mythologized in the name of creativity to a society that stresses the manipulation of what already exists, be it capital or cultural signs. This is the culture that structuralism describes or which can at the same time be said to create structuralism. The conditions of such a post-industrial society have existed in Europe since the end of World War II, when the first structuralist texts appeared there. In the United States, the conditions of post-industrialism have only appeared in the last few years, in the wake of Vietnam (with the curb it imposed on American colonial ambitions) and of the oil crises of the '70s, which effectively brought to an end the growth of the American economy. Along with the arrival of post-industrial conditions, a new structuralist-oriented art practice has appeared in the United States.

The advent of post-industrialism has also seemed to make obsolete the very concept of nature, giving rise to a critique of the idea of nature in post-structuralism and bringing to an end the reign of nature in art. If the industrial period represents the era in which nature was viewed as real, society can today be seen as entering an era in which bourgeois culture is severing its bond with this nature and completing the process by which it has established its own mode of thought, its own consciousness, as referent. Increasingly, the important "others" of the industrial period have been eliminated—wilderness is bracketed by law, while tribal and folk modes of social organization have been almost completely assimilated (there remains only the difficult question of the subconscious).

Baudrillard, in particular, has advocated a historicization of the idea of nature. He describes the "triumph of nature" in the industrial period as an historical occurrence:

> Nature appeared truly as an essence in all its glory under the sign of the *principle of production.* This separation also involves the *principle of signification.* Under the objective stamp of Science, Technology, and Production, Nature becomes the great Signified, the great Referent. It is ideally charged with "reality"; it becomes Reality. . . .[1]

Bourgeois culture is increasingly seizing the opportunity to "simulate" (in Baudrillard's terminology) the crucial powers that were assigned to nature's dominion—the power of thought, repeated in the computer, which "realizes" bourgeois dualism; the ability to create life, accomplished chemically and mechanically; and the ability to create space itself in the binary circuitry of computer animation devices. Thus the circle of bourgeois thought is finally completed; the bourgeois world is made to refer back only to itself. Recently even the human heart, perhaps the most natural object in the old order, has been reconstituted according to the thought processes of bourgeois consciousness.

Advertising's recent appropriation to the vocabularies of nature and post-war modernism makes apparent the extent of this change, which is a triumph of the market over nature. That beer, detergent, and make-up are now called "natural" is significant. Today the name "Nature Valley" refers to a kind of breakfast cereal; cigarettes have been given such transcendentalist labels as "True," "Light," and "Now."

Yet a number of troubling questions are provoked by recent structuralist art practice. First, there is the question of how artists can address the world of the simulacrum. If indeed the post-industrialist world is characterized by signs that simulate rather than represent, how can an artist communicate this situation? Is it possible to represent a simulation? If not, it only remains for the artist to engage in the practice of simulation himself or herself. But by so doing an uncertain situation is set up. The practice of simulation by the artist can be seen as an endorsement of the culture of simulacra. But one wonders if such an endorsement is desirable if, as Marxist critics believe, post-industrial culture constitutes a further level of social alienation. Artists who ascribe to a serious structuralist practice still seem to be in the process of answering this question. But, as Hal Foster has pointed out,[2] the work of the so-called neo-expressionist artists clearly validates the new social conditions by its simulation of the modernist notion of the masterpiece.

Fredric Jameson has observed that cultural analysis is today dominated by two separate trends.[3] On one hand, there is the theory of the simulacrum, as developed by Baudrillard. On the other, there is the work of Michel Foucault, which sees contemporary culture not as a shimmering surface of autonomous signs but as a place in which the technologies of surveillance, normalization, and categorization have ever broadening control over social life. In contrast to Baudrillard's vision of the detached signifier, Foucault finds hidden behind the various signifiers of contemporary society the veiled signified of power, in the form of the consolidation of class position. One questions why artists and art theorists today have been attracted so exclusively to Baudrillard's rather than to Foucault's interpretation of social relationships. One wonders if perhaps Baudrillard's brilliant world of surfaces is not more seductive than Foucault's bleak excavation of the spaces of regimentation. And one wonders if artist and audience, seduced by this shimmering world, have not been deflected away from the investigation of crucial issues about society's structure.

Finally, one finds oneself turning away reluctantly from poststructuralism's promise—its potential for sweeping away the mythologies of so many deceptive humanisms—to a consideration of what negative results it may engender. For ultimately structuralism, whether Baudrillard's, Foucault's, or Barthes', cannot be separated from certain misinterpretations to which it inherently gives rise. To misinterpret structuralism is to arrive at a single reality, the reality of power—not the power with which one class controls another, but the single remaining power to understand and manipulate the codes.

Currently on television there is an advertisement for an investment services company admonishing the viewer that "Some investments require discipline, some require courage." Clearly this advertisement addresses the potential "investor" as if he were a kind of warrior needing the traditional martial traits. Here, as in so many sectors of contemporary society, including perhaps the present art world, the successful manipulation of the codes to gain social power is treated as if it were a life and death matter. To acknowledge only the existence of language has created an unfortunate limitation on the range of actions that are thought to make sense.

The final image that emerges from these reflections is the image of destruction. One thinks of the Second World War, that "natural disaster" brought about by social players, and one shudders at imagining the torrent of destruction that may be unwittingly released by the inhabitants of our own empire of signs if, in their struggles to gain power over the codes, they unleash forces beyond everyone's controlling.

Peter Halley is an artist who lives in New York. Halley is considered to be one of the most prominent theorists and spokesman for "simulation" and "appropriationist" modes of art.

NOTES

1. JEAN BAUDRILLARD, *The Mirror of Production,* Telos Press, St. Louis, 1975, p. 54.
2. HAL FOSTER, "Between Modernism and the Media," *Art in America,* vol. 70, no. 6, 1982, p. 17.
3. FREDRIC JAMESON, *The Political Unconscious,* Cornell University Press, Ithaca, New York, 1981, p. 92.

12

Art as a Human Behavior: Toward an Ethological View of Art

Ellen Dissanayake

It should be a matter of some interest and concern to those who teach and contribute to humanistic studies such as the philosophy of art that their work is founded on a heritage of philosophical speculations about the nature of knowledge and the mind that was formulated by men who had no reason to suspect that human consciousness and mental activity have had a long evolutionary history. Although modern linguistic philosophy postulates inherited predispositions for language and hence for mental functioning, most branches of philosophy continue their investigations without regard for the implications of recent palaeo-anthropological discoveries which imply that the human mind is of a remote antiquity or that it has evolved (and is evolving) within certain biological limits and that its varied abilities have necessarily and primarily been of importance to man's survival as a species.[1]

Aesthetics is one of the branches of Western philosophy that has generally, even resolutely, held itself aloof from scientific encroachment or

This essay was originally published in the *Journal of Aesthetics and Art Criticism,* summer of 1980. Reprinted with permission of the publisher.

scrutiny. In Western thinking art resists methods of science such as categorization, definition, or precise measurement. Its complex workings whether of construction or appreciation are private, unobservable and usually fleeting, and therefore do not lend themselves to scientific perusal.

Viewing art from the perspective of biological evolution, as in the present paper, is not quite the same thing as subjecting it to scientific analysis. More accurately, it is a *way of looking*[2] at art as a human behavior, based on the assumption that human beings are a species of animal like other living creatures, which further implies that their behavior like their anatomy and physiology has been shaped by natural selection. Such a viewpoint may suggest new avenues for thinking about some of the problems with which aesthetics has traditionally been concerned: the nature, origin, and value of art, not as an abstraction, not *sui generis,* but as a universal and intrinsic human behavioral endowment.[3] As this is, as far as I know, the first attempt to examine art closely in this way, my effort is in the nature of a preliminary inquiry, with the hope that others will be encouraged to modify, refine and extend the ideas presented here.
Ethology and Art

I. ETHOLOGY AND ART

The biology of behavior—or as it calls itself, ethology—is a relatively new science that is concerned with what living creatures *do* in their normal, everyday existence. General and specific activities, particularly those that contribute to the unique way each animal fits into its larger world of natural environment and other creatures, can be defined and observed. Recognizing that behavior is as characteristic of and dependent on an animal's way of life as his anatomy and physiology, ethologists observe (and compare, in order to better understand an individual species) universal behavioral phenomena and tendencies such as courtship and mating, territorial maintenance and spacing mechanisms, or communicatory behavior.

It is possible to view human beings from an ethological perspective if one accepts—as seems undeniable—that man is an animal species who has evolved and whose behavior as well as his biological organs and systems has had adaptive or selective value in that evolution. Human ethologists propose that certain ubiquitous behavioral features or tendencies in man's life are an intrinsic, relatively unchangeable part of his nature and have arisen and been retained because they contribute positively to his evolutionary success, his survival as a species.

Those who attempt to view humans ethologically are often dismissed as being sensationalists, reductionists, or mechanists. They are accused of being slipshod, or simplistic, or spinning theories heavier than the facts will bear. It is easy to find counter-examples that appear to refute broad, speculative theories, particularly where man is concerned, who for the last 25,000 years has—unlike any other animal—displayed a prodigious *cultural* evolution whose amazing variety of manifestations has tended to obscure the more broadly-based limits of biological evolution on which they are undoubtedly based.

Yet limits undeniably exist, and in order to understand these it is necessary to collect and compare examples of universal human behaviors from many societies. Accounts from anthropological studies of a wide variety of human groups show that in spite of wide lability in details, human beings universally display certain general features of behavior that ethologists have identified in most animal societies as well. For example, both human and animal societies tend to form and maintain some kind of social hierarchy. Both humans and animals (including reptiles, birds, and even insects) use ritualized nonverbal communicatory signals that formalize emotional responses, channel aggression, and reinforce social bonds. Like many young animals, all human children play. Fundamental universal human patterns and behavioral sequences have been observed in courtship and mating practices or in the mother-infant association, although these are overlaid with individual cultural variations. Similarly, in both animals and humans, an individual zone of physical distance from others is maintained, and relaxed with certain intimates or in certain situations.[4]

There are in addition behaviors that seem unique to the human species. Among these is art.[5] No human society has been discovered that does not display some examples of what we, in the modern West, are accustomed to call "art." It is worth investigating whether we can identify a universal "behavior of art" and, if we can, attempting to determine what its selective value has been in human evolution. Such an approach may seem distasteful or irreverent: the field of thinking about art, now that the subject matter of theology is usually handed over to the social and behavioral sciences, remains the last bastion of those who assume that man and his works are "above" or at least unconcerned with biological imperatives. One may argue, however, that regarding art as a fundamental manifestation of human nature with its roots in biological processes is not to reduce it to these roots, or to denigrate it, but rather to better appreciate its essential value. Awareness of man's connectedness with all life need not mean a denial of his uniqueness. Indeed it indicates more clearly where that uniqueness lies.

The paper will address three aspects of an ethological view of art: (1) the setting out of fundamental assumptions that such a view demands; (2) the attempt to identify a "behavior of art"; and (3) a discussion of a posited contribution of art to human evolutionary success.

II. ASSUMPTIONS

1. The ethological view of art presumes that the history of art as a behavior predates by far what is today considered to be the history of art. Chipped

stone tools, cave paintings, and fertility statues may be the earliest artistic artifacts that are extant, but they are not the beginning of art as a behavior, whose origin must be at least in the pre-palaeolithic phase of hominid evolution. Art is a manifestation of culture and in that sense is a concern of anthropologists, but one can claim that like other specific cultural behaviors such as language or the skillful making and use of tools it will have its roots in earlier, less differentiated, genetically determined behavior and tendencies. An ethological approach should attempt to examine and delineate these.[6]

2. Another assumption, alluded to in the introduction, is that the behavior of art has (or has had) selective value, that it in some way enhances the survival of a species whose members possess that behavior. Such an assumption appears to controvert the premiss that generally obtains in modern views of art since Kant, i.e., that it is "for its own sake" and has no practical or extrinsic value. An ethological view generally assumes that any widely prevalent behavior has a function and is the way it is for a reason. Art would not exist universally if it did not possess positive selective value, and we must ask ourselves what it could be about art that is essential to the survival of the human species or to individuals in it, or to the genes of individuals.[7]
3. Although the qualifying features of a behavior of art remain to be identified and discussed in the next section, we must mention here that the concept of art as a behavior does not refer only to specific artistic acts of making and enjoying artworks. Instead it comprises a broad general phenomenon which (like other general "behaviors," e.g., aggressive behavior or sexual behavior) is characteristic of all human beings, not just the special province of a minority called "artists."
4. Similarly, all human societies will have art, although it is accepted that no society need demonstrate or emphasize equally all the kinds of manifestations of this behavior.
5. Concern with the nature, origin, and history of the behavior of art does not include any assumption about the value (other than "selective value") of its result. "Art" does not, as in so many discussions of aesthetics, presuppose or mean "good art."
6. The manifestations of a universal behavior in one human group in one spot in time and space are certain to be limited. Art in our Western view will have to find its place as one of a number of manifestations that have existed and do exist.
7. Making art and recognizing (or "appreciating") and responding to art are more easily considered separately, although they are related and must each be understandable within the ethological purview.

III. ART VIEWED ETHOLOGICALLY

The Problem

At one time discussions of art by philosophers and critics assumed that it was defined by a quality (e.g., beauty, harmony, proportion, representational accuracy, significant form) inhering in an object that was recognized by a kind of predisposition in the attitude of the beholder. As aesthetic theory has developed, the number of apparently undeniable qualities or characteristics of art that have been suggested and must somehow be incorporated into any definition has become decidedly unwieldy,[8] and today it is generally agreed that definitions of art, if one desires them at all, must be either injunctive or open-textured.

Although the attendant problems and difficulties are of a different kind, an ethological approach to art is perhaps no less complex or daunting—at least initially—than a philosophically-based inquiry. To begin with, the assumptions listed above must not be contravened. What we call art must be universally applicable to all men (not only "artists") and societies past and present (not only modern Western society), and must have plausible adaptive value. At the same time we must hope that what we eventually choose to regard as artistic behavior will be neither so labored nor so broad that it is meaningless.

Secondly, one who proposes an ethological view of art is as it were breaking new ground.[9] To be sure others have made suggestions about the origin of art and about its significance or necessity to mankind. However, these offerings have rarely come from evolutionists or biologists (who tend to omit art from their speculations), but from writers on philosophy, history, criticism, and aesthetics. On inspection they turn out to be of little use to an ethological inquiry, for they are not based on the essential premise that art is a behavior that is the handiwork of biological evolution, and therefore they do not meet the assumptions listed above.

Regarding art's origin, for example, quasi-evolutionary views in the past have tended to trace it to one source: to play,[10] to body ornamentation,[11] to a "configurative urge,"[12] a creative or expressive impulse,[13] to sympathetic magic,[14] to relief from boredom,[15] or to motives of self-glorification[16]—any one of which can be shown to be inadequate to explain the genesis of more than a few of the varieties of art. Attempts to decide what art is, not by speculating about its origin but by isolating some essential X-factor that art provides to human life (e.g., adornment or decoration; "practice" for real life, "escape" from real life; sensuous or "aesthetic" satisfactions; order; disorder) have been made, but on inspection are partial and thus inadequate as well.

It is art's stubborn and irrepressible variety—of objects, activities, attitudes, effects—that causes grief to ethologists in search of first principles no less than to hapless philosophers of art. This variety is so in other human societies no less than in our own.

When we survey primitive societies in the Americas, in Africa and in Oceania we discover a wide variety of artistic and aesthetic conceptions.[17] For some societies art is extremely important and in others it has little or no importance. In some groups artists are specialists; in others art is considered to be an ability of everyone. Art may be in the service of specific communal ends or performed as a personal expression of feeling. Art objects may be carefully looked after or casually discarded; they may be considered sacred and valuable in themselves, or their value may reside in the supernatural power they embody. Value may accrue to novelty or to conventional formulaic repetition of tradition. Depiction may be abstract or representational. The artist may be admired or revered, or he may be regarded as deviant or socially inferior. Some groups consider that art comes from a special or divine realm, or that it is widespread, occurring gratuitously. Although usually one person creates one work, in some groups several persons may work on the same object.[18]

Our own Western notion of art is far from uniform or clear. When one examines writings on art he finds that, depending on the author, the word refers to a bewildering array of meanings. Art may be viewed variously as *artifice* (both in the sense of skillfulness or craft and of artificiality); as *fantasy* (make-believe, wish-fulfillment, illusion, the ideal, play); as *creativity* (exploration, invention, innovation, self-expression); as *form or order* (the psychological, perceptual and mental need to discover or impose a formal order on experience; pattern-making; recognition of beauty as order); as *heightened existence* (emotion, ecstasy, extraordinary experience, entertainment); as *disorder* (deviance or dishabituation); as *sense* (the immediate fullness of sense-experience as contrasted with abstract thought, or the sensuous qualities of things such as color or sound); as *revelation* (or innately-compelling symbols, of God, of reality); as *adornment or embellishment* (the wish or tendency to beautify, a decorative or configurative urge); as *self-expression,* as *significance or meaning* (interpretation) and as combinations of two or more of these.

It is evident that art is somehow concerned with all these things, but when they are more carefully examined from an ethological standpoint, the concept "art" tends to evaporate. Each of the above-mentioned aspects of experience can be subsumed under another psychological or biological need or propensity, without invoking a special behavior, "art," at all. For example, the well-studied behavior of play is able to cover all nonutilitarian making, as well as fantasy, illusion, make-believe, ornamenting and decorating. Exploratory and curiosity behavior can account for instances of innovation and creativity, if they are not simply called problem-solving behavior. Sensory experiences can be studied as examples of perception. All animals require formal order and predictability: cognition cannot occur without them, and some would say that cognition *is* perceiving or imposing order. Similarly, all animals require disorder and novelty: behaviors that include or provide these need not be called art. Heightened existence is frequently sought and obtained in experiences few would call artistic or aesthetic—e.g., sexual orgasm, successful acknowledgement or exercise of power, achieved ambition, sporting events, catastrophes, carnival rides, even childbirth. Revelation and a sense of significance are components of religious experience, or of loving and being loved—not only of art.

It would seem that by assuming any of these is art or is provided by art, a specific identifying feature still eludes us. To say that art is any of these one must say what it is that is *different* about "artistic" play, "artistic" order, "artistic" perception, "artistic" significance. In other words, one must still determine what is artistic about art.

Identifying a Behavior of Art

If there is such a thing as a "behavior of art" we must assume that it developed in human evolution from an ability or proclivity that our pre-palaeolithic ancestors could have shown. I should like to suggest that this root proclivity is the ability to recognize or confer "specialness," a level or order different from the everyday.

In every case, even today, when giving artistic expression to an idea, or decorating an object, or recognizing that an idea or object is artistic, one gives it (or acknowledges) a specialness that without one's activity or regard it would not have. One renders it special, recognizes that it is extraordinary. This characteristic of art has been referred to by other names by other thinkers, e.g., transformation,[19] aesthetic transposition or promotion.[20] It is a sort of "jacking-up," a saltation or quantum leap[21] from the quotidian reality in which life's vital needs and activities occur, to a different order, an "aesthetic order"[22] which has its own kind of motivation or intention and a distinctive attitude or response.

This root proclivity may also be identified in two other kinds of behav-

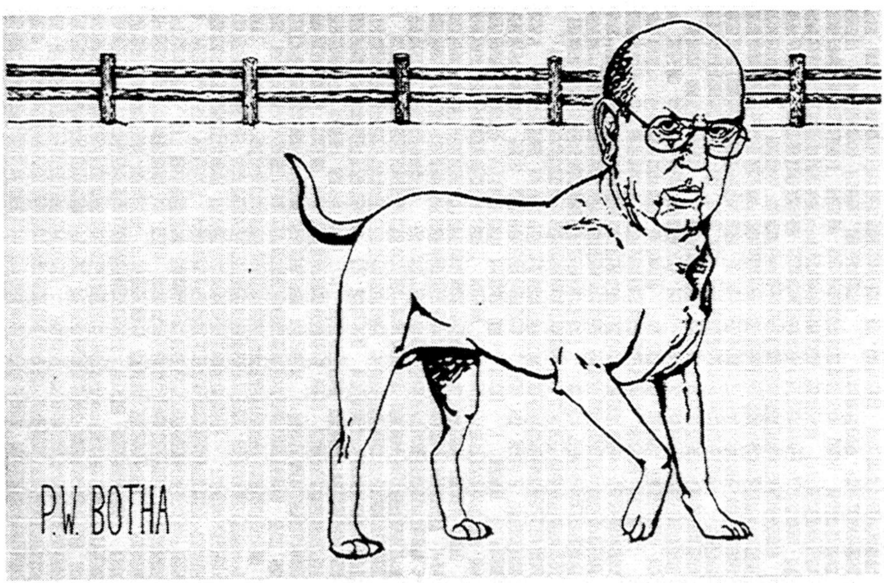

Tim Rollins & K.O.S., *From the Animal Farm: P.W. Botha (III)* 1984–89, acrylic on bookpages on linen. *Courtesy of Jay Gorney Modern Art, N.Y.*

ior whose similarities to art have indeed frequently been noted: Play and Ritual. For example, in most instances both play and art[23] use make-believe, illusion, and metaphor; neither is directly concerned with primary ends of direct survival (like eating, fighting, escaping danger) but is performed "for its own sake"; as behaviors they are labile and relatively unpredictable; they make use of novelty, incongruity, surprisingness, complexity, change, variety; they have an inherent dynamic of tension and release, arousal and relief, deviation and recurrence or restatement.[24]

As behaviors, ritual and art[25] are similar in that both formalize and shape emotion; communicate in a symbolic "language"; and for expressive effect make use of out-of-context elements, of exaggeration, and of repetition. Many rituals are expressly concerned with another level or realm from the ordinary, and art is used by ritual as a means to the end of revealing this special, extraordinary reality.[26]

The close relationship even today between art and play and art and ritual suggests that in human evolutionary history they were once intimately related if not indistinguishable. Acted upon by different evolutionary requirements and molded by different emergent physical and mental endowments, the root proclivity of making special could diverge into related but usually distinct currents: play, ritual, and art.

Art as we are accustomed to think of it, then, should be considered as an instance of the broader proclivity of making special. In our ethological view, *artistic behavior shapes and/or embellishes everyday reality with the intention*[27] *of constructing or manifesting (or recognizing) what is considered to be another "level" from quotidian practical life.*

Yet, although according to this view all societies and people have art, we cannot assume that all societies and people regard works of art with the distinctive aesthetic attitude that is usually presupposed by modern Western theories of art. The usual human responses to art, to things made special or the act of making special, are reactions such as being impressed by power or size or opulence or skill or monetary value; sharing the excited reactions of a crowd; feeling satisfaction at the carrying out of a known practice or observance; sensuous or kinaesthetic pleasure; vicarious enjoyment; catharsis; and so forth.

Although these may be ingredient in our Western response to art as well, we usually insist that there be an added "aesthetic" regard—that the work of art be experienced not only as it has been translated into another plane, set apart from the everyday world, but by an awareness and acknowledgement of the *way* in which this has been done. Although non-Western peoples are certainly capable of making such judgments (e.g., recognizing that a tale is not only a good tale, but that it is "well told";[28] agreeing that a dispute is not only settled, but "settled artfully,"[29] and some persons of leisure and cultivated taste in all higher civilizations have most likely been able to appreciate the "art" in art), such discrimination is in general not observably a widely-held ability or proclivity.

In other words, we can propose that it is the behavior of making things special and appreciating that some things are special which is fundamental, universal, and which has had selective value, but not the ability to appreciate how this specialness is achieved. Appreciating "how," the *way* something is done, demands a cognitive awareness—a more or less self-conscious discriminating, relating, recognizing and following manipulations within an acquired code. This type of awareness is of course biologically useful in human communication and in the processes of cognition and perception generally. But it seems safe to say that when developed to the degree necessary to appreciate a Bach fugue or Cézanne landscape, such an ability is biologically irrelevant.

IV. THE VALUE OF ART

Although it has just been stated that art as we are accustomed to understand the term—the fine arts—is not biologically necessary, there are those who would claim that art is still in some sense vital. Apart from biologists who might attribute a general adaptive value to art, poets and philosophers have often expressed their conviction that art is necessary, that it makes a qualitative difference to human life.

Let us examine some of the ways in which art has been said to have functional or selective value to human societies, and thus presumably to the human species.

Anthropologists frequently claim that art contributes essential social benefits to primitive societies: it expresses or relieves or canalizes feelings, reiterates social values, mirrors the social code, provides an avenue for shared experience, and the like—all of which are socially useful activities.[30] In historic times in the West, too, art has served social ends such as documentation, illustration of precepts and stories that are significant to society, pictorial reinforcement of traditional beliefs, distraction and entertainment, impressive display of wealth and power, facilitation in a group of a dominant mood, and so forth. Even today with much of art existing ostensibly for its own sake, art has socially observable practical and social as well as aesthetic consequences.

Yet there arises a difficulty with attributing the selective value of art to these or other social functions that it serves. The ethological view of art is not surprised that art is socially useful. But it is interesting to note that in some instances the socially significant function of art is to represent custom and tradition, that is, to uphold the status quo and maintain concord; in others, art provides an "escape valve" through license and heightened or diverted feeling. Art may be orderly and disorderly, immanent and ideal, emotional and intellectual, Apollonian and Dionysian—which suggests that it can be all things to all social and individual requirements.

Additionally, the biologically adaptive functions that have often been proposed for art (like the oft-cited characteristics of art that were mentioned above) refer upon closer examination not to *art,* but to characteristics art shares with other behaviors or to these behaviors themselves. Thus, for example, when people suggest that art is therapeutic,[31] or gives us direct unselfconscious experience,[32] provides paradigms of order,[33] trains our perception of reality,[34] gives a sense of significance or meaning to life,[35] and so forth, it is arguable that what is being referred to is not what is "artistic" about art, but rather what art shares with play, exploration, ritual, order-giving, and so forth.

It might be suggested that although other behaviors may contribute to our practical life, our sense of fulfillment and meaning, our psychological or social integration, it is the *degree* to which art embodies and communicates experience that makes it unique[36] and irreplaceable. For those who are receptive to works of art in the modern sense this is probably so. Yet, as we have implied, great numbers of people appear to get along psychologically and practically without assistance from the more complex and refined arts, and in addition they seem to find their greatest emotional sense of significance to come from nonaesthetic experiences such as parenthood, achievement and successful practice of a skill, power, recognition, being praised and needed, and so forth.

It has been only a very short time, speaking in evolutionary terms, that art has been detached from its affiliates, ritual and play, and that its various components have coalesced to become an independent activity. Until less than a hundred years ago the primary tasks of artists were not to "create works of art" but to reveal or embody the divine, illustrate holy writ, decorate shrines and private homes and public buildings, fashion fine utensils and elaborate ornaments, accompanying ceremonial observances, record historic scenes and personages, and so forth. The artist, in our terms, made these things "special," but specifically aesthetic considerations were no more important to most observers than other functional requirements—although it is not to be denied that artists of all times have been highly skilled in marrying the two.

Although space does not allow a detailed reconstruction of the way in which the behavior of art could have originated and evolved, it is my contention that only in historic times did the behavior of art become increasingly detached from the rest of life, regarded and valued primarily for its own sake. Although today in advanced Western society we acknowledge that it is possible to shape and embellish other human behaviors—sex, eating, communicating by word or gesture—in order to make them special, and the relationship of art and life can be said to be a major preoccupation in advanced contemporary thought,[37] it is not often appreciated that in a quite unselfconscious way art actually appears to inform all of life in some traditional societies.[38]

It would seem that in its rudimentary beginnings, the activity of giving shape to and embellishing life was not an impractical, leisure-time activity, but the way the human mind worked: it was a way of prehending and comprehending the world. Looked at in this way it was not separated from the activities of formalization (embodied in such activities as cognitive orientation, conceptualization, cognitive structuring, systematizing, giving narrative relationship in time or perceptual shape in space) and of the propensity—inherent in the ability to symbolize—to recognize or imagine an order other than the mundane. Such a proclivity demonstrates simply that man cannot bear, individually or as a species, senselessness or lack of meaning.

Our minds still "work" the same way. We still need a sense of meaning. But rather than finding this meaning exclusively in explanations provided by traditional social institutions (e.g., tribe, clan, family, caste, religion, a body of tradition, language, rituals) that are expressed and reinforced in symbols which have been given artistic form and embellishment, as have most human beings throughout the ages, many of us in the modern world are in a position of not accepting traditional meanings, or finding that they are inadequate.

The ways in which meaning was apprehended by our ancestors were not divided into separate entities called "art," "science," "metaphysics." Our attribution of the name "art" to tribal singing or dancing or to cave paintings is artificial and misleading. More simply, these are ways of finding meaning in life or giving it, making it special, ways that were inextricably bound to social institutions and practices whose fundamental assumptions are no longer accepted unquestioningly. By looking back and identifying elements, activities, and artifacts that suit our categories of what is artistic, we are in danger of giving an interpretation that was not known to the people who used these elements, engaged in these activities, and produced these artifacts.

Is there any reasonable way in which we can assign selective value to a behavior—making special—that was not independent? Only by acknowledging that what *has* had selective value is "giving meaning" so that aesthetic elements, activities, and artifacts, insofar as they have accompanied and reinforced meaning-giving have themselves had selective value.

Another way of looking at it is to recognize that *meaning is aesthetic.* Ordinary day-to-day life is formless, incoherent. When shaped and embellished or transformed as in ritual or play or art it takes on a greater or more significant reality so that when we find something to have coherence it seems to be "aesthetic." When we feel something to be aesthetic we recognize that it is coherent. This seems such a fundamental part of man's nature that the question of its "selective value" is beside the point. What is unprecedented today is that for modern man aesthetic meaning, bracketed, and removed from everyday life, does not invariably reflect a reality shared by his fellows, as it has for most of the human species throughout human history. In large part modern man must be his own artist and find or create his own meanings, meanings which do not necessarily cohere with other meanings.

It is my suspicion that the widespread Western axiomatic notion of the incompatibility of art and life, as well as the more recent concern with the shared boundaries and interpenetration of the two, are symptoms or results of this broad and gradual change in the locus of human meaning. Although their congruence with the concerns and values of human life remains an important consideration in our response to works of art, some persons in the twentieth century in the modern West have nevertheless been able to accept self-contained objects or events, isolated from the rest of experience, as art and to respond to them "aesthetically."

Indeed, this attitude—that detached self-containment is a defining and even universal feature of art (at least "great art") and that one's response to works of art is primarily or preferably a detached one—seems to be strongly embedded in contemporary advanced Western thought. I would like to suggest that although writing and theorizing about art in this sense may well be a fascinating and satisfying endeavor, it is however likely that like its subject it is a self-referential activity performed for its own sake and ultimately has no bearing on the wider consideration of art as a universal human behavior. We must be aware that our pronouncements about the nature of art derived from the culture-bound preconceptions of modern Western aesthetics may apply only to art produced and appreciated by persons of an infinitesimal number in both time and space, who appear in their conceptual framework and way of life to be unprecedented and without parallel in human evolutionary history.[39]

After living in Kandy, Sri Lanka, Ellen Dissanayake now teaches at the New School for Social Research in New York City.

NOTES

1. J. Z. Young, *Programs of the Brain* (Oxford University Press, 1978).
2. J. H. Crook, "Social organization and the environment: aspects of contemporary social ethology," in C. L. Brace, and J. Metress (eds.), pp. 100–115 *Man in Evolutionary Perspective* (New York, 1973), p. 112.
3. This paper does not address the fascinating and important question of the possibility of innate "biological" propensities for considering certain things to be beautiful. Investigations of preferences for certain proportions, colors, musical intervals and the like suggest that there may be some very broad, general innate or universal bases for taste and judgment, but these are not likely to illuminate our understanding of "aesthetic" responses to works of art which seem to be responses to subtle complexities that inhere in specific or even unique circumstances and that do not lend themselves to precise analysis and measurement. What is generally called "aesthetic" response seems to be based upon

at least tacit acquaintance with a "code" of symbolic representations—i.e., requiring an intellectual learned or cognitive element—which in itself suggests that reflexive or innate actions would be of limited significance in the total response, though they may well influence its general outlines.

4. These and other fundamentals of human behavior can be found described, with an extensive bibliography, in L. Tiger, and R. Fox, *The Imperial Animal* (New York, 1971). Also see D. Morris, *Manwatching* (London, 1977) for a compendium of universal human gestures and signals.
5. Whether or not animals make art is, essentially, a matter of definition. Some have claimed that the decoration of his nest by the bower bird, or birdsong itself, are examples of a rudimentary artistic sense. But see below, note 27.
6. There is not space for such an endeavor here, though in a still unpublished manuscript I have attempted to identify and draw together art's antecedents.
7. Resolution of the current controversy concerning the basic unit of evolution—gene, individual, or species—will not affect the theory presented here of the selective value of art.
8. See, e.g., H. Kreitler, and S. Kreitler, *Psychology of the Arts* (Duke University Press, 1972). Definitions of art usually include at least some of the following elements, claiming that art: is the product of conscious intent; is self-rewarding; tends to unite dissimilar things; is concerned with change and variety, familiarity and surprise, tension and release, bringing order from disorder; creates illusions; uses sensuous materials; exhibits skill; conveys meaning; conveys a sense of unity or wholeness; is creative; is pleasurable; is symbolic; is imaginative; is immediate; is concerned with expression and communication. None of these, however, is characteristic only or primarily of artistic behavior. Monroe Beardsley's insistence on the presence of elements such as these "to an unusual degree" in a work of art (see M. Beardsley, *Aesthetics* [New York, 1958], p. 528) seems to me the only way to include these ingredients, which art shares with other human activities and attitudes, in a definition of art. The present analysis of artistic behavior does not deal with such traditionally ascribed attributes of art.
9. Others have treated art from bio-evolutionary perspective but do not attempt to identify what their subject includes, or to treat it within a specifically ethological framework. See, e.g., A. Alland, Jr., *The Artistic Animal* (Garden City, N.Y., 1977); R. Joyce, *The Esthetic Animal* (Hicksville, N.Y., 1975).
10. Authors who have espoused "play" theories of art include F. Schiller, *Letters on the Aesthetic Education of Man* (1795), E. H. Wilkinson and L. A. Willoughby, eds., (Oxford University Press, 1967), 14th Letter; H. Spencer, *Principles of Psychology*, 2nd ed. (London, 1870–72); S. Freud, *Creative Writers and Daydreaming* (1908) (London, 1959); J. Huizinga, *Homo Ludens* (London, 1949).
11. A number of authors who hold this view are listed in O. Rank, *Art and Artist* (New York, 1932), p. 29.
12. H. PRINZHORN, *Artistry of the Mentally Ill* (1922) (New York, 1972), p. 13.
13. See O. Rank., op. cit., and Yrjo Hirn, *The Origins of Art* (London, 1900).
14. This view is espoused by numerous investigators of Upper Palaeolithic cave painting. See the discussion in P. Ucko, and A. Rosenfeld, *Palaeolithic Cave Art* (London, 1967).
15. P. VALERY, *Aesthetics* (London, 1964), p. 214.
16. Proposed by W. Perceval Yetts, *The Cull Chinese Bronzes* (London, 1939), p. 75.
17. Many primitive societies have no word for or concept of art, although many others do. Until art is defined ethologically we have no recourse but to look at their activities and artifacts and identify what we in the West are accustomed to call works or kinds of art: e.g., carvings, paintings, decorated vessels, dancing, singing, theatre, and the like.
18. A provocative discussion of philosophical and other questions raised by considering the manifestations of art in primitive societies can be found in Richard L. Anderson, *Art in Primitive Societies* (Englewood Cliffs, N.J., 1979). Accounts of various non-Western attitudes towards and practices of art may be found in Carol F. Jopling, (ed.), *Art and Aesthetics in Primitive Societies: A Critical Anthology* (New York, 1971); Charlotte M. Otten, (ed), *Anthropology and Art: Readings in Cross-Cultural Aesthetics* (Garden City, N.Y., 1971); and in Warren L. d'Azevedo, (ed.), *The Traditional Artist in African Societies* (Indiana University Press, 1973).

19. A. ALLAND, JR., op. cit., p. 32 *et seq.*
20. G. CHARBONNIER, (ed.) (1961) *Conversations with Claude Lévi-Strauss* (London, 1969), pp. 123–24.
21. My use of the terms "up" and "leap" and "more" does not imply that I consider this different order to be higher in the sense of more exalted than everyday reality. It means, really, "removed from" everyday reality.
22. P. VALERY, op. cit., pp. 148–49.
23. In the Gola of northwest Liberia, one word is used to designate the two kinds of activities that we call art or play. To the Gola, the distinguishing feature of this activity is to be an end in itself, and they include play, festiveness and entertainment, display, pastime, the making of images, elaborate decorated personal adornment, and a strongly desired by frivolous object as instances of this world. See Warren L. d'Azevedo, "Sources of Gola Artistry," pp. 282–340 in Warren L. d'Azevedo, op. cit., p. 306.
24. E. DISSANAYAKE, "A hypothesis of the evolution of art from play," *Leonardo* 7: (1974) 211–17.
25. In most primitive and traditional societies art objects are usually not even to be seen or considered apart from their ritual context.
26. E. DISSANAYAKE, "An ethological view of ritual and art in human evolutionary history," *Leonardo*, 12 (1979) 27–31.
27. According to the present view, art is never produced unintentionally. For this reason as well as others we will not attribute art to animals.
28. J. H. VAUGHAN, JR., "*ənkyangu* as artists in Marghi society," in W. L. d'Azevedo, (1973) op. cit., pp. 162–93.
29. J. W. FERNANDEZ, "The exposition and imposition of order: artistic expression in Fang culture," in W. L. d'Azevedo, (1973), op. cit., pp. 194–220.
30. This point of view is called "functionalist" and has been criticized as being tautological. The controversy need not concern us here.
31. E.g., A. Stokes, *The Image in Form* (New York, 1972), pp. 80, 86, 96, 105.
32. S. BURNSHAW, *The Seamless Web* (New York, 1970).
33. A. STORR, *The Dynamics of Creation* (London, 1972), p. 139.
34. H. READ, *Icon and Idea* (London, 1955); H. Read, *The Forms of Things Unknown* (London, 1960); J. Dewey, *Art as Experience* [1932] (New York, 1958), p. 200.
35. J. Z. YOUNG, *An Introduction to the Study of Man* (Oxford University Press, 1974), p. 360; E. Cassirer, *An Essay on Man* (Yale University Press, 1944), Ch. IX.
36. H. KREITLER, and S. KREITLER, op. cit.
37. For some examples of this preoccupation see A. Berleant, "Aesthetics and the contemporary arts," *Journal of Aesthetics and Art Criticism* (Winter, 1970), 155–68.
38. See, e.g., L. Thompson, "Logico-aesthetic integration in Hopi culture," *American Anthropologist* 47: (1945) 540–53; C. Geertz, *The Religion of Java* (Glencoe, Ill., 1960), pp. 233–34.
39. For a discussion of the "cognitive structures" underlying the making and appreciation of much of twentieth-century Western art, see S. Gablik, *Progress in Art* (London, 1976).

13

The Marriage of Art and Money

Carter Ratcliff

The Whole Business of Man Is The Arts.
—William Blake, *The Laocoön,* ca. 1820

The chief business of the American people is business.
—Calvin Coolidge, 1925

Imagine that art and money are characters in a novel. If they were to marry, which novelist would best convey the motives of their union? Henry James, undeniably, for he understood that marriage is a market transaction, and that no market, not even the most crass, confines itself to monetary exchange. A financial deal always has an aspect of the social, in the large and the small senses of that word, and the social entails the esthetic. James's heroes and heroines often read like allegorical figures of art and money, nowhere more clearly than in *The American* (1879), the story of Christopher Newman, who comes out of nowhere and makes a fortune, chiefly in copper. By the age of 35 he has accumulated so much money that more would be pointless, so he sails to Europe.

In the Old World, Newman visits churches—470 of them, roughly—and contemplates marriage. As he says in Chapter Three, "I have succeeded, and now what am I to do with my success? To make it perfect, as I see it, there must a beautiful woman perched on the pile"—i.e., on his money—"like a statue on a monument. She must be as good as she is

This essay originally appeared in *Art in America,* July 1988. Reprinted with permission of the author and publisher.

beautiful, and as clever as she is good. . . . I want to possess, in a word, the best article on the market." If Newman gets his wish, he will acquire not merely a distinguished wife but a living art work, a statue marking the pinnacle of a fortune so monumental it has its own esthetic aspect. I believe James means us to understand that, like the western prairies, the American's money is sublime in its vastness. Newman zeros in on Madame de Cintré, an aristocratic young widow endowed with complex and subtle loveliness. Their marriage would join the sublime and the beautiful, an esthetic event so devoutly to be wished that when Newman's proposal is accepted he seems to have achieved the ultimate coup, a deal so gloriously profitable that it transmutes money, mere lucre, into something ethereal—a medium not of exchange but of life lived as if it were a work of art.

Though some characters in the story believe in this transformation, the hero, as far as I can tell, does not. James appears to let Newman understand that he can move from one market to another, but never escape the realm of the economic. To belong to Western culture, in the Old World or the New, is to compete. Four years as a Civil War officer left Newman "with an angry, bitter sense of the waste of precious things—life and time and money and 'smartness' and early freshness of purpose; and he had addressed himself to the pursuits of peace with eagerness and zest." He turned from military competition, which tears things down, to the commercial kind, which builds them up. However, on a trip to New York to clinch a bit of particularly sharp dealing, he suddenly feels "a mortal disgust for the thing I was going to do. . . . I couldn't tell the meaning of it; I only felt that I loathed the whole business and wanted to wash my hands of it." So he travels to Europe to find a third market, the one where Madame de Cintré, an allegorical figure of art, is the prize offered for successful competition.

In his art criticism, James writes of portraits and landscapes as if he were describing the characters of his novels and supplying them with scenic backdrops. The most refined of James's invented personages are emblems of art, and he wrote that art works are at their best when the emblemize people.[1] James's novels join with his criticism to suggest that emblems of both sorts take their value from marketplace transactions, some delicate and others not. In James's *The Awkward Age* (1899), toward the end of the Book I, a character says that "in London. . . . staring, glaring, obvious, knock-down beauty, as plain as a poster on a wall, an advertisement of soap or whiskey, something that speaks to the crowd and crosses the foot-lights, fetches such a price in the market that the absence of it . . . constitutes . . . a sort of social bankruptcy."

This is brutal commentary and not applicable now precisely as it was in James's day. The economics of marriage and of personal image have changed. Nonetheless, his narratives still convince with their arguments that individuals are economic units, that every variety of meaning and value is generated by market transactions. Though Christopher Newman's aristocratic in-laws are particularly good at calculating the rates of exchange that transform cash into supra-monetary value, that knack is not the exclusive property of their class. William Blake, a social and esthetic radical shunted to the margins of the English art world, worked out such transactions with minute care. He began his annotations to the *Discourses* of Joshua Reynolds by announcing: "This Man was Hired to Depress Art"—with emphasis on the word "Hired." Blake saw the Academy as a monopoly that prevented deserving artists from finding their way to a fair market. Isolated from patronage, Blake devised complex strategies to compensate him, in imagination, for his hardships. Always in need of money, he never gave up hope for "a Fair Price & Proportionate Value & a General Demand for Art"[2] from a public somehow made indifferent to the snobbish authority of aristocratic connoisseurs.

When the hope of a fair market collapses, artists sometimes affect scorn for money. In our century Futurists ranted against "the slovenly and facile commercialism which makes the work of our most highly respected artists throughout Italy worthy of contempt"; Francis Picabia led the Dadas in their assault on "this odious trade: Selling art expensively"; André Breton tried to encourage the artist who works to satisfy not his need for money but "the personal needs of his mind." Offended by Salvador Dali's commercial shenanigans, Breton dubbed him "Avida Dollars" and expelled him from the Surrealist movement.[3] In the 20th century, whenever art and money threatened to marry, certain avant-gardists militantly refused to hold their peace. Despite their objections, the works of the European art movements—including products of the most violently anti-market stances—became valuable commodities. So did paintings and sculptures by the leading New York School artists, among them Jackson Pollock, Mark Rothko and others who nurtured phobias about selling out.

Pop artists sold well and seemed not to object. Taking consumer products as subject matter, their works gave those products back to the culture at large as images aglow with the aura of fine art. In a bliss of willful ignorance about compunctions that had tormented artists for more than a century, Andy Warhol reconciled Blake and Calvin Coolidge with the remark that "Being good in business is the most fascinating kind of art."[4] During the '60s, devotees of Pop art enjoyed a utopian state of affairs, a giddy sense of a world—or at least a world of images—made right by a union of art and money that appeared to degrade neither party. Things were not so simple for admirers of Color-Field painting.

Clement Greenberg's criticism didn't so much establish a credible rate for the exchange of money and "correct" pictorial form as it defined "correct" form as utterly pure, hence impossible to conceive in even the most tenuous relationship with money. Thought on the subject was—officially, at least—extinguished, so sales could go forward without a thought, or at least none for the difficult meanings stirred up by the marketplace. That Greenberg served—unofficially—as a sort of dealer-curator made matters all the simpler. The power broker who issued pronouncements on "quality" also stood ready to assure collectors that certain paintings were extremely good buys. As members of the Color-Field salon assumed a posture of condescending distaste for the marketplace where Greenberg's judgments were, for a time, so persuasive, others on other scenes began cranking up the horror of lucre to the point where it inspired a new vision of art somehow freed from commerce.

In 1965 Barbara Rose praised Minimalist objects that "blatantly assert their unsaleability and functionlessness, . . . difficult, hostile, awkward and oversize" art works that flaunt a "refusal to participate, either as entertainment or as whimsical ingratiating commodity (being simply too big or too graceless or too empty or too boring to appeal)."[5] Minimalism displayed a strong and almost immediate market appeal, however, suggesting that collectors could not be deterred even by an object's complete lack of qualities traditionally thought seductive. So, a new tactic was proposed: art must fend off commerce by displacing esthetic intent from the object to something less substantial. Antimarket radicals imagined—or put on a good show of imagining—that with none of the usual goods to sell, the market could no longer impose a money taint on the artist's work.

In 1969 the Kunsthalle in Bern sponsored "When Attitudes Become Form," an exhibition with a motto: "Live in your head." Scott Burton's catalogue essay suggested that "art and ideas are becoming indistinguishable."[6] Concept, in other words, was replacing thing. Kynaston McShine wrote of the artists included in the "Information" show he organized for the Museum of Modern Art, New York, in 1970, that they employ "concepts . . . broader and more cerebral than the expected 'product' of the studio. . . . they are interested in ways of rapidly exchanging ideas, rather than embalming the idea in an 'object.'"[7] Moving at the speed of thought, the new art would not—could not—be snared by market mechanisms.

Of course the "Attitudes" show in Bern included plenty of salable work—paintings by Robert Ryman and Richard Tuttle, sculpture by Richard Serra. Featuring Rafael Ferrer's blocks of ice and scads of scruffily typewritten pages by Barry Le Va, Sol LeWitt and others, "Information" looked more resistant to commerce—but only at first glance. Not long into the 1970s, a bustling market for ostensibly unmarketable art works developed, as buyers developed a taste for the texts of the Conceptual artists and the photographic relics of performance pieces. Earthworks bore no price tag, but their aura of unsalability generated a demand for documentation. As if to close, at long last, this chapter on art's failure to resist the usual market machinery, Michael Heizer's *Double-Negative,* an earthwork built in 1969–70, recently passed into the possession of the Los Angeles County Museum of Art.[8]

The marriage of art and money seems blissful these days, when artists like Jeff Koons and Haim Steinbach do well, critically and commercially, with works that celebrate consumerism at least as enthusiastically as they question it. Avida Dollars is the moment's unsung culture hero, yet blasé attitudes about money obscure a persistent uneasiness. Still half-consciously fearing that a union with commerce besmirches art, we put the blame on art dealers. After all, when art and money marry, dealers are the brokers. Cast in that questionable role, they look resilient and smooth.

Weathering the 1973–74 recession without much trouble, dealers in contemporary art glided to the end of the decade more than ready to cash in on Neo-Expressionism's "return to the figure."[9] Galleries have boomed and multiplied in the 1980s. New York's East Village scene invented itself, sprawled, then contracted as a new art neighborhood appeared at the intersection of Broadway and Prince Street. Partly a SoHo annex, partly an economically upward migration from the East Village, this outpost on Lower Broadway does not yet feel permanent. It does look prosperous. Paradoxically, as the '80s art market flourishes, galleries seem to come in for less blame. Flashier, more aggressive players have begun to assume some of that burden. Sleek with profits, they inspire moralistic fingers to shift direction, like weathervanes. Dealers, too, have begun to point. Their targets are the auction houses.

Auctioneers are charged, first, with inflationary mischief that divorces esthetic merit from any reasonable assessment of market value. In what sense is van Gogh's *Irises* worth the $53.9 million it fetched at Sotheby's last November 11th? Why not $5.39 or $539 million? The circus atmosphere of an auction encourages decimal points to leap about like wayward acrobats. Records are set, but not for all artists, all styles, all periods. Hence the indictment's second count: auctions narrow the art world's focus to the sort of object that goes well off the block. Much art is ignored, while a few varieties begin to glitter like financial instruments of a new kind—bearer bonds made of oil on canvas or sculpted metal. This is the weightiest charge: more effectively than gallery sales, bidding scrimmages on the auction floors don't simply taint art with a commercial flavor; they turn paintings and sculpture into a kind of money.

When the bidding sets a record, the event is news, and in any case auction houses must make their prices public. Though dealers are now required to post the prices of works on view [see pp. 86–87], that is all—absolutely all—the monetary information they must or will provide. They will disclose no details about discounts to favored clients, the number of exhibited works actually sold, or the nature and extent of their back-room business in unexhibited works. In contrast to auction houses, the galleries form an unexamined and largely unregulated market. This permits discretion, a valuable commodity in itself. As Andre Emmerich puts it: "Galleries offer clients the opportunity to collect art in the absence of publicity." Though the nature of the case thwarts proof, it seems sensible to assume that certain collectors reap measurable benefits from this pecuniary hush. Buyers may also gain a less tangible advantage from the ambiance that accompanies financial tact: with no auctioneer's hammer threatening, a client can consult with the dealer, get to know a work of art, make an informed choice. A personal relationship with the dealer and his staff may develop, and this can lead to friendships with artists, with other collectors and with curators avid to borrow the works one has acquired. From the stillness of the dealer's viewing room, a way of life elaborates itself.

I have of course presented an idealized view of the advantages of buying from a gallery, but it would be too cynical to suppose that the ideal is wildly at variance with the facts. Many collectors report themselves pleased with buying from dealers, a satisfaction they owe in part to the friendships fostered by the privacy that galleries are so careful to preserve. When a dealer in the secondary market emerges as a collector, as they often do in the '80s, friendship between entrepreneur and client is strengthened by a cluster of converging interests.

Friendship aside, much of the art seems united in distaste for the high-glitz commercialism of the auction houses. If art is to redeem money, shouldn't that redemption confer, at the least, a measure of genteel elegance? Some collectors revel in the journalistic clatter set off by record prices. Others prefer their consumption to be less conspicuous. They appreciate the power of a gallery's social ambiance to take the sharp commercial edge off the marriage of art and money. The finesse of the New York galleries sometimes permits buyers to believe, almost, that art-dealing is not a business like any other. Commercial realities fade or, if they insist on remaining visible, are cast into a flattering light.

Adam Smith argued that in seeking profits, a merchant is "led by an invisible hand to promote an end that was no part of his intention. . . . pursuing his own interests he frequently promotes that of the society more effectually than when he really intends to promote it."[10] Good businessmen unconsciously do good for the community, said Smith. The "invisible hand" is not market manipulation, as some commentators have thought. A benevolent force beyond any merchant's influence, Smith's "invisible hand" is a secular version of divine Providence. Guiding ordinary business people to provide social benefits above and beyond personal profit, this agent of a capitalist divinity settles matters so that a by-product of art-dealing is a transcendent *cultural* good. Or so dealers subtly encourage us to believe. No dealer claims outright that Providence has extended to the art market an "invisible hand" more refined and sophisticated than the one that guides ordinary markets. But all the dealers I interviewed make the claim implicitly with the observation that, by its very nature, the gallery business performs public services of an elevated sort, and their yearly rounds of free public exhibitions, some of museum caliber, give this claim a degree of plausibility.

To hear some dealers tell it, no "invisible hand," crude or sophisticated, shapes the auction market. Once the bidding starts, there is only raw acquisitiveness, a Hobbesian state of war that pits each against each and God—or the auctioneer—against all. No higher good emerges, just the spectacle of art works converted directly into lucre. Pushed to extremes, this argument would conclude that there are two art markets, one beneficial, the other not. Of all the dealers I interviewed, only Phyllis Kind came close to saying this. The others confined themselves to expressing reservations, mild or vigorous, about the auction houses' effects on the market and on art itself. Few dealers claim to inhabit an art market separate from the auction market, yet they all imply, more or less straightforwardly, that they operate in a shared market in a calmer, more constructive way. The dealers claim in effect that when they arrange marriages between art and money, the outcome is more favorable to esthetic value that it is at auction.

The auction houses naturally do not accept this view. Martha Baer, the director of Christie's 20th-century fine arts department, says, "Many collectors make purchases both from dealers and at auction. There's a great deal of overlap in the two sets of clientele. In fact, galleries will often make purchases at auction for clients, and would be remiss if they didn't, assuming that an appropriate piece had appeared on the block. Dealers are very active participants in the auction market." To the charge that galleries provide personal attention that auction houses do not, Baer says, simply, "It's nonsense. We talk to clients all the time." Furthermore, the major houses present lectures and offer art appreciation courses.

Lucy Mitchell-Inness, vice-president of Sotheby's contemporary department, acknowledges that vigorous bidding creates certain problems for galleries. When unnamed Japanese corporations and other mega-bidders enter the fray, prices can quickly climb beyond a dealer's reach—or at least beyond what they expected to pay. Moreover, dealers who can afford to buy at auction find that certain clients shy away from paintings recently knocked down at heavily reported prices. Other clients have no such qualms, and, in general, says Mitchell-Inness, "There is a wide group of collectors who buy at auction and from dealers. Naturally some make all their purchases from galleries, but another group only participates in auctions. We make it easy for busy people to acquire art. They study our catalogues, attend the twice-yearly sales, and build a collection that way. It isn't necessary for them to go running around in the rain or enter into discussions about price with a seller. There are no negotiations in the salesrooms. Some people simply enjoy the sport of bidding at auction."

Only the most indignant dealers would disagree with Baer that "there's room enough for everyone—and not only enough room. Also interdependence. Galleries often consign works to auction houses, and of course the contemporary pieces we sell usually came onto the market originally in gallery exhibitions" [before passing through their consignors' hands]. Yet, as dealers often told me, "The art market revolves around resale." Auctions

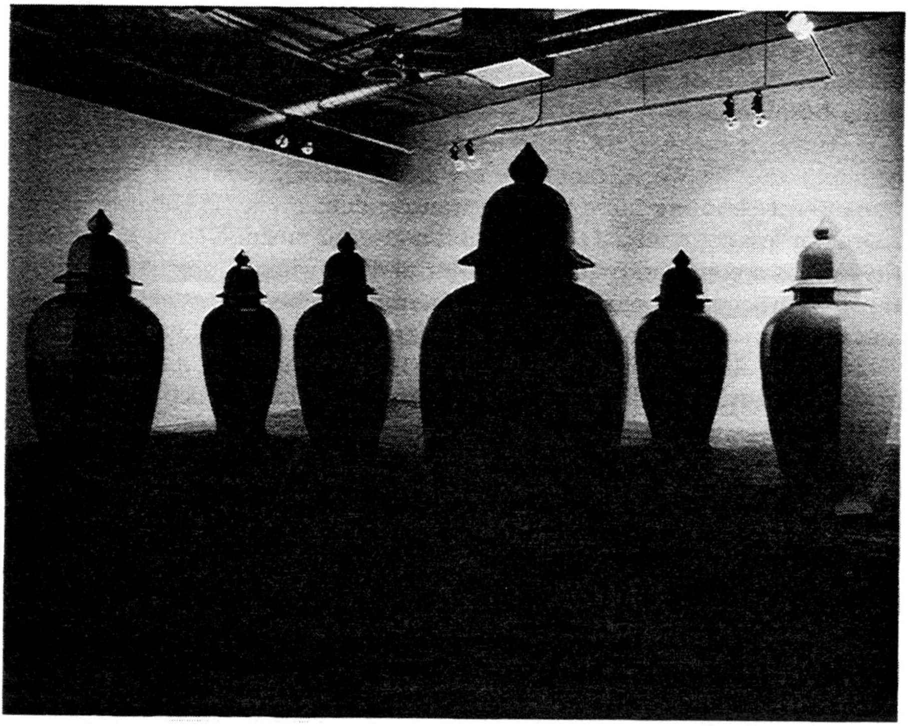

Allan McCollum, *Perfect Vehicles 1988*, Mixed Media. Installation view: Richard Kuhlenschmidt Gallery, Santa Monica. *Photo: James Franklin.*

have been indispensable to this resale—or secondary—market in contemporary art at least since Sotheby's sold off the Scull collection in 1973. For nearly two decades, the auction houses and the galleries have worked the same market on shared economic terms. If dealers wish to set themselves apart from the turmoil of the auctions, they must stress differences of style and method. Galleries are orderly places where advance schedules are determined in detail. Auction houses must take what turns up on consignment or whatever they, as art-stalkers, can drive from cover. So even as they boost the market in contemporary art, the auction houses must follow paths blazed by the galleries—or by some of them.

All high-powered dealers and many still gathering their strength are guided by some more or less articulate notion of what the history of art has been and ought to be, and these notions generate trends. The works on view at the auction houses' presale exhibitions of contemporary art can reflect current developments in only the roughest, fun-house way. Because of that roughness, because the auction houses can follow the contemporary market but not lead, and because they've made such a financial success of this tagging-after, some dealers accuse the auction houses of opportunism.

These polemics are effective in shifting the money taint from dealing to auctioneering, yet it seems clear to me that, despite their wish to accomplish an elevated sort of good for the culture, galleries are as commercial as any other business.

If this is so, then the galleries might as well shelve their attempts to convince the art world that they are better than auctions at redeeming money—at elevating lucre to some transcendent plane. If galleries are no more nor less commercial than auction houses or business firms in general, then art is a commodity like any other and we will no longer have to go through the motions of shock or enlightenment when artists like Steinbach and Koons present works that reveal (yet again) the commodity status of art.

Above all, we will no longer have to feel qualms about the marriage of art and money. We will no longer have to wonder if it is possible to separate the esthetic value of an art work from its commercial value. For, as nonchalant about art and money as we have become, we still try to make that separation. We still assume that a price tag is one thing and a critical evaluation is another thing entirely. They are not, though it might be helpful to say at the outset that I am not going to argue that esthetic value is merely a function of market value, or that a critical judgment is a commercial judgment in disguise. My argument is expansive, not reductive.

I believe that our persistent habit of trying to separate market value from esthetic value is misguided, like the struggle to extricate a picture's content from its form—an impossible feat, and not because form and content are so intimately intertwined that we can't disentangle them. They are simply not separate things: "form" and "content" are the names of aspects—facets, if you like—of a single thing. As our interests shift, we focus on one aspect or another. Sometimes the criticism properly called formalist focuses on shape and color exclusively enough to convince us that the aspect of art we call content is somehow extraneous—added on—to an essence called form. But it is not. Content, no less than what we call form, is integral to every art work. The space in Claude's paintings makes no formal sense unless we acknowledge that he painted landscapes. The space in Mondrian's paintings makes no formal sense unless we acknowledge that an aspect of its form is its content of De Stijl polemics, and, moreover, that those polemics did not banish from Mondrian's art all vestiges of Claudian landscape. Likewise, Western art since the Renaissance makes no esthetic sense unless we recognize that what we call "esthetic" is only one aspect of art works whose other aspects include those called "entrepreneurial" or even "commercial." At its most "esthetic," art as we know it is always "selling" something—or many things, its own vision of the world first.

Somewhere near the top of the list of an art work's offerings is its physical presence. Even the Conceptualist's scrap of onionskin paper wants to get bought, in the narrow sense, by a collector. But just as there is no conflict between form and content, there is none between an art work's wish to make itself attractive, a must-have item, in the eyes of collectors and its attempt to persuade a general audience to accept its larger meanings. The two appeals are more than compatible, they are identical—different aspects of the same invitation to understand, to accept, to buy the work and its meanings, figuratively and literally. Some art looks so obscure or outrageous that it seems designed to repel collectors even as it makes a bid for critical notice. Think of Jackson Pollock's drip paintings when they were new or Leon Golub's horrific tableaux. If critics do take note of "difficult" work—if, in other words, there is an exchange between writer and artist on the level of analysis—a marketplace exchange often follows.

Western art gains its entrepreneurial flavor from the Western self. We define ourselves in competition for economic profits that, thoroughly examined, reveal other aspects—social, cultural, esthetic.[11] Likewise, the most transcendentally esthetic behavior or image reveals motives in some sense economic. The esthetic is an aspect of the economic, as the economic is an aspect of the esthetic. So to carry on—as some still do, in however desultory a way—the project of isolating the market value of an art work in the hope of excluding that supposedly crass, vulgar consideration from the realm of the esthetic is as misconceived a procedure as the formalist protocol that tries to banish content from the realm of form. We often say things like, "X is a good artist even though nothing was bought at the last show"; or, more to the point, "Y is brilliant, *even though* her works are fetching absurdly high sums." I'm suggesting that such remarks, not to mention our allegorical images of the marriage of art and money, rest on a nonexistent distinction.

But what, you might ask, about the $53.9 million paid for van Gogh's *Irises?* Surely here is an instance of economic value added to a painting with no, or little, bearing on its esthetic worth. Time and again I hear it said that van Gogh is great but prices like that are absurd. I agree with this chorus of protest but not wholeheartedly. *Irises* fetched a nonsensically high price, but it doesn't mean van Gogh was any less entrepreneurial than other Western individuals, or that his art was not intent, in its way, on selling itself, figuratively and literally. [For more on van Gogh and the market, see Carol Zemel's article in this issue, p. 88.] Even William Blake wanted to make sales, as his many prospectuses make obsessively clear. In 1793 he published an announcement of a series of etchings with this note: "The Labours of the Artist, the Poet, the Musician, have been proverbially attended by poverty and obscurity . . . owing to a neglect of means to propagate such works as have wholly absorbed the Man of Genius." But now, Blake continues, he has discovered a printing process that makes his illuminated poetry available cheaply; he is, he announces, "sure of his reward." But 15 years later, his reward had not come, and he rails against "the Oppression of [Sir] Joshua [Reynolds] & his Gang of Cunning Hired Knaves."[12] Blake saw in himself a modern individual, and in Reynolds a representative of a guild authority on a medieval model, the Royal Academy, whose chief purpose was to drag art and individuals backward.[13] As Adam Smith objected to the constraining effects of old-fashioned mercantilism, so Blake argued that the Royal Academy was outmoded the moment it appeared.

It may seem odd to pair the sober Adam Smith with the visionary Blake, but if we can get over the habit of seeing the commercial and the esthetic as separate orders of value, it will become clear that Blake and Smith shared the modern entrepreneur's faith that, with providential certainty, free markets generate the best outcome for all. There is an image of Blake as an archetype of the Romantic individual who defined personal freedom as a value independent of marketplace demands. If we set aside this long-standing image, we will see that Blake did the opposite of what is routinely supposed; that is, he defined freedom not in defiance of commerce, but rather in marketplace terms that, when looked at from another angle, become the terms of untrammeled Romantic self-expression.

Artists like Blake and van Gogh—I mean visionaries of the kind we too readily see as untainted by money or the thought of it—feel a particularly urgent need to win in the marketplace, to have their visions accepted in as many ways as possible, by purchasers, viewers, critics, historians, everyone. That is because they, more than others, feel marginal and unaccepted. Of course it is the nature of modern institutions to make us all feel that way to some extent. The forms of feudalism, by contrast, molded themselves to the human material at their disposal in a way that the forms of modern factories and bureaucracies do not—or so we have believed ever since Horace Walpole began to play games with the Gothic at Strawberry Hill. However warped our view of the Middle Ages may be, our nostalgia for that era and for supposedly primitive, non-Western cultures is a strong sign that we feel bereft in our own times. Our institutions provide only so much acceptance and there are so many of us to compete for it. Look at the hordes of young people who come out of art school seeking the glamour of recognition as artists. How can we understand them—or our interest in art, for that matter—unless we acknowledge that esthetic aspirations cannot be formulated in our culture without formulating, in the same instance and with the same act, a desire for market success across the board, from the review columns to the collectors' living rooms? The entrepreneurial self looks nowhere without seeing a prospect for a sale.

But, I seem to hear, this doesn't quite dispose of the *Irises* problem. Surely economic value occasionally soars to a point where it splits off from any other sort of value, meaning that if we want to look at van Gogh's *Irises* as art, we must put its price tag out of mind. Maybe, but such compartmentalizing tactics remind me of Roger Fry's attempt to see the "plastic beauty" of Rembrandt's *Christ Before Pilate* apart from the "psychological truth" of the painting's narrative.[14] He set aside the narrative to concentrate on what, by his faulty logic, was leftover. I call his logic faulty because by removing one aspect of a painting from consideration he removed the entire work;

aspects, by their nature, belong to a whole. Seeing *Christ Before Pilate* as form divested of content, Fry saw something other than what Rembrandt intended. Thus he didn't see the work, nor will we see *Irises* or think about it clearly if we try to purify the picture of the astonishing knowledge that someone paid $53.9 million to own it.

If we are to live in our historical moment, we have to look at *Irises* (or a reproduction of it) with a full sense of the price it fetched and try to see that outrageous number as part of what the painting means now. Maybe we can't do that. If we cannot, the painting will go unseen in its fullness. We will see in its place an image lacking that aspect we call "intention," for van Gogh intended this painting to sell, and it has, ten times since his death.

I hope it doesn't sound as if I am making common cause with laissez-faire ravers and all the other theodicists who assure us that whatever is, is right.[15] I don't say that every price is fair, any more than I would say that every critic's degree of emphasis on form or on content is just. A market is a species of discussion, and any lively discussion is full of extravagances, irrelevancies and outright silliness. What I am saying is that in these matters fairness and unfairness, justice and injustice, turn on the same question: how well balanced is the market's or the critic's treatment of an art work? Does it account for all the work's aspects? Does it bring those aspects into an equilibrium that reflects the wholeness of the work, its unity, such as it is? Balance may not occur but it remains possible. If we think the latest price for *Irises* was thrown out of whack by a grotesque overemphasis on van Gogh's myth, we must also believe, consciously or not, that some price for the painting would be proper. And some price (don't ask me what) *would* be proper, for in our culture art works are commodities, as well as all the other things that they are.

Born beyond the clutches of the market, art must be seduced and prostituted to become a fit object for commerce—this melodramatic story is tattered now and often neglected, but still strong in a way, for it still provides a basis for our definitions of the esthetic. In rejecting the image of art as money's innocent victim, I don't deny that an entrepreneurial esthetic can produce abuses, in painting or sculpture or the marketplace, just as I don't deny that our entrepreneurial culture produced Blake's "dark Satanic Mills" and now expands the oppressive dreariness of the corporate bureaucracies. I agree with antimarket critics that for a quarter of a century the American art world has paid too much attention to money and the crasser forms of power. It's as if we had spent the last 25 years looking at the stars and stripes—and the auction prices—of Jasper Johns's Flags and ignoring the subtler sales pitch of the brush work.

Those paintings of Johns, especially the monochromes, have textures as luxurious as the exquisitely tanned hides of endangered creatures. Johns gave the anxieties of Action Painting the supple allure of melancholy. His Flag paintings offer death in a seductive mode—the death of an icon, the

Stars and Stripes; the death of Action Painting, an all-American style; the death of the New York artist as a two-fisted esthetic brawler. The offering was accepted, Flag paintings were bought, and in exchange Johns received a degree of legitimacy to apply to the account of the new model of the American artist he was bringing forth from the death of the old. He received a larger measure of legitimacy when museums bought his works literally and their curators bought, in a figurative way, Johns's claim to be not the only but nonetheless the most significant descendant of the New York School's first generation.

Meanwhile, the markets, both literal and figurative, for first generation figures like Willem de Kooning and Jackson Pollock boomed. They continue to boom. Only in markets for things like detergents or toothpaste does the acceptance of one commodity lessen another's chances. Detergents are all alike. Individuals and their works of art are not. The market for distinctive commodities, for emblems of individuals powerful to the point of defiance, is expansive—so expansive that, as we've seen, there has long been a demand among collectors, curators, critics and the general public for images that insist, sometime belligerently, that they don't want to be consumed. This makes them irresistibly consumable, for we experience our world as a marketplace where the most vivid presences, the offerings most in demand, include artists and art works that make the most fuss, sincere or not, about never capitulating to the market. Likewise, Marxism has currency among Western critics not because it shows a way beyond the mechanics of capitalism but because, with their challenges to that market machinery, certain Marxist critiques take on a particularly salable aura of courageous individuality. Each new Marxist challenge, no less than the most off-putting innovations of Carl Andre or Hans Haacke, is an alluring image of an entrepreneurial self. When we learn to see this not as an ironic peculiarity but as a straightforward fact, we will have begun to get a clear view of our culture and its art.

Carter Ratcliff is a contributing editor to Art in America *and the author of numerous monographs on contemporary artists. His most recent book profiles the work of Soviet-American artists Komar and Melamid and was published in 1989 by Abbeville Press.*

NOTES

1. "There is no greater work of art than a great portrait," said Henry James in "John S. Sargent" (1893), reprinted in *The Painter's Eye: Notes and Essays on the Pictorial Arts,* ed. John L. Sweeney, London, Rupert Hart-Davis, 1956, p. 227. For James's way of han-

dling what might be called the economics of response, the exchange of approbation for meaning, when faced with landscape painting, see "The Norwich School" (1878), *The Painter's Eye,* pp. 152–57. A notable point here is that an observer of James's authority determines not only what degree of approbation to give to works of art, but the amount and nature of meaning he is to receive from them.

2. WILLIAM BLAKE, "Annotations to Sir Joshua Reynolds's *Discourses*" (ca. 1808), *William Blake: Complete Writings,* ed. Geoffrey Keynes, London, Oxford University Press, 1969, pp. 445, 446.
3. UMBERTO BOCCIONI et al., "Manifesto of the Futurist Painters 1910," reprinted in *Futurist Manifestos,* ed. Umbro Apollonio, New York, 1973, p. 25; Francis Picabia, "DADA Manifesto" (1920), reprinted in *Dadas on Art,* ed. Lucy R. Lippard, Englewood Cliffs, N.J., 1971, p. 166; André Breton, "The Relationship Between Intellectual Work and Capital" (1930), reprinted in *What Is Surrealism? Selected Writings,* ed. Franklin Rosemont, New York, 1978, pp. 66–69.
4. ANDY WARHOL, *The Philosophy of Andy Warhol,* New York, 1977, p. 92.
5. BARBARA ROSE, "A B C Art" (1965), reprinted in *Minimal Art: A Critical Anthology,* ed. Gregory Battcock, New York, E. P. Dutton, 1968, pp. 294, 297.
6. SCOTT BURTON, "Notes on the New," *When Attitudes Become Form,* Kunsthalle Bern, 1969, n.p.
7. KYNASTON L. MCSHINE, "Essay," *Information,* New York, Museum of Modern Art, 1970, p. 139. See also Carter Ratcliff, "SMS: Art in Real Time," *SMS: A Collection of Original Multiples,* New York, Reinhold-Brown Gallery, 1988, n.p. Organized by the American Surrealist William Copley in 1968, SMS ("Stop More Shit") was a utopian attempt to transform works of art from luxury goods into mass-produced objects available through the mail for a nominal fee. Two decades later, it is difficult to determine how ironically the project's participants espoused its utopianism. Among the contributors to SMS were such gallery stars as Roy Lichtenstein and Claes Oldenburg.
8. For a summary of antimarket agitation in the late 1960s and early '70s, see Lucy R. Lippard, *Six Years: The Dematerialization of the Art Object,* New York, Praeger, 1973. In her "Preface" (1969), pp. 7–8, Lippard wrote that "dematerialization" is "introducing a drastic solution to the problem of artists being bought and sold so easily, along with their art. Not, God knows, that the artists making conventional objects want that any more than anyone else, but their work unfortunately lends itself more easily to capitalist marketing devices." But in her "Postface" (1972), p. 263, she notes that "dematerialization" did not free artists "from the tyranny of a commodity status and market-orientation." One wonders if they wanted that freedom, for, as she acknowledges, artists who in 1969 had looked to her like antimarket radicals were in 1972 "selling work for substantial sums here and in Europe; they are represented by (and, still more unexpected, showing in) the world's most prestigious galleries. Clearly, whatever minor revolutions in communication have been achieved by the process of dematerializing the object . . . art and artist in a capitalist society remain luxuries."
9. Of course the return to the figure was a non-event. The figure never went away. See Carter Ratcliff, "Stampede to the Figure," *Artforum* 22, no. 10, Summer 1984, pp. 47–55.
10. ADAM SMITH, *An Inquiry into the Nature and Causes of the Wealth of Nations* (1776), Chicago, University of Chicago Press, 1976, vol. 1, pp. 477–78.
11. See Carter Ratcliff, "Dramatis Personae: Proprietary Selves," *Art in America,* Feb. 1986, and "Dramatis Personae: Rulers of Sensibility," *Art in America,* May 1986, on the interior realm—the sensibility—that must be discovered, mapped and, so to speak, improved for this competition to go forward in a thoroughly satisfying way; in other words, the self competes best on a playing field where, as the only effective player, it holds Napoleonic sway. Thus does the entrepreneurial self, spawned by marketplace competition, become, in private, a totalitarian monopolist.
12. BLAKE, loc. cit, and "Prospectus: To the Public" (1793), *Complete Writings,* p. 207.
13. Blake saw Joshua Reynolds and Thomas Gainsborough as England's delegates to the party of artists, such as Rubens and Rembrandt, who "Blotted & Blurred" their way to contemptibly generalized images ("Annotations to Reynolds's *Discourses*" [ca. 1808], *Complete Writings,* pp. 445, 469, 477). "All Sublimity," Blake says, "is founded on Minute

Discrimination," and so the "great golden rule of art, as of life, is this: That the more distinct, sharp and wirey the bounding line, the more perfect the work of art" (p. 453). So far, it could be said, Blake has merely stated a preference for the linear over the painterly. But he claims that the "rule of art" also applies to life, and later in this passage he gives formal matters a moral significance: "What is it that distinguishes honesty from knavery, but the hard and wirey line of rectitude and certainty in the actions and intentions? Leave out this line, and you leave out life itself; all is chaos again" ("A Descriptive Catalogue of Pictures" [1809], *Complete Writings,* p. 585). Painterly painters try to sell us a false, generalizing picture of reality, according to Blake, who scorns their wares but not the market; he wants to sell us images of the truth, which, as he sees it, requires particulars to be discriminated with a sharp line. These economics of the image have a political aspect. Particulars establish individuality, in things and in human beings, an important point in Blake's view, for only the individual's imagination can grasp the "Infinite & Eternal"—that is, the truth ("A Vision of the Last Judgment" [1801], *Complete Works,* p. 605). Each individual must be free to see the truth in his own way, for none but the vision of a liberated individual can establish truth: "As the Eye, Such the Object" ("Annotations to Reynolds's *Discourses,*" p. 456). Only democratic government can tolerate such diversity, he believes, and only free markets can reward it. Politics and economics mix in Blake's diatribe against backward, monopolistic commerce that tries to preserve its power and oppress "Individual Merit" by imposing obscure, generalizing standards ("A Public Address" [ca. 1810], *Complete Works,* pp. 593–94)—for example, the standard of taste that leads to favorable judgments on the "Blotted & Blurred" images of painterly painters. Matters of politics are also matters of pictorial form. Consciously or not, every artist links form to economics to politics and back again to form. Adequate criticism traces those links in all their particularity.

14. ROGER FRY, "Some Questions in Esthetics" (1920), reprinted in *Transformations,* Garden City, N.Y., Doubleday Anchor Books, 1956, pp. 28–29.
15. See Alexander Pope, "Essay on Man" (1733–34), l. 289.

14

Suspicious Art, Unsuspecting Texts

David Carrier

What every serious critic is saying is that we are suspicious about the belief that reality can be represented, suspicious about the claim of art to be authentically personal expression, suspicious about the institutional role of the artist. And these suspicions appear both the product of historical developments within the artworld and the awareness that the writers who matter the most—Barthes, Baudrillard, Derrida, Foucault, Lacan, etc.—are themselves suspicious of representations. And yet, our critics are all too unsuspicious about the claims made in their own texts, for even as they deconstruct visual representations they almost unfailingly trust their own verbal representations, as if those texts could be immune to all the doubts they express.

THE POSTFORMALIST HISTORY NARRATIVE

Thomas Lawson's "Last Exit: Painting" (*Artforum,* October 1981) has a clear and forceful narrative line. We start with the (apparent) end of painting and ask: how can we continue? If the Russian modernist revolutionaries failed; if minimalism simply took Greenberg too literally; if the interest in radical action "remained only a posture, rarely developing into a deeper commitment to social change"; if neo-expressionism is smug, "acceptable to those who seek only entertainment"; then what is left to be done? Some false

This essay originally appeared in *Arts* Magazine, November 1985. Reprinted with permission of the author.

solutions are listed. Daniel Buren is master of "an elegant device" whose repetition already trivializes it; Sherrie Levine is the converse of Schnabel, her "appropriations" matched to his "misappropriations." Still, a positive suggestion appears "paradoxically" in Crimp's account of Buren. If painting's function depends upon the "mythology of individuality," it can be used to criticize that myth. "For since painting is intimately concerned with illusion, what better vehicle for subversion?"

The 'paradox' here is only apparent, for given the way Lawson poses these questions, what we inevitably expect, and get, is some answer to them. Since his sentence about illusion and subversion introduces that answer, it's worth observing how the rhetoric here involves an equivocation. Painting traditionally mimes reality; painting can be used to subvert beliefs about what is real. Understood literally, that is as problematic as Lawson's later suggestions that for Picasso Cubism and camouflage are "one and the same, a device of misrepresentation," but as a narrative device for introducing answers to his questions, it functions brilliantly. For now Lawson can contrast all the would-be photographers to the most radical, and so best artists, those who "place" critical esthetic activity at the center of the marketplace"; for example Lawson himself.

Notwithstanding its (by now traditional) critique of formalism the strategies here are thoroughly traditional. Just as Pollock was said to continue Cubism, and Stella to critique Abstract Expressionism, so now Lawson continues the tradition of painting. That this claim is so easily generated by the structure of such an historical narrative is one reason to be as suspicious of its claims as Lawson is of visual representations. Begin with a seemingly insoluble problem; point out its history, note ways that it cannot be resolved; and conclude with a more accurate solution. Even if we think that "our very liberty is at stake," note how the order of such a text generates pressure to produce a seemingly inevitable conclusion. It is hard to distinguish between these problems as they are represented by Lawson and how they really are apart from thus being represented. Imagine a reply by Crimp in which Buren and Levine were said to be more radical than Lawson; an article arguing that the radical artist is an outmoded figure; an essay by a formalist asserting that all these approaches are irrelevant. Each narrative structure would enforce a different view of the issues, for whatever we believe, how we describe our beliefs determines, in part, how what we say is understood.

If the central issue in "Last Exit: Painting" was constructing a story solving the dilemmas posed by modernism's end, Lawson's concern in "The Dark Side of the Bright Light" (*Artforum,* November 1982) is the representation of artists. Who has the authority to speak about art? If Kuspit lacks, as Lawson argues, authority to synthesize his, Lawson's, projects, then who can describe the role of such a critic-editor-painter? His work is like Robert Smithson's, and so, not surprisingly, he offers a very Smithsonian description of "that lethargy of progressive entropy in which everything seems to grind slowly to a halt and thereby crack." This sounds like Smithson on geology, but Lawson wants to narrate an illustrated history of the representation of Pollock, Warhol, and Mary Boone. If the present danger is that we are overloaded "with staggering amounts of information of all sorts then order may be created by this historical sequence. For just as (so Michael Fried said in the 1960s) Morris Louis is a figure in the sequence Cubism-Pollock-Louis, so here Mary Boone is a figure in Lawson's sequence. And just as Fried offered a formal analysis of Louis' paintings so Lawson analyzes the spatial arrangement of Boone's gallery.

To object that, unlike Pollock and Warhol, she is not an artist would miss the point; what counts in the contemporary artworld is less what a figure does than how he or she is represented. The pictures of Pollock working show "the spectacle of a grown man engaged in a manifestly daft gesture"—is this true?—and thus assimilate him into Warhol posing in an airline advertisement and a *Life* photograph depicting Boone doing her toenails. The danger Lawson describes, "all forms of representation . . . (become) inert," arises here within his context of representation of artists and dealers as depicted by the mass media. If this worry seems a puzzling one to present in *Artforum,* few of whose readers know Pollock or Boone primarily through *Life* articles, still Lawson's strategy provides an alternative to a more traditional account which might analyze the style of the art of Pollock, Warhol, and some painters associated with Mary Boone. If Lawson's conclusion that "art loses its autonomy" seems less a claim proven by this analysis than a result fore ordained given his narrative strategy, so, equally well, a formalist who assumes that content is irrelevant will construct an art history validating that assumption. Boone is here "one last, brilliant" master of these publicity techniques, as in "Last Exit: Painting" Lawson was the last post-Salle painter—less because no new dealers will come after her than because Lawson, like every good writer, aims to give his narrative an air of inevitability, achieving closure by identifying the end of the text with the end of those traditions represented in that text.

REPRESENTING THE POST-STRUCTURALISTS

Much contemporary criticism involves the explicit appeal to poststructuralist texts, and since the aim of those otherwise diverse theorists is to deny that representations are ever unproblematic, the representation of such theories themselves is complex. When, for example, Kate Linker ("From Imitation to the Copy to Just Effect: On Reading Jean Baudrillard," *Artforum,* April 1984) asserts that now "signs no longer refer to a 'subjective or objective reality' " because "there is no reality left to re-present," one should ask how that, if true, can be said. The claim that signs refer only to "an artificial universe without meaning" is, if true, problematic, since here the familiar word 'reality' is being used even as its normal meaning is rejected. To generalize: To think that the claims of Baudrillard, or Derrida, Foucault, Lacan, etc., can be paraphrased is to assume what they perhaps deny, that form and content are separable.

This problem occurs frequently in the texts of *Octoberists* like Hal Foster and Craig Owens. Consider Foster's account of Barbara Kruger and Jenny Holzer ("Subversive Signs," *Art in America,* November 1982). Though they are said to "call language into crisis," that crisis is confined to their work, whose nature Foster's language can clearly describe, and if for Holzer "language is the site of pure conflict," yet that site is represented without any conflict. Foster elegantly makes a general contrast between (everyday) passive sign manipulation and the practice of these artists "that renders the viewer an active reader of messages," a practice here subtly undermined by being so clearly described. Even in saying "neither photo nor text is privileged as truth," similarly, Foster seemingly contradicts himself, for though in Kruger's art photo and text interplay, in this exegesis of that unity the (critic's) text is privileged. The assertion that Holzer's truisms show that "only through contradiction can one construct a self that is not entirely subjected" must also seem puzzling, for unlike her, Foster does not play with contradictions. If the aim of these artists is to underline the distinction between active and passive use of language, the (unavoidable) effect of criticism about them is to break down those very distinctions. Even when in his closing sentence Fosters talks about "a critical task," of "setting the stereotype at a distance," he himself is involved in such problems, for here his text is a quotation of Barthes' words which have become well enough known to themselves be a stereotype. The effect of supplementation of such artwork texts is to remind us that Kruger and Holzer are artists, that their special use of language can be explicated by being placed within the context established by the non-artistic use of language as in Foster's commentary.

Craig Owens' "Representation, Appropriation & Power" (*Art in America,* November 1982) raises the very issues mentioned in its title by using texts of Foucault and Louis Marin to criticize orthodox art history. Owens describes a conference at which those Frenchmen were not present where "their arguments were, however, represented . . . by two art historians," Svetlana Alpers and Michael Fried. His narrative strategy is to contrast Alpers and Fried, who he says misrepresent the Frenchmen, with Leo Steinberg, whose "sensitivity to the viewer" validates their claims. For Marin, Owens says, "representation is . . . appropriation and is thereby constituted as an apparatus of power," and here in Owens' representation of Marin, Steinberg, and also Alpers and Fried, their texts are appropriated to argue for a conclusion none of them have argued for, Owens' claim that "postmodernist artists demonstrate that . . . 'reality' . . . is a fiction." To say that because they repudiate Marin and Foucault, Fried and Alpers "testify to art history's distance from contemporary artistic practice" is, similarly, to enlist them in Owens' argument. To treat Steinberg as a pro-Foucaultian critic of Alpers may, also, attribute to him ideas he would question, but within his text he is represented as an American art historian sympathetic to Owens' view of the discipline who thus functions as the link between the two absent Frenchmen and the two American art historians who misunderstand post-structuralism.

Earlier Owens follows Derrida in criticizing Meyer Schapiro and Heidegger for treating what paintings represent as a "stand-in or replacement for someone who would not otherwise appear," words which well describe his own procedure in appropriating the texts of these five figures. Certainly Owens' conclusion, "connection to the vital present . . . is absolutely prerequisite for all historical investigation," is interesting, and may be true, but the argument he gives for that claim, that Walter Benjamin believed it, is conclusive only if we already believe that Benjamin was correct. Like the postmodernist works it describes, Owens' text illustrates how narrative is ideological, how "the apparent absence of an author" ultimately is a fiction. For the author who assembles and uses these quotations, thus demonstrating that "representation is an inextricable part of social processes of domination and control," is Owens himself.

SUBTLE RHETORIC, STYLISH CRITICISM

One obvious question raised by my discussion is how I can consistently pose such questions since even as I question how Foster and Owens can represent other writers, I must myself represent their texts in ways, no doubt, they would in turn question. To begin to answer it, consider texts which avoid the problems inherent in either Lawson's historical sequences or the *Octoberists'* representation of absent authorities.

What is subtle rhetoric? Criticizing Hilton Kramer's critique of the NEA art criticism program, Donald Kuspit begins with a long quote from Goebbels and then notes how "however unwittingly" Kramer's views "unexpectedly" resemble Goebbels' ("Forum," *Artforum,* May 1984). But of course these resemblances cannot be unexpected nor unwitting, for they are created by Kuspit's juxtaposition, and what is unsubtle is the pretense that Kuspit discovered the comparison. (For whatever view one takes of American conservatives and German Nazis, their claims—as a reader who looks at the full context can discover—are pretty different.) If such unstable rhetoric is commonplace, what is rare is the stylish criticism of Carter Ratcliff; his texts, because they rely more on literary structure than reference to theory, pose most interesting questions for my narrative analysis.

Consider "Stampede to the Figure" (*Artforum,* Summer 1984). Presented with this new development, the figure's return, we are also told that the figure "never went away"; if Friedrich and Turner use the figure, so also do Pollock and Newman. For the 'figure' here stands for the artist's 'will' and that space, pictorial and/or real, the will seeks to dominate. This history of the will in art may be contrasted to the "always amusing and sometimes revealing" attempts of outmoded analysis, formalist ones for example, to explain such historical changes. What is compelling in this virtuoso performance is Ratcliff's own display of will, as when he illustrates his theory of appropriation by borrowing a quotation from a most unlikely source, Ronald Firbank, to explain the struggle among Pollock's heirs, or in his recurrent, deliberate paradoxes, as when he concludes that today figure painters are pertinent just because their claims are dubious. What does he mean by 'will', and how does appeal to it tie together Delacroix, Van Elk, Baudelaire's view of China, subway graffiti, Baron Haussmann's Paris boulevards, Rothko's suffering, Richard Long's landscape walks? (And here I merely list names without, like Ratcliff, elegantly weaving them together.) The answer of course is that 'will' is such a flexible, all-purpose concept that it cannot, and is not, meant to be defined. When Kruger and Holzer, for example, are said to be like Pollock, creators of works whose "boundaries have a strong feeling of the arbitrary to them," we have transcended any merely historical analysis or description.

What has "enchanted me," he wrote elsewhere, is the use in criticism of utterly inappropriate language, which may have "the allure of sheer willfulness" ("Critical Thought, Magical Language," *Art in America,* Summer 1980). Equally well, I am enchanted by his willfulness, and it takes a moment before I am ready to analyze his account. Ratcliff resented the presentation of the claims of formalism, which "were fictions, and poor ones at that," as truths. When he adds that "our resentments lay a trap for us, persuading us to define ourselves in simple opposition to what we resent," I begin to understand why he finds the 'will' so important. Faced with "the confusion, fragmentation, doubt of the moment," how is criticism to be written? To tell a history in which Pollock leads to Warhol and to Mary Boone, or give a debate in which Foucault and Marin argue with Alpers and Fried, is to offer accounts whose outline provides an armature which needs but to be filled in to produce the text. Admittedly, speaking of that arduous process as if it were straightforward is misleading, but the contrast I want to make is between texts which require such conceptual frameworks and Ratcliff's which does not. If what he thus gains is giving up narrative techniques which are, so we have seen, problematic, then how is unity to be achieved? What act of will holds his narratives together?

Look at his David Salle catalogue (Museum Boymans-van Beuningen, Rotterdam, 1983). Ratcliff flirts with an historical narrative; he introduces references to minimalist color fields, the glamor of sheer image (Warhol), the materiality of Salle's materials (thus like Pollock's enamel). But this genealogy is deliberately half-hearted, for before long he opposes the attempt of color-field painters and their critic-supporters to speak of visual

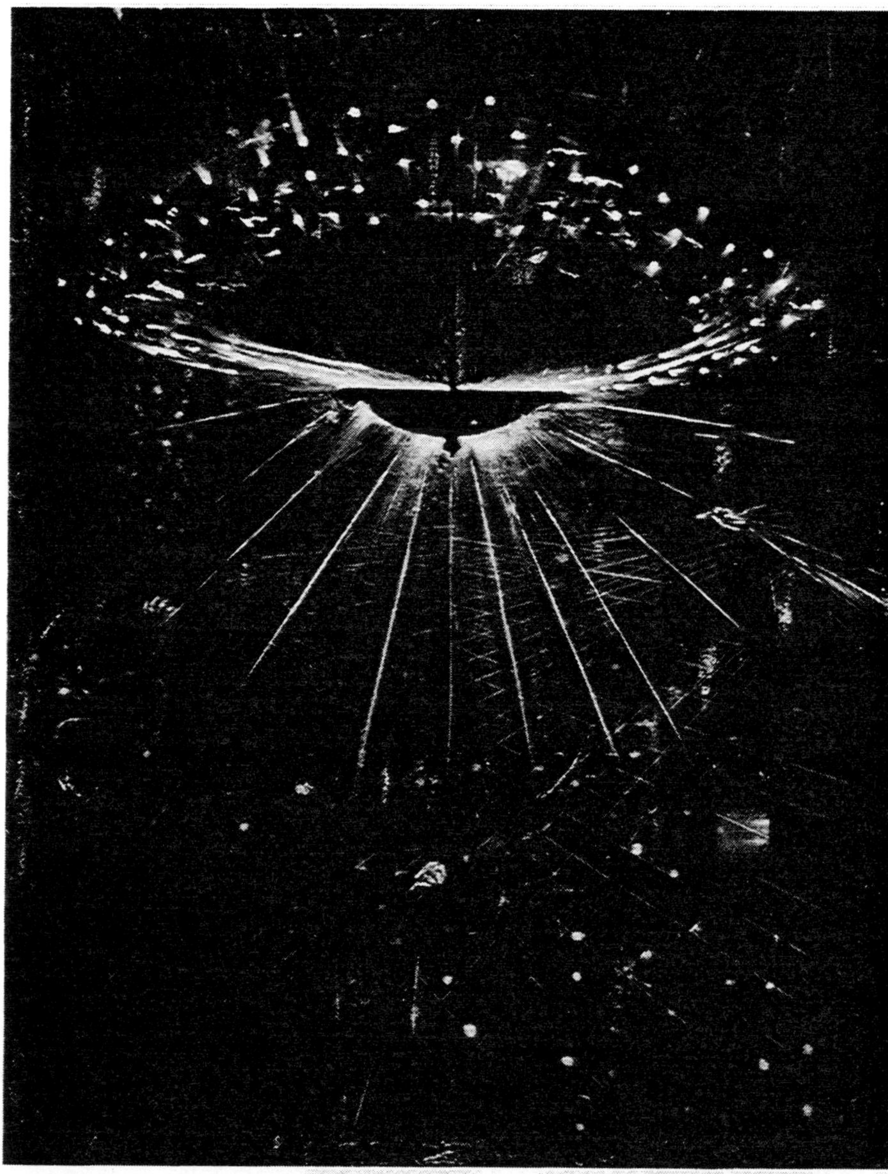

Ross Bleckner, *Examined Life*, 1988, oil on canvas. *Courtesy of Mary Boone Gallery, N.Y.*

necessity to Salle's refusal to do that. If we immediately start again running through history—Northern Romanticism's sublime, Smithson, Pollock—once again, even more quickly, Ratcliff brings us up short: "Once again, Salle is not a storyteller." Nor of course is Ratcliff. From Vasari to Fried, most sustained art criticism involves telling some story, whether of the artist's life, or the *ekphrasis* in which the text told in the painting is retold by the critic, or the historical narrative in which a painter's precursors are identified. Such stories provide frameworks for criticism. Take away that structure and what remains?

Ratcliff rhetorically asks, "we might ask how Salle himself manages to survive in the face of the anxieties and ambiguities he cultivates in his art." That question, which he answers by saying that the artist "begins every painting under pressure to devise a given of his own," describes his own strengths and limitations as critic. If Ratcliff's virtue is that he eschews all too familiar narrative techniques, the disadvantage is that he is left frankly dependent upon what he calls fictions. The Salle essay concludes by asserting that the paintings "permit us to entertain two vital fictions," and so "take on the air of the simple, the self-evident, the given." But since we have earlier learned about Salle's complexity, and been told that the 'given' is a fiction, this conclusion must seem paradoxical. A text which so openly questions its own conclusion is fascinating, but also problematic. To speak of the fiction that art criticism is coherent discourse on works and values or to identify the critic as a needed magician—"We can't shield our selves from his power. Nor is there any reason to want to"—is to be skeptical about this enterprise ("Critical Thought, Magical Language").

But how can that be consistently done? For in that essay Ratcliff appeals to the sort of cliché he elsewhere denounces—"Magical thinking is in league with the fragmentary nature of modern experience"—and he too provides that familiar fictional device, an upbeat conclusion by proposing that the best critics exchange "magical enchantment for imaginative language of a more sophisticated kind." Art criticism, he has said, "is a fiction . . . its unverifiable judgments are neither right not wrong, but useful, appropriate, moving or not" ("Art Criticism Other Eyes, Other Minds," *Art International,* December 1974). But if such talk about fiction constitutes part of his rhetoric, as in this attack on Greenberg's confusion of fictions with facts, how then are we to understand Ratcliff's own analysis, a fiction about fictions? So many novels, poems, and films both entertain us with illusions and remind us that they themselves are just representations; hence stories in which the characters tell us that they are characters in a story, and films about their own making. The trouble with Ratcliff doing that in art criticism, still, is that the art he describes exists apart from his representation of it in ways that fictional characters usually do not. And though much criticism involves fictions, as when Diderot narrates his promenades into Vernet's landscapes, the idea that such writing is itself a branch of is more difficult to grasp. If Ratcliff's texts are only fictions how can he tell us that without contradicting himself?

By now I am playing both sides of this fiction/reality division, since after criticizing Lawson, Foster, and Owens for making the distinction too rigid, I complain that Ratcliff makes it too vague. How can we understand the way art criticism stands somewhere between a truthful description and those fictions related to reality only as the town in which Marcel lives relates to Proust's hometown? Here an historical perspective is helpful, for it will help us to place Ratcliff's criticism.

THE TRIUMPH OF *ARTFORUM*

How can we describe our artworld in which such prose, suspended between fact and fiction, constitutes a meaningful system of discourse? What, to invoke Foucault's vocabulary, is the origin of such an 'archive'? In the late 1960s leadership in art criticism passed from the traditional belletristic journalism of *Artnews* to the severely professional style of *Artforum.* Two examples—many more might be given—can mark this break.

William Rubin's sequence of texts on Jackson Pollock published in *Artforum* in 1967 discussed that artist in novel ways. Earlier the subject of many brief, journalistic accounts, now Pollock is treated like an old master, a figure whose influences, life story, and critical literature are studied in depth. But what distinguishes Rubin's account from Greenberg's, Rosenberg's, and even Fried's is not only its length and elaborateness, but also its assumption that a near-contemporary artist deserves the in-depth treatment that would be given to Raphael. The search for precedents for Pollock's scale or drip techniques; the comparison of his color with that of the Impressionists; the concept of 'all-over' composition: all these issues, discussed briefly by Pollock's partisans, now can be analyzed in a text which itself aims for scholarly completeness by providing comprehensive references to the earlier literature on the artist. Because Pollock's importance is established, the analysis need no longer be partisan; the advocacy of the journalist is replaced by the objectivity of the scholar.

Such an account records the consensus that Pollock is an important figure in art history. The presentation of young, not-so-well-established artists in a similar format is a further innovation. Compare John Ashbery's account of Brice Marden ("Grey Eminence," *Artnews,* March 1972) with the discussion by Jeremy Gilbert-Rolfe (*Artforum,* October 1974). In many ways these texts overlap. Both talk about Marden's interest in Godard and Robert Ryman—say, that he responds to minimalism and Johns—and place his art in a larger historical context. But where Ashbery's first paragraph moves from a description of Marden's collection of art reproductions to asserting that in his art "the urgent articulations of Kafka, Dylan or Cézanne" are somehow being reworked, Gilbert-Rolfe takes nineteen pretty dense paragraphs of art-historical analysis to get a personal account of the artist. Where Ashbery merely invokes names of Marden's immediate precursors, Gilbert-Rolfe elaborately analyzes their work. Ashbery's graceful commentary on a studio visit is akin to the early 1951 "Pollock paints a picture"

Artnews articles; Gilbert-Rolfe assumes that Marden is already, like Rubin's Pollock, an art-historical figure.

"All of the pictures seem to be keeping a weather eye on Doomsday while asserting in various ways that there are important things still to be done"; Ashbery's words are sufficiently vague as to be undebatable. The same is not true of Gilbert-Rolfe's. To assert that Marden redoes Cézanne after Johns—"Marden has taken the dialectic implied in Cézanne's technique to be a characteristic of the physical object"; that his analysis of painting's institutions is absolutely opposed to Stella's; that where for Kelly "color stands for an entirely conceptual and abstract space (for) Marden it denotes things and also brings them together"—is to make specific claims of a sort which today seem problematic. Gilbert-Rolfe's analysis is not so different from Fried's claims in the 1960s that Stella's deductive structure relates him to Mondrian, and that Olitski's color is akin to van Eyck's.

The trouble with such talk, skeptical critics like Ratcliff have urged with great success, is that it is not so much false as fictitious. For if the aim of such writing is to lend status to a new artist's work by persuading us that it is the natural and inevitable outcome of earlier art, we now recognize that the only necessity here is 'narrative necessity', that the relationship between these works is defined largely by how they are represented in such texts. Such art-historical genealogies seem fictions created by the critic, which is why Ratcliff is so hesitant in presenting Salle as the successor of the Minimalists and Pop artists, and also why nowadays Marden's work is written about differently.

The art history of which I speak is itself a relatively recent creation, for a contrast analogous to that of Ashbery's and Gilbert-Rolfe's accounts appears in late 19th-century texts. Compare, for example, Wölfflin's *Classical Art* (1899) with *The Cicerone* (1855) of his teacher, Jacob Burckhardt. Where Burckhardt says that in Raphael's *Sistine Madonna* "the expression of the supernatural is produced not merely by the idealized form, but by the visionary treatment of space, the advancing forward upon the clouds, and the grand, solemn flow of the drapery"—and that is his full account—Wölfflin has an extended formal analysis. A recent article ("The Curtain in Raphael's *Sistine Madonna,*" Johann Konrad Eberlein, *Art Bulletin,* March 1983) summarizes 78 accounts of just the curtain in that picture, and itself, predictably, generated in response a 79th account ("Raphael's Curtain," Richard Cocke, *Art Bulletin,* June 1984). What marks art history is posing questions about pictures in a detailed enough way that such ongoing debate is possible. In this transition from texts of poets or tour guides to that of professors, the difference between Vasari's and Goethe's impressionistic remarks on *The Last Supper* and Leo Steinberg's staggeringly complex book-length article is not just that Steinberg tells us much more about Leonardo's picture, but that such close analysis is an altogether new phenomenon. This birth of professional art history introduces problems, I am suggesting, not unlike the triumph of *Artforum.*

For the transition from the journalism of Burckhardt or Ashbery to the art history-style writing of Wölfflin and Gilbert-Rolfe raises altogether novel questions about the capacity of such texts to truthfully represent the artworks described. Burckhardt's discussion of the *Sistine Madonna* and Ashbery's of the early 1970s Mardens are sufficiently brief and vague that one would be hard-pressed to explain how they could be false. The texts of Wölfflin and Gilbert-Rolfe, so the subsequent vast literature debating with them shows, are specific enough to provide starting points for such debate, for it is when artworks are described in great detail that later writers may object to both parts of that interpretation and its methodological presuppositions. Yet, paradoxically, it is just when the debate does proceed at great length that concerns about whether any interpretation can be true become pressing. If 78 interpretations have failed to establish the significance of Raphael's depicted curtain, if so much Pollock criticism has not produced agreement about his significance, could that be because such accounts are less true or false than convincing or not? This is of course what Ratcliff says when he calls art criticism 'rhetoric'. If art historians have failed to draw the equivalent lesson about their field, perhaps that is because nowadays few of them are much interested in concerns about theory.

In the study of contemporary art, in any case, what constitutes the triumph of *Artforum* is the general acceptance of the belief that serious criticism should be written in such a dense, art-historical-type style. Of course, not every text in this journal is so written, and many accounts elsewhere imitate this style; but the consensus about the importance of *Artforum* marks a sea-change in how art criticism is evaluated. Compared with what Lawson, Owens, Foster, or Ratcliff usually write, what appears today in *Artnews* is by comparison merely popularization. "Pollock paints a picture" (Robert Goodnough, *Artnews,* May 1951) was an important account, but the recent *Artnews* coverage of Salle is, by contrast, a simplified version of earlier, more influential accounts like Ratcliff's. This belief that serious discussion of contemporary art is a specialized enterprise, initially accessible to only a relatively limited audience, is the assumption which defines the role of *Artforum,* and thus distinguishes it from more widely read, easier-to-understand journals.

My strategy at each stage in this account has been to note how what critics say about visual representations can be applied also to their verbal representations of those images. What justifies this approach is recognizing that suspicions about the capacity of pictures to represent should also be extended to questioning texts. What is inconsistent in the writing of Lawson, Foster, Owens, and others, I urge, is the failure to press their skepticism far enough. And yet, Ratcliff's frank admission that all criticism, his own included, involves fictions also, so I have argued, leaves problems. For though the search for truthful art-critical descriptions may in the end turn out to be a chimera, if we believe that such a quest is not even possible, how can criticism be written at all? What is so interesting about this history of criticism is that it thus mimics the development of recent art itself, as if we all gradually began to realize that our questions about art are also questions about how that art may be described. What then is the meaning of 'the triumph of *Artforum*'? The answer to that question can only be determined by an analysis which takes up, and takes further, this discussion.

David Carrier, who teaches philosophy at Carnegie Mellon, is a contributing editor to Arts Magazine *and a co-editor of* Leonardo. *His books include* Artwriting, *a study of the history of American art criticism, and a history of art history to be published by the Pennsylvania State University Press. He is completing a book on Poussin.*

Bibliography

ANDERSON, RICHARD. *Arts in Primitive Societies.* Englewood Cliffs, NJ: Prentice-Hall, 1979.
BARTHES, ROLAND (trans. Annette Lavers). *Mythologies.* New York: Hill & Wang, 1972.
BAUDRILLARD, JEAN. *For a Critique of the Political Economy of the Sign.* Telos Press Ltd., 1981.
BENJAMIN, WALTER. *Illuminations.* New York: Schocken, 1969.
BERGER, JOHN. *About Looking.* New York: Pantheon, 1980.
———. *Art in Revolution.* New York: Pantheon, 1969.
———. *Ways of Seeing.* New York: Penguin, 1977.
CARRIER, DAVID. *Artwriting.* Amherst, MA: University of Massachusetts Press, 1987.
DANTO, ARTHUR. *The Transformation of the Commonplace.* Cambridge, MA: Harvard University Press, 1981.
DEMETZ, PETER, ed. *Reflections: Essays, Aphorisims, Autobiographical Writings* (of Walter Benjamin). New York: Schocken, 1986.
FISH, STANLEY. *Is There a Text in This Class? The Authority of Interpretive Communities.* Cambridge, MA: Harvard University Press, 1982.
FOSTER, HAL, ed. *The Anti-Aesthetic: Essays on Postmodern Culture.* Bay Press, 1983.
———. *Vision & Visuality,* Bay Press, 1988.
FOUCAULT, MICHEL. *The Archeology of Knowledge.* New York: Pantheon, 1982.
———. *This is Not a Pipe: Illustrations & Letters by Rene Magritte.* Berkeley, CA: University of California Press, 1982.
GABLIK, SUZI. *Progress in Art.* New York: Rizzoli, 1977.
GALLOP, JANE. *The Daughter's Seduction: Feminism & Psychoanalysis.* Ithaca, NY: Cornell University Press, 1988.
———. *Thinking Through the Body.* New York: Columbia University Press, 1988.
GOLDBERG, ROSELEE. *Performance: Live Art 1909 to the Present.* New York: Abrams, 1979.
HAUSER, ARNOLD. *The Philosophy of Art History.* Evanston, IL: Northwestern University Press, 1985.
———. *The Social History of Art,* Volumes 1–4. New York: Random House, 1985.
HERTZ, RICHARD. *Theories of Contemporary Art.* Englewood Cliffs, NJ: Prentice-Hall, 1985.
HUIZINGA, JOHAN. *Homo Ludens: A Study of the Play Element in Culture.* Boston, MA: Beacon Press, 1955.
JAMESON, FREDRIC. *The Political Unconscious: Narrative as a Socially Symbolic Act.* Ithaca, NY: Cornell University Press, 1982.
KLEIN, MELANIE. *Envy and Gratitude and Other Works 1946–1963.* New York: Macmillan, 1984.
KOSTELANETZ, RICHARD, ed. *Esthetics Contemporary.* Buffalo, NY: Prometheus, 1978.
KRAUSS, ROSALIND. *Passages in Modern Sculpture.* New York: Viking, 1977.
KUSPIT, DONALD. *The Critic is Artist: The Intentionality of Art.* Minneapolis, MN: UMI Research Press, 1988.
LACAN, J. (trans. A. Sheridan). *Ecrits: A Selection.* New York: Norton, 1977.
LINKER, KATE, ed. *Difference: On Representation and Sexuality.* New York: New Museum, 1985.
———. *Individuals: A Select History of Contemporary Art, 1945–1986.*
LIPPARD, LUCY R. *Changing: Essays in Art Criticism.* New York: Dutton, 1971.
———. *Get the Message? Activist Essays on Art and Politics.* New York: Dutton, 1983.
———. *From the Center.* New York: Dutton, 1976.

———. *Overlay: Contemporary Art and the Art of Prehistory*. New York: Pantheon, 1983.
———. *Six Years: The Dematerialization of the Art Object*. New York: Praeger, 1973.
NOCHLIN, LINDA. *Women, Art & Power*. New York: Harper-Row, 1989.
PARKER, ROSZIKA and GRISELDA POLLOCK. *Old Mistresses: Women, Art and Ideology*. New York: Pantheon, 1981.
POSTER, MARK, ed. (trans. Jacques Mourrain). *Jean Baudrillard: Selected Writings*. Stanford, CA: Stanford University Press, 1988.
RISATTI, HOWARD. *Postmodern Perspectives: Issues in Contemporary Art*. Englewood Cliffs, NJ: Prentice-Hall, 1990.
ROSENBERG, HAROLD. *Art & Other Serious Matters*. Chicago: University of Chicago Press, 1983.
———. *The De-Definition of Art*. Chicago: University of Chicago Press, 1983.
———. *The Tradition of the New*. Chicago: University of Chicago Press, 1982.
ROSKILL, MARK and DAVID CARRIER. *Truth and Falsehood in Visual Images*. Amherst, MA: University of Massachusetts Press, 1983.
ROTH, MOIRA, ed. *The Amazing Decade: Women and Performance Art in America 1970–1980*. Astro Artz, 1983.
SELTZ, PETER. *Art in Our Times: A Pictorial History 1890–1980*. New York: Abrams, 1981.
SMAGULA, HOWARD. *Currents: Contemporary Directions in the Visual Arts*, second edition. Englewood Cliffs, NJ: Prentice Hall, 1989.
SONDHEIM, ALAN, ed. *Individuals: Post-Movement Art in America*. New York: Dutton, 1977.
SPITZ, E. H. *Art and Psyche: A Study in Psychoanalysis and Aesthetics*. New Haven, CT: Yale University Press, 1985.

Index